IEG WORLD BANK | IFC | MIGA
INDEPENDENT EVALUATION GROUP

I0120184

The World Bank's Country Policy and Institutional Assessment

An IEG Evaluation

2010
The World Bank
Washington, D.C.

http://www.worldbank.org/ieg

© The International Bank for Reconstruction and Development / The World Bank
1818 H Street NW
Washington, DC 20433
Telephone: 202-473-1000
Internet: www.worldbank.org
E-mail: feedback@worldbank.org

1 2 3 4 13 12 11 10

This volume is a product of the staff of the International Bank for Reconstruction and Development / The World Bank Group. The findings, interpretations, and conclusions expressed in this volume do not necessarily reflect the views of the Executive Directors of The World Bank or the governments they represent.

The World Bank does not guarantee the accuracy of the data in this work. The boundaries, colors, denominations, and other information shown on any map in this work do not imply any judgment on the part of The World Bank concerning the legal status of any territory or the endorsement or acceptance of such boundaries.

Cover image: Unisphere at Flushing Meadows – Corona Park. New York, New York. © Rudy Sulgan/Corbis. The Unisphere was built as the theme symbol for the 1964–65 World's Fair.

ISBN: 978-0-8213-8427-5
e-ISBN: 978-0-8213-8429-9
DOI: 1596/978-0-8213-8427-5

Library of Congress Cataloging-in-Publication data have been applied for.

World Bank InfoShop
E-mail: pic@worldbank.org
Telephone: 202-458-5454
Facsimile: 202-522-1500

Independent Evaluation Group
Communications, Strategy, and Learning
E-mail: ieg@worldbank.org
Telephone: 202-458-4497
Facsimile: 202-522-3125

Printed on Recycled Paper

Contents

vii   **Abbreviations**

ix   **Acknowledgments**

xi   **Foreword**

xiii   **Executive Summary**

xix   **Management Response**

xxv   **Chairman's Summary: Committee on Development Effectiveness (CODE)**

xxvii   **Advisory Panel Statement**

1   1   **Introduction and Evolution of the CPIA**
          4   Evolution in the Content of the CPIA
          8   Other Changes in the CPIA
          9   Role of the CPIA in IDA Allocation

13   2   **Relevance of the CPIA for Growth, Poverty Reduction, and Effective Use of Development Assistance**
          15   The CPIA and Determinants of Sustained Growth
          25   The CPIA and Determinants of Poverty Reduction
          29   The CPIA and the Effective Use of Development Assistance
          31   Findings and Recommendations

39   3   **Reliability of the CPIA Ratings**
          41   Comparability with Other Indicators
          48   CPIA Ratings Generation Process

57   4   **Findings and Recommendations**
          59   Overview
          59   Main Findings
          62   Recommendations

65   **Appendixes**
          67   A: 2008 Country Policy and Institutional Assessment Criteria
          71   B: Public Sector Literature Review
          81   C: 2007 CPIA Criteria on Economic Management, Structural Policies, and Policies for Social Inclusion/Equity and Evidence in the Literature
          91   D: Literature Review on Aid Effectiveness
          93   E: Examples of Positive Impacts of Aid Projects from Randomized Evaluations in Education, Health, Infrastructure, and Agriculture
          95   F: Review of Financial Sector Criterion
          99   G: Country Policy and Institutional Assessment (CPIA) and Loan Performance

103 H: Comparing Country Policy and Institutional Assessment Ratings by the World Bank, African Development Bank, and Asian Development Bank

105 I: Comparator Indices of the CPIA

109 J: Number of IDA and IBRD Countries for Which External Data are Available

111 K: Comments by Network on Regional CPIA Rating Proposals, 2007

113 Endnotes

119 References

Boxes

4   1.1   Changes to the CPIA Criteria in 1998 That Reflect the Emphasis on Institutions

11   1.2   The Governance Adjustment in IDA's Country Performance Ratings, FY1998–2008

19   2.1   Channels through Which Inequality Affects Growth

44   3.1   Comparator Indicators

50   3.2   The Process of Preparing CPIA Ratings

51   3.3   The Network Reviews of CPIA Ratings

Figure

25   2.1   Relationship between Changes in PBA and the Ratio of Cluster D Ratings to Ratings on Other Clusters for "Core IDA" Countries

Tables

5   1.1   CPIA Criteria 1998–2008

10   1.2   Evolution of IDA's Performance-Based Allocation Formula and the Adjustment for Governance

16   2.1   Mapping of the "Consensus" Determinants for Sustained Growth and the CPIA Criteria

22   2.2   Correlations between Ratings of CPIA Clusters, 2007

22   2.3   Correlations between CPIA with Different Cluster Weights and CPIA with Equal Cluster Weights, 2007

23   2.4   Simulation Results: Effects on Performance-Based Allocations for "Core IDA" Countries Arising from a Larger Weight on the "Governance" Cluster Compared to Equal Weights on All Clusters

33   2.5   Simulation Results: Changes in PBA from Dropping q8

34   2.6   Simulation Results: Changes in Trade Ratings Arising from Changes in Weights of Trade Subcriteria by Numbers and Shares of IBRD and IDA Countries

35   2.7   Simulation Results: IBRD and IDA Countries That Would Experience Changes in Trade Ratings due to Changes in Weights for Trade Subcriteria

37   2.8   Simulation Results: Changes in PBA Arising from Changes in Weights for Trade Subcriteria

42   3.1   Rank Correlation Coefficients between CPIA Ratings and Comparator Ratings for 2007

45   3.2   Other Indicators—Expert Judgment or Hard Data?

46   3.3   Are Other Comparator Indicators Closer to the Bank or to AfDB and ADB?

47   3.4   Comparison of Changes in CPIA Ratings 2006–07 between the Bank, AfDB, and ADB

49 3.5 Rank Correlations between the CPIA and Other Indicators: IBRD versus IDA Countries

52 3.6 Numbers and Shares of Initial Regional Rating Proposals on Which the Networks Disagreed with the Regions, by Criteria, for 2007

53 3.7 Number and Share of Initial Regional Rating Proposals on Which the Networks Disagreed with the Regions, by Region and IBRD and IDA Countries for 2007

53 3.8 Network Disagreements with Initial Regional Rating Proposals

54 3.9 Share of Instances Where Networks Prevailed When Networks Disagreed with Regions over Proposed Increases in Ratings from 2006

54 3.10 Share of Instances Where Networks Prevailed When Networks Disagreed with Regions, 2007

55 3.11 Shares of Countries on Which Networks Commented in 2007 When Regions Proposed the Same Ratings as in 2006

Energy transmission and power lines, Tajikistan. Photo by Gennadiy Ratushenko/World Bank

Abbreviations

ADB	Asian Development Bank
AfDB	African Development Bank
AML-CFT	Anti-money laundering and combating the financing of terrorists
ARPP	Annual review of project performance
BCP	Basel core principles
CGAP	Consultative Group to Assist the Poor
CPIA	Country policy and institutional assessment
CPR	Country performance ratings
DAC	Development Assistance Committee of the Organisation for Economic Co-operation and Development
DB	Doing Business
ESI	Environmental Sustainability Index
ETI	Enabling Trade Index
GCI	Global Competitiveness Index
GDP	Gross domestic product
GNIpc	Gross national income per capita
GNPpc	Gross national product per capita
HIV-AIDS	Human immunodeficiency virus-acquired immunodeficiency syndrome
IBRD	International Bank for Reconstruction and Development
ICP	IDA country performance
ICRG	International Country Risk Guide
IDA	International Development Association
IEG	Independent Evaluation Group
IMF	International Monetary Fund
IP	Implementation progress
ISR	Implementation Status and Results Report
IT	Information technology
MDGs	Millennium Development Goals
NGOs	Non-governmental organizations
NPLs	Non-performing loans
NTB	Non-tariff barrier
OECD	Organisation for Economic Co-operation and Development
OED	Operations Evaluation Department (the previous name of IEG)
OLS	Ordinary least squares
OPCS	Operations Policy and Country Services
PBA	Performance-based allocation
PRMED	Economic Policy and Debt Department
QAG	Quality Assurance Group
SMEs	Small and medium enterprises
UNDP	United Nations Development Programme
VAT	Value-added tax
WGI	Worldwide Governance Indicators

Harvesting rice fields, Vietnam. Photo by Tran Thi Hoa/World Bank

Acknowledgments

This evaluation of the World Bank's Country Policy and Institutional Assessment was prepared by the Country Evaluation and Regional Relations division of the Independent Evaluation Group.

The evaluation was led by Helena Tang, the author of the report. Saubhik Deb carried out the statistical and econometric analyses for the report. Background papers were prepared by Julia Cage, Shailaja Fennel, Patrick Honohan, and Biaoyun Qiao. Inputs were provided by Carla Pazce, Rupa Ranganathan, and Dusan Vujovic. Production and logistical support was provided by Agnes Santos. Barbara Balaj copy edited the study for publication.

The peer reviewers were Victoria Elliott, Aart Kraay, and Steven Webb. The team received guidance and support from the IEG management team, and also benefited from the comments received from the various IEG units.

The evaluation team extends its thanks to the staff from all six Regions, the various networks, Operations Policy and Country Services, and Resource Mobilization who were interviewed for the report.

Director-General, Evaluation: *Vinod Thomas*
Director, Independent Evaluation Group – World Bank: *Cheryl Gray*
Senior Manager, IEGCR: *Ali M. Khadr*
Task Manager: *Helena Tang*

Woman in India. Photo by Curt Carnemark/World Bank

Foreword

The Bank's Country Policy and Institutional Assessment (CPIA) assesses the conduciveness of a country's policy and institutional framework to poverty reduction, sustainable growth, and the effective use of development assistance. The CPIA enters the calculation of country performance ratings that, since 1980, have been used to allocate International Development Association (IDA) resources to eligible client countries. This evaluation was undertaken at the request of Board members to assess the appropriateness of the CPIA as a broad indicator of development effectiveness and as a determinant of the allocation of IDA funds. As indicated in the Approach Paper, this evaluation reviews the effects of the CPIA ratings on IDA allocations but does not review the IDA allocation formula itself.

The evaluation finds that the CPIA content broadly reflects the determinants of economic growth and poverty reduction identified in the economics literature, but some criteria need to be revised (such as the *trade* criterion that places much greater emphasis on imports than exports) and streamlined, and one criterion (assessment of disadvantaged socioeconomic categories other than gender) added. The CPIA ratings also correlate well with ratings of similar indicators, and more so for International Bank for Reconstruction and Development than for IDA countries. In part, this could be caused by the CPIA exercise's practice over the past several years of taking into account a country's stage of development, which also means that the CPIA is no longer an index in the true sense of the word. It is difficult to establish an empirical link between the CPIA and economic growth outcomes, although CPIA ratings are found to be positively associated with aid effectiveness in the narrower sense—specifically, the performance of Bank loans.

The CPIA's 16 criteria are grouped into four clusters—economic management, structural policies, policies for social inclusion and equity, and public sector management and institutions. These clusters are weighted equally to derive the overall CPIA rating. In contrast, the IDA allocation formula weights the clusters unevenly—the first three clusters are each given a weight of 8 percent, and the last cluster (the governance cluster) a weight of 68 percent and portfolio performance the remaining weight of 8 percent. The literature offers no evidence to justify any particular set of weights on the four clusters, whether in deriving the overall CPIA rating or in calculating the IDA allocation. Neither is there justification for why the clustering is as it is—having all social sectors combined with the environment in one cluster, for example. There is also insufficient evidence to conclude that the governance cluster associates better with Bank loan performance than the other three clusters.

The report lays out four recommendations: disclose International Bank for Reconstruction and Development ratings; discontinue the "stage of development" adjustment to the ratings; review and revise the content and clustering of the criteria; and discontinue the current aggregation of the criteria into an overall index.

Vinod Thomas
Director-General, Evaluation

Girl in classroom, Mexico. Photo by Curt Carnemark/World Bank

Executive Summary

The World Bank's Country Policy and Institutional Assessment (CPIA) assesses the conduciveness of a country's policy and institutional framework to poverty reduction, sustainable growth, and the effective use of development assistance. It plays an important role in the country performance ratings that have been used for allocating resources from the International Development Association (IDA) to eligible countries since 1980.

The CPIA consists of 16 criteria grouped into four clusters—economic management, structural policies, policies for social inclusion and equity, and public sector management and institutions—weighted equally to derive the overall CPIA rating. Since the beginning of fiscal 2009, IDA has made transparent the weights of the clusters used in the IDA allocation formula—24 percent on the first three CPIA clusters combined and 68 percent on the fourth (governance) cluster, with the remaining 8 percent weighted on portfolio performance. In other words, the governance cluster has eight and a half times the weight of each of the other three clusters in the formula. This has also made transparent the weak link between the overall CPIA index and IDA allocations, with a country's governance performance (particularly relative to its performance in the other clusters) being more important in the latter.

The content of the CPIA broadly reflects the determinants of growth and poverty reduction identified in the economics literature. However, some criteria need to be revised and streamlined and one criterion added. The literature offers no evidence to justify any particular set of weights on the four clusters used for IDA allocation or the way the criteria are clustered (for example, having social sectors and environment in one cluster). The literature offers only mixed evidence

regarding the relevance of the content of the CPIA for aid effectiveness broadly defined—that is, that it represents the policies and institutions important for aid to lead to growth. However, the CPIA is associated with aid effectiveness defined more narrowly as the better performance of Bank loans. But there is insufficient evidence to conclude that the most heavily weighted CPIA cluster associates better with loan performance than the other three clusters.

The CPIA ratings are generally reliable and correlate well with similar indicators, but it is difficult to establish an empirical link between the CPIA and growth outcomes. Network reviewers' validation of ratings helps guard against potential biases in having Bank staff rate countries on which their work programs depend. The CPIA ratings correlate better with similar indicators for International Bank for Reconstruction and Development (IBRD) than for IDA countries. This correlation could in part be because more information is available on IBRD countries, and in part because the CPIA ratings are meant to take into account the stage of development (which is more pertinent for IDA countries and which means ratings for these countries are more subject to judgment than those for IBRD countries). This tendency is exacerbated by the different practices with respect to accounting for the stage of development, as none of the regional reviewers of the CPIA do this, whereas network reviewers vary in their practices.

The International Evaluation Group (IEG) makes four recommendations. First, disclose the ratings for IBRD countries in the interest of accountability and transparency. Second, remove accounting for the stage of development in the rating exercise to reduce subjectivity. Third, undertake a thorough review of the adequacy of each criterion, including a review of experience and the literature, and revise as necessary, based on, among other things, the findings of this evaluation. Fourth, consider not producing an overall CPIA index although continue to produce and publish the separate CPIA components.

Overview

This evaluation takes the premise that beyond informing IDA allocation, the CPIA is useful as a broad indicator of development effectiveness. It reviews the appropriateness of the CPIA as an indicator that assesses the conduciveness of a country's policies and institutions to fostering poverty reduction, sustainable growth, and the effective use of development assistance. It assesses the relevance of the content of the CPIA through a review of the economics literature. It also assesses the reliability of CPIA ratings in two ways— through comparing CPIA ratings with similar indicators, and through reviewing the CPIA ratings generation process. Based on these assessments, the evaluation derives recommendations for enhancing the CPIA.

Relevance of CPIA

The contents of the CPIA are largely relevant for growth and poverty reduction. The CPIA criteria map well with the determinants—policies and institutions—of growth and poverty reduction identified in the literature, although some criteria can usefully be revised and streamlined and one can be added (see recommendations).

The evidence is mixed regarding the relevance of the content of the CPIA for aid effectiveness as broadly defined in the literature. Indeed, the review of the literature indicates there is little consensus on the impact of aid on growth itself and on the conditions under which aid can have a positive impact on growth.

However, the CPIA is associated with aid effectiveness in a narrower sense—that is, with respect to the performance of World Bank loans. Empirical analysis finds that the overall CPIA ratings are negatively associated with the share of problem loans that in turn is correlated with loan outcomes.

Empirical analysis indicates that there is insufficient evidence to conclude that the governance cluster associates better with loan performance than with the other clusters. Based on this finding, as well as the lack of consensus in the literature on the conditions under which aid has an impact on growth, it can be surmised that the way in which the CPIA enters the formula for the allocation of IDA funds is driven much more by fiduciary and possibly other concerns of donors than by the objectives of achieving sustained growth and poverty reduction.

The CPIA strives to allow for country specificity, that is, that different sets of policies and institutions can achieve similar outcomes. However, there are some pitfalls. The CPIA instructions to staff indicate that outcomes need to be taken into account when assessing policies and institutions, which helps to account for country specificity. Indeed, outcome indicators are included in the assessment of some criteria. They could also be added to other criteria, in particular trade.

The *trade* criterion does not adequately allow for country specificity. The specification of particular tariff rates for different ratings reflects a one-size-fits-all approach to trade liberalization that is not supported by country experience. Export performance (an outcome indicator) needs to be included in the assessment and would help to allow for country specificity.

The *trade* criterion also does not reflect the importance of complementary institutions for successful liberalization. The two-thirds weight on trade restrictiveness and one-third weight on trade facilitation is not supported by country experience that shows that at moderate tariff levels (which practically all countries currently have), complementary factors (macroeconomic stability and trade facilitation) are more important than further tariff reduction to promote integration into the global economy.

The CPIA is missing an assessment of disadvantaged socioeconomic groups other than gender. Currently, only gender is being assessed with respect to equality, yet country evidence indicates that social exclusion of other marginalized groups could have severe poverty and growth implications.

Important linkages among certain criteria are not reflected in the CPIA. Except for the three *economic management* criteria, all of the CPIA criteria are assessed independently. This could be problematic in two instances. First, the assessment of trade liberalization needs to take into account the extent of intersectoral labor mobility because liberalization in the absence of labor mobility could exacerbate poverty. Second, fiscal policy needs to be assessed in conjunction with the quality of budgetary and financial management to ensure that the fiscal condition of the country in its entirety is realistically captured.

Reliability of CPIA Ratings

The Bank has made efforts over time to improve the definition of the CPIA rating scale to enhance the reliability of the ratings. These efforts have been aimed at reducing staff discretion in providing ratings.

The CPIA ratings correlate well with similar indicators in terms of relative rankings of countries and direction of change. For each of the 16 criteria, the rank correlation coefficients of CPIA ratings with similar indicators average between 0.7 and 0.8. Other indicators correlate better with the Bank's CPIA ratings than with

those of the African Development Bank and the Asian Development Bank, the closest comparators to the Bank, as they use almost exactly the same CPIA guidelines.

CPIA ratings correlate better with similar indicators for IBRD than for IDA countries. This could be due in part to the greater amount of information available on IBRD than on IDA countries, which increases the likelihood of different institutions having similar assessments on IBRD countries. It could also be due partly to the fact that the CPIA rating exercise takes into account the stage of development (introduced since 2004). This is more pertinent for IDA countries and hence would subject ratings of those countries to more judgment in an exercise that is already centered on staff judgment.

Accounting for the stage of development in the CPIA ratings is problematic. In addition to the judgment involved, accounting for the stage of development is also problematic because of the different practices adopted across the Bank. Regional reviewers do not take this into account, whereas network reviewers vary in their practices. Further, accounting for the stage of development means that the CPIA is no longer an index in the true sense of the word.

The review process for the CPIA, which gives the networks responsibility for validating the ratings, helps to guard against potential biases in ratings, although there are exceptions. A major advantage of the CPIA exercise is having well-informed professional judgment of staff as the central determinant of the ratings. At the same time, however, having staff rate the countries on which their work programs depend could lead to rating biases.

Analysis of the 2007 review process indicates that for instances where the networks challenged the regions' initial proposals of a rating increase from 2006, the networks prevailed 73 percent of the time for IDA countries. They prevailed more often—86 percent of the time—for IBRD countries. However, these instances made up only 6 percent of the ratings for IDA countries and 5 percent of the ratings for IBRD countries; hence, there does not seem to be a strong upward bias in ratings for either group of countries.

Recommendations

Based on its findings, IEG has derived recommendations to enhance the CPIA as an indicator of policies and institutions that are important for growth, poverty reduction (or welfare more broadly), and the effective use of development assistance.

Adoption of these recommendations could result in a discontinuity in the CPIA ratings, which Bank management has been trying to avoid. However, it is important that the CPIA reflect the latest thinking in development as well as lessons learned—both of which are stated intentions of the Bank. It would also provide the opportunity to address an issue that some network reviewers have raised regarding the quality of the ratings for some criteria because of what they perceive as inflated baseline ratings from a few years ago. The recommendations are as follows.

First, disclose the ratings for IBRD countries. Disclosure is important for accountability and transparency and would further enhance the quality of the ratings.

Second, remove accounting for the stage of development from the CPIA exercise. If this cannot be done, at the very least it is important to clarify and justify in the guidelines which criteria need to take into account the stage of development and how such adjustments need to be made.

Third, undertake a thorough review of the CPIA and revise the criteria as necessary. IEG recommends that the review entail an in-depth literature review for each criterion and reflect the latest thinking on development and lessons learned. The review needs to reflect an appropriate balance between liberalization and regulation. The review needs to also examine whether the clustering of criteria is appropriate. In particular, it needs to examine the appropriateness of combining the social sectors with the

environment, which limit the emphasis accorded to these aspects. Guideposts for assessing the criteria need to be reviewed at the same time. The following points also need to be taken into account in the review and revisions:

- Revising the *trade* criterion to include a subcomponent on exports that evaluates performance as well as policies and institutions to reduce anti-export bias. This subcomponent and those on trade restrictiveness and trade facilitation need to all get equal weights. The trade restrictiveness subcomponent needs to be revised to reflect country experience that at moderate levels of tariffs (which almost all countries have), any further reduction would be less important than complementary factors for global integration.
- Dropping or reformulating the criterion on *equity of public resource use*, as much of its content is already covered by other CPIA criteria (specifically, property rights, access to education and to credit, income transfers) or information is lacking for an adequate assessment (specifically, the progressivity or regressivity of taxes).
- Adding an assessment of other disadvantaged socioeconomic groups to the CPIA. This could either replace the criterion on *equity of public resource* use or be added to that criterion if it were to be reformulated.
- Revising the *financial sector* criterion. This needs to entail (i) revising of the weights for the three subcomponents—stability, depth and efficiency, and access—in light of the importance of financial stability as reflected by recent global evidence, and the mixed evidence on the importance of microfinance; (ii) adding assessment of policies, regulations, and institutions for fostering an enabling environment for the financial sector taking into account lessons learned, notably from the current crisis; and (iii) strengthening the assessment of financial stability.
- Combining the assessment of tax policy with fiscal policy.
- Streamlining the assessment of judicial independence and the assessment of corruption in the public sector management and institutions

cluster, as they are currently assessed in more than one criterion in this cluster.

- Strengthening the assessment of the *environment* criterion and making the process more efficient. Currently, staff need to answer 85 questions for only one rating.
- Reporting only one consolidated rating for the three *economic management* criteria to avoid confusion.

Fourth, consider not producing an overall CPIA index, and continue to produce and publish the separate CPIA components. The overall CPIA index is not used as such for the allocation of IDA funds. With respect to the broader use of the CPIA as an index of policies and institutions, country specificity implies that the appropriate weights of the different clusters could differ depending on a country's initial conditions and stage of development. Producing the different components of the CPIA without assigning weights to them to arrive at an aggregate index would allow for different weights to be applied according to country contexts and use.

Students building houses in Kahyelitsha township, South Africa. Photo by Trevor Samson/World Bank

Management Response

Management welcomes the Independent Evaluation Group (IEG) report on the World Bank's Country Policy and Institutional Assessment (CPIA). In management's view the findings of the review include several useful insights that will contribute to further strengthen the CPIA.

The report makes four recommendations:

- Disclose the ratings for International Bank for Reconstruction and Development (IBRD) countries.
- Remove accounting for the stage of development from the CPIA exercise, or, if this cannot be done, clarify and justify in the guidelines which criteria should be subject to the adjustments and how the adjustments should be made.
- Undertake a thorough review of the CPIA and revise the criteria as needed (the evaluation contains recommendations regarding a few specific criteria, such as trade and financial sector).
- Consider not producing an overall CPIA index although continuing to produce and publish the separate CPIA components. Except for the recommendation on disclosing the CPIA ratings for the IBRD countries, management broadly concurs with the recommendations emanating from this evaluation.

Relevance of the CPIA. The evaluation finds that the contents of the CPIA are largely relevant for growth and poverty reduction and that they map well with the policies and institutions that are identified in the literature as relevant for growth and poverty reduction. On the basis of a review of the literature, the IEG evaluation concludes that there is little consensus on the impact of aid on growth and poverty reduction and on the conditions, including the role of policies and institutions, under which aid can influence growth. The IEG evaluation finds, however, that the CPIA is associated with aid effectiveness in the narrower context of the performance of World Bank loans. Poor CPIA scores are correlated with the share of problem loans, which in turn is correlated with loan outcomes.

CPIA criteria. The evaluation also contains recommendations on a few CPIA criteria, such as the criteria covering trade, the financial sector, and the equity of public resource use, which IEG finds could be streamlined and revisited. Management considers these recommendations useful and intends to use them to inform the next review of the CPIA. After assessing gaps in coverage, the IEG evaluation notes that the CPIA is missing an assessment of disadvantaged socioeconomic groups other than gender. Management intends to address this issue in the context of the CPIA review.

Reliability. The IEG evaluation notes the efforts the Bank has made over time to strengthen the CPIA and enhance the reliability of the scores. It finds that in terms of relative ranking and directions of change, the CPIA scores are correlated well with existing indicators, but it notes that the correlations are higher for IBRD than for International Development Association (IDA) countries. The report also analyzes the process used by the World Bank to generate the CPIA scores—a process in which the regions put forward a set of proposals for country scores that are then subject to review by the networks and central departments. IEG finds that this internal review process gives the networks an important role in validating the scores, helping to prevent potential bias in the scores and to address possible conflicts of interest. The review concluded that there is no strong evidence of upward bias for either the IDA or IBRD country scores. Management welcomes these findings and views them as useful inputs for further strengthening the CPIA process.

General Comments

Disclosure of IBRD scores. The objective of the CPIA exercise is first and foremost to provide an assessment of country performance that will be used to determine IDA allocations. To underscore this point, by the suggestion of the Board, these scores are disclosed as the IDA Resource Allocation Index. IEG argues that disclosure of the IBRD scores is important from an accountability and transparency standpoint and will strengthen the ratings. The report neither elaborates on the argument nor discusses trade-offs. Accountability and transparency are important, but there are other issues to consider.

A major reason not to disclose the IBRD scores is the possible effect on market perceptions and credit ratings and associated financial consequences for the countries concerned. Moreover, the Bank would not want to be seen as a credit rating agency. Unlike the scores for IDA countries, the scores are not discussed or shared by Bank staff with their IBRD counterparts; the IBRD country scores do not play a role in lending decisions, and their confidentiality limits their use. They have been used internally in analytic work and by the Quality Assurance Group and IEG on portfolio-related issues. When the 2004 external panel reviewed the CPIA and discussed these issues, it leaned toward dropping the IBRD countries from the exercise. IEG notes (chapter 4) that the report recommendations are aimed at enhancing the CPIA beyond its use for IDA allocations, and that if the CPIA is viewed only in an IDA-allocation context, the need to include IBRD countries can be questioned.

Management disagrees with the recommendation to disclose the IBRD scores and prefers restricting the coverage of the CPIA exercise to the IDA-only countries. In the context of the forthcoming CPIA review, management will analyze in more depth the value added and the costs of preparing CPIA scores for IBRD countries for internal Bank uses, as well as other relevant aspects. The conclusions of this work will inform management's decision on how to go forward, namely regarding the coverage of the CPIA, and, if warranted, the consideration of alternative approaches to disclosure. In the meantime the CPIA exercise will continue to cover the IBRD countries.

Accounting for development stage. The CPIA guidelines state that staff may need to take into account the size of the economy and its degree of sophistication in their assessments. The criteria were developed so that higher scores could be attained by a country that, given its stage of development, has a policy and institutional framework that fosters growth and poverty reduction. This approach recognizes that in many areas, countries cannot be judged by the same yardstick if they are at very different stages of development. Some of the policy objectives may be considered to be invariant to income—for example, the desirability of having a well-managed budget. But others depend, for example, on the sophistication of the financial system (expectations regarding regulatory capacity would be different for a high-income country than for a low-income country) or on the degree of urbanization. Social protection in a largely urban, formal economy (unemployment insurance, pensions, and so on) is fundamentally different from the problem of protecting a poor rural subsistence economy from weather-related harvest shocks.

The report raises a number of concerns regarding the CPIA treatment of the stage of development. At the same time, the evaluation and the recommendations (including those concerning the revision of the *financial sector* criterion) recognize that stage of development considerations are important (appendix box F.1).

Unless this dimension is considered, some of the criteria scores may be linearly correlated with income—which is not the objective of the exercise. Controlling for a country's stage of development seems necessary, as what constitutes good policy in many of the areas covered by the CPIA is linked to stage of development as well as to country-specific characteristics. The report points out that accounting for the stage of development in the CPIA exercise may not always have been uniformly applied. It suggests that, if the approach continues to be used, the guidelines should clarify and provide the rationale for its use in specific criteria, showing how the adjustment should be carried out in determining the final scores. Management agrees with this recommendation and in the context of the review of the CPIA will revise the guidelines accordingly.

Review of the CPIA criteria. Periodic reviews of the CPIA to update and refine the content of the criteria and the conduct of the exercise have been a mainstay of the CPIA's history, and they should continue to remain so going forward. But these reviews should also be done at sufficient intervals so that the CPIA scores have some validity over time. Consensus on development thinking moves slowly. As the IEG report notes, these periodic reviews resulted in several breaks in the CPIA series, as some criteria were dropped, some were added, and some were revised. As the report notes, the last major revision took place in 2004, informed by the recommendations of an external panel that undertook an in-depth review of the CPIA.

The IEG report suggests that perhaps the time has come for Bank management to undertake a thorough review and revision of the CPIA. Management generally concurs with this suggestion and plans a revision of the CPIA, to be completed by the time IDA 16 is launched. Management wishes to point out, however, several important considerations to take into account in planning the timing of the review. First, in revising the CPIA, it is important to balance making the instrument flexible enough to reflect new developments with maintaining some stability in the criteria that will allow for comparisons of scores over time. Revisions will create another break in the CPIA series, and, as in 2004, there will be substantial cost in reworking the country scores and in explaining to the governments and external audiences the new criteria, the differences in relation to the previous criteria, and the rationale for the changes. Second, following the introduction of a new set of criteria, changes in some scores do not necessarily reflect a deterioration or improvement in performance, but result from the changes in the criteria. Because the scores are used for IDA allocations, the revisions of the criteria could result in aid volatility. And third, the CPIA criteria are used by other multilateral development banks, and management also intends to consult them throughout the process of revising the instrument. Management would add, however, with respect to the IEG report's detailed recommendations on how some criteria could be revised, that it finds these suggestions useful and intends to use them to inform the next revision.

Caveats. Although management broadly agrees with the thrust of the findings of the IEG evaluation, it would like to point out that the report contains a few examples of statements—specifically, regarding the interpretation of some of the findings—that would have benefited from further elaboration or qualification. Overall, management agrees with most of the IEG findings and, with the exception noted above, accepts its recommendations. Management's specific responses to the IEG recommendations are given in the Management Action Record.

Management Action Record

Independent Evaluation Group (IEG) Recommendations Requiring a Response	Management Response
Disclose ratings for International Bank for Reconstruction and Development (IBRD) countries.	***Disagree.*** The objective of the Country Policy and Institutional Assessment (CPIA) exercise is first and foremost to provide an assessment of country performance that will be used in determining International Development Association (IDA) allocations. IEG argues without elaboration that disclosure of the IBRD ratings is important for accountability and transparency and would further enhance the quality of the ratings. Whether "disclosure" will further the quality of the ratings is not self-evident. Accountability and transparency are important in their own right, but there are other issues to consider. A major reason not to disclose the ratings is the possible effect on market perceptions and credit ratings and the associated financial consequences for the countries concerned. IEG notes (chapter 4) that the report recommendations are aimed at enhancing the CPIA beyond its use for IDA allocations. It suggests that if the CPIA is viewed only in an IDA-allocation context, the need to rate IBRD countries can be questioned. Management disagrees with the recommendation to disclose the IBRD scores and prefers to limit the coverage of the CPIA to the IDA-eligible countries only. Given that the IBRD scores are used internally by the Bank, the forthcoming CPIA review will include a more in-depth analysis of the value added and the costs of preparing for internal uses CPIA scores for IBRD countries. The conclusions of this work will inform management's decision on next steps. In the meantime the CPIA exercise will continue to cover the IBRD countries.
Remove accounting for the stage of development from the CPIA rating exercise.	***Partially agreed.*** As the report notes (for example, chapter 2), there is relative consensus in the literature that there is no single recipe for growth and that country specificities, including the stage of development, need to be taken into account. Some of the policy objectives may be invariant to income (for example, desirability of well-managed budgets), but others are not (for example, expectations regarding regulatory capacity in low-income countries versus middle-income countries; social protection in a largely urban formal economy versus a poor rural subsistence economy). The IEG report suggests (the recommendations in the executive summary and chapter 4) that if accounting for the stage of development stage cannot be removed, then it is important to clarify in the guidelines which criteria should take into account the stage of development, what the rationale is for doing so, and how the adjustments should be made. Management agrees with this suggestion. Therefore, as part of the broad review of the CPIA (see below), the guidelines will be revised to clarify which criteria should be adjusted to account for stage of development and how the adjustment should be made.
Undertake a thorough review of the CPIA and revise the criteria as necessary. This needs to entail a detailed review of the literature for each criterion and needs to reflect the latest thinking on development and lessons learned. It also needs to take into account the recommendations of IEG on specific changes to the criteria that were derived from the evaluation.	***Agreed.*** Periodic reviews of the content and methodology have been a fixture of the evolution of the CPIA, and going forward they should continue to be. As the IEG evaluation recognizes, these reviews create discontinuities, as some criteria are added, dropped, or revised. The last major revision took place in 2004, informed by the recommendations of an external panel that undertook an in-depth review of the CPIA. Consensus on development thinking moves slowly, and revisions should be undertaken with sufficient intervals so that the CPIA scores have some consistency over time. From the standpoint of country relations and aid volatility, it is also important to avoid situations where changes in scores result from modifications in the criteria rather than from a deterioration or improvement in country performance. The CPIA is used by other multilateral development banks and an extensive consultation process would be necessary. The IEG evaluation found that "perhaps the time has come… for a thorough review of the CPIA" (chapter 2). Management broadly agrees but underscores that such a review needs to be carefully planned and done in the context of IDA 16. The specific suggestions provided in the IEG evaluation will inform this review, to be completed by the time IDA 16 is launched.

(continued on next page)

Management Action Record

Independent Evaluation Group (IEG) Recommendations Requiring a Response	Management Response
Consider not producing an overall CPIA index although continue to produce and publish the separate CPIA components.	***Agreed.*** Management will take this IEG recommendation into consideration in the context of the review of the CPIA mentioned above. IEG's rationale for this recommendation is that producing the different components of the CPIA without assigning weights to them in order to arrive at an aggregate index would allow different weights to be applied according to country context and uses. In management's view, in the absence of robust evidence as to what these weights should be, there is value in applying a uniform weighting scheme across all countries and producing an overall index that summarizes the information contained in the different criteria and provides a clear reference point. Moreover, because the scores for all the criteria are disclosed, nothing prevents the users from creating an alternative index based on their preferred set of weights. As part of the review of the CPIA, management will consider whether or not to produce an overall index.

Young boy sitting by centuries-old cistern, Hababa, Republic of Yemen. Photo by Bill Lyons/World Bank

Chairman's Summary: Committee on Development Effectiveness (CODE)

The Committee on Development Effectiveness (CODE) considered the report *The World Bank's Country Policy and Institutional Assessment (CPIA) – An Evaluation*, prepared by the Independent Evaluation Group (IEG), and the draft Management Response. A statement by the external advisory panel on the IEG report was distributed as background document for the meeting.

Summary

The Committee welcomed the timely discussion of the IEG report, which confirms the usefulness of CPIA as a broad indicator of development effectiveness. The Committee noted that the CPIA is not only being used for allocation of International Development Association (IDA) resources, but also for other purposes such as the debt sustainability framework, for which an assessment on the impact of the CPIA review was requested. In this vein, there was an agreement that the purpose of the CODE discussion was not to address the use of CPIA in the performance-based allocation formula for IDA.

The discussion focused on the four recommendations in the evaluation. Members and management broadly agreed with IEG's findings on the content of the CPIA and the recommendation to review the individual CPIA criteria. There was extensive discussion about IEG recommendation to disclose International Bank for Reconstruction and Development (IBRD) ratings. Some members questioned the value added of disclosing CPIA for IBRD and stressed the importance of consultations with the countries being rated
before further considering the matter. Others endorsed the recommendation and the benefits of disclosure for accountability and transparency, although they recognized the complexity of this issue. There was general consensus that further review and consultations would be needed with a view to consider improving transparency over time. Regarding "accounting for the stage of development" in the CPIA exercise, some members believed that this dimension should still be incorporated in CPIA and supported management's proposal to clarify the relevant staff guidelines.

Recommendations and Next Steps

The Committee recommended to management the following:

The review of the CPIA should take into account the comments and suggestions raised at the meeting to enhance its quality. This would include reviewing the CPIA criteria as called for in the evaluation—for example, with respect to trade and finance, social and environmental components, and incorporation of criteria on disadvantaged groups in addition to gender, and engaging client countries. The next steps are:

- Management will undertake a thorough review of the CPIA in the context of IDA 16.
- IEG will disclose its report together with the Management Response and the summary of CODE discussion.

Main Issues Discussed

Disclosure of IBRD ratings. Differing views were expressed on this recommendation. Some speakers disagreed and recommended a more prudent and cautious approach to consider the value added of CPIA for IBRD countries. It was noted that the disclosure of CPIA for IDA countries was related to its use for the allocation of IDA resources, that the CPIA did not play a role in determining IBRD lending envelopes, and that IBRD countries were not consulted on their CPIA. Others supported the IEG recommendation to extend disclosure to IBRD countries in the spirit of transparency and accountability, suggesting that this may be done on a voluntary basis or for selected clusters of indicators, and always consulting the concerned countries before moving to disclosure. There was also a proposal to extend the indicator to industrialized countries. One speaker underscored that the CPIA is an indicator that tries to measure very different countries against a single benchmark.

Stage of development. Some members agreed with management on the importance of clarifying the staff guidelines rather than removing the "accounting for the stage of development" in the CPIA exercise as recommended by IEG. Others pointed out the need to know the effect of removing the "accounting for the stage of development" on IDA allocations before endorsing the recommendation. One speaker stressed the need for CPIA to guide allocations in a fair, transparent, and effective manner. In this regard, members raised questions on how to synthesize effectively or prioritize specific issues such as governance, and how to strike a balance on "soft" versus "hard" macro issues. In particular, there was support for strengthening the "soft" indicators in the CPIA.

Review of CPIA. Members broadly encouraged management to undertake a thorough review of the CPIA and revise the content and criteria as recommended by IEG. In this regard, there were comments on the lack of agreement in the literature on the impact of aid assistance on growth and on the evidence to justify the large emphasis on governance; the need to avoid overlaps and further enhance the reliability of CPIA ratings; the linkage with Country Assistance Strategies and single country exposure framework; and disclosure of the CPIA methodology. Management indicated that the review of the CPIA will also analyze the issues of the value added and cost of preparing a CPIA for IBRD countries. The conclusion of this work will inform management's decision on how to go forward.

Overall CPIA Index. There were different views expressed on the need to produce an overall CPIA index although continue producing and publishing the separate CPIA component. Some speakers noted that it was inevitable to have one overall index.

Giovanni Majnoni, Chairperson

Advisory Panel Statement

Comments by Jürgen Zattler on some of the recommendations
Deputy Director General, Federal Ministry of Economic Cooperation and Development, Germany

The Independent Evaluation Group (IEG) suggests removing accounting for the stages of development from the Country Policy and Institutional Assessment (CPIA) exercise:

- It is much more difficult for a small fragile state to account for all standards that the CPIA demands than for India. Hence, there would be an unfair treatment for less-developed countries to receive a fair allocation.
- Alternatively to accounting for stages of development by regional and network reviewers, there could be a more differentiated weighting of the various criteria. The most important criteria to fulfill for a least-developed country in fragility should be weighed higher. Hence, fragile states can achieve a higher rating quickly if they concentrate on the most urgent criteria first. This measure also provides an incentive system to sequence measures for development.

IEG recommends that it should be considered not to produce an overall CPIA index although continue producing and publishing the separate CPIA components.

- If the separate clusters should be weighed individually according to the individual country situation, then this would be in line with my proposal above to weigh criteria according to their importance for development.

IEG recommends a thorough review of CPIA and revise criteria if necessary. This I can fully support.

- Criterion 8 can be dropped or reformulated possibly measuring policies aimed at poverty reduction such as agriculture (as proposed in the review) or even infrastructure.
- Assessment of other marginalized socio-economic groups besides gender should be definitely integrated. In general, participation and minority protection could be integrated (possibly in the governance cluster).
- There should be a separation of social sectors and environment, possibly creating a separate environmental cluster with more differentiated criteria, but with a reduced number of questions for the reviewers.

IEG suggests that there is no proof that the high weight of the governance cluster increases loan performance.

- Establishing good governance is one of the core and most difficult tasks for a fragile state or a least-developed country and managing to do so could be especially rewarded by weighing the governance cluster higher.

IEG suggests the disclosure of CPIA ratings for International Bank for Reconstruction and Development (IBRD) countries to increase transparency. I support this.

- However, there might be many further issues where transparency and accountability can be better addressed (such as publishing the margin of error, and increased use of external sources for double-checking). The review could have touched upon more issues.

We would like to emphasize our support for the contents of the articles in chapter 2 regarding revising the *trade* and *financial sector* criteria.

Comments by K.Y.Amoako
Executive Secretary,
Economic Commission for Africa
United Nations Under-Secretary General

The IEG report should provide a sound basis for streamlining the structure, criteria and indicators of the CPIA to enhance its alignment to the goals of economic growth, poverty reduction and development effectiveness. The report also provides the basis to discuss where to position the CPIA's process and results in the World Bank's toolkit for improving the effectiveness of its support for economic growth and poverty reduction.

The recommendations for changes in the criteria for trade to include exports and reduce the weight given to trade protection, and for the inclusion of agriculture as a criteria in the CPIA, are welcome. These are particularly germane for growth and poverty in Sub-Saharan Africa. On trade, indicators of export diversification and compliance with regional integration obligations would be useful. Indicators for the agriculture criterion should not only focus on public expenditures on agriculture, but should also seek to reflect progress in research and extension services, adoption of new technologies, strengthening land tenure, provision of credit to farmers, as well as marketing, distribution and pricing issues.

Expanding microcredit and developing microcredit institutions can help to enhance financial intermediation and to develop financial services and contribute to the deepening of the financial sector in general. Thus, the inconclusive evidence on the growth impact of microfinance notwithstanding, its place in the CPIA should be retained.

The overarching nature of governance would justify the large overweighting. Besides, for those countries with long periods of poor governance, the potential impact of improvements in governance may be large compared to other clusters. However, the indicators in the governance cluster, particularly in q15 and q16, may not be the most relevant indicators to assess progress in governance in low-income countries,

particularly since governance challenges tend to be country specific. Furthermore, reliable information may not exist to make objective assessments, and staff of the World Bank may not possess the required skills/competencies to make the right calls on these issues that require deep appreciation of the political economies. There is a need for more work on the governance criteria to strengthen the relevance of governance indicators, identify gaps in information and take steps to close those gaps. Work in this area would gain from the use on national and regional governance experts that are close to the scene.

The recommendation that the Bank not produce an overall CPIA index, although continuing to produce and publish the separate CPIA component, is a good one. An aggregate index is not likely to be a basis for informed policy discussions and probably takes away the focus on the component ratings, where debate and analysis would be most useful.

The report notes that "the strength of the CPIA ratings is Bank staff professional judgment." Thus the process through which the Bank harvests its considerable expertise for the CPIA is important. The evaluation report assumes that the process is fine. Nonetheless one may question whether the existing process, which could be viewed as overly bureaucratic, is best for tapping the expertise in the World Bank. Other related issues include the nature of consultations with governments and other informed stakeholders, support for economic and sector work and the quality of the statistical information base. For low-income countries, the Bank is the main source of economic and sector analysis and support for statistics development invariably depends on external assistance. Countries with a combination of relevant World Bank staff with limited experience, limited recent economic and sector work and lack of good statistics, may end up with unreliable CPIA ratings.

The CPIA is carried out every year. This could be too frequent as the policies, institutions and performance do not change that rapidly. Furthermore, the annual revisions of the International

Development Association (IDA) allocations cannot be helpful to country programming by the World Bank and budget planning by the governments. Although the CPIA does stimulate thinking about a range of development issues, it is not a substitute for detailed policy and institutional analysis that would help the countries make policy and build institutions. Is the CPIA crowding essential country work in the environment of constrained administrative budgets? In particular, there is the question of value addition of the CPIA for non-IDA countries and thus the need for CPIA for non-IDA countries.

Comments by Ravi Kanbur
T.H. Lee Professor of World Affairs and Economics
Cornell University

I welcome this report on the CPIA. It is a thorough assessment and it raises a number of important issues that Bank management needs to address. Moreover, given the key role played by the CPIA in the IDA allocation process, and in many analytical contributions to the development literature, the report's assessments are of interest to the broader development community as well. By and large, I support the analysis and the recommendations of the report. However, in my comments I will highlight where I think the conclusions could have been much sharper.

I will structure my comments around the four principal recommendations of the report.

First, disclose the ratings for IBRD countries.

I agree. But the report could call for more transparency all around.

One suggestion is that *all* previous ratings, IBRD and IDA, in *all* previous years, should be made public. There is no reason why this cannot be done. This will allow analysts in general, and not just Bank researchers, to analyze the relationships between the different components of the CPIA and development performance. The debate will serve to strengthen the review of

CPIA components that this report calls for (see below). I think the report should make this an explicit recommendation (or subrecommendation) to get management's response to it.

A second suggestion is that when the ratings are disclosed each year, the Bank should engage in a debate and discussion with local scholars and analysts on a country's ratings. A group of us did this a couple of years ago in Ghana, with some surprising results—some local scholars thought the Bank was being too soft on some scores.

A more radical option is to bring in local expertise at the time of rating—perhaps in the form of a standing panel of distinguished country experts who can provide their inputs to the Bank country team.

Second, remove accounting for the stage of development from the CPIA exercise.

The central issue here is country specificity (see also my comments on the third recommendation below). The conceptual foundation of the CPIA is a cross-country econometric regression of a development outcome (usually growth but it could be a social indicator as well) against a number of "right hand side" (RHS) variables. It is these RHS variables that the CPIA clusters and categories are meant to capture. But in any regression there are points above and below the line. The question is, do these deviations contain information, or are the deviations purely random, with no information content whatsoever? The difficulty for a CPIA type exercise arises because we think that there is indeed information content in the deviations—that the "Bangladesh paradox" (why does a country with such poor governance ratings does so well on social indicators?) is indeed a paradox.

As noted in the report, the "stage of development" accounting is a way of trying to put back country specificity. The intention is good but, as documented by the report, the way it is done is not. I support the recommendation to remove accounting for the stage of development as it is currently done, but this still leaves open the question of how country specificity is to be brought in to the assessment (see below).

Third, undertake a thorough review of the CPIA and revise the criteria as necessary.

I support this recommendation strongly. Indeed, after this major review I would suggest something like a cycle of three-year reviews. An alternative is to have a standing committee of external experts keep a watch on the CPIA process, with a major review every three-to-five years to incorporate new knowledge of the development process.

By and large I support the specific subrecommendations under this category. However, I would like to highlight a point which, although it is present in the report, is not emphasized enough. This is the importance of bringing in actual outcome variables in the CPIA. I have argued elsewhere (Kanbur 2005) —that bringing in the evolution of outcome variables is one way of factoring in country specificity that, for whatever reason, is not easily captured by the CPIA variables (think again of the Bangladesh paradox). As noted in the report, some outcome variables are already brought in to the CPIA assessment. The report itself argues for some more outcome variables, for example when it recommends "Revision of the trade criterion to include a subcomponent on exports that evaluates performance as well as policies and institutions."

My basic point is that the major review of the CPIA that is recommended in the report must explicitly address the question of systematic inclusion of outcome variables in the assessment as part of an overall investigation of how country specificity is to be brought into the assessment, which itself is part of the fundamental question which the review must start with—"What observable variables are good predictors of development performance along the dimensions we are interested in?"

Fourth, consider not producing an overall CPIA index although continuing to produce and publish the separate CPIA components.

I support this recommendation. It will then render transparent how different uses, for example the IDA allocation process, weight the different components. It will allow researchers to try out different weights for different purposes and advance the development debate in that way. But (see my comments on the first recommendation), in order for the research and the debate to be comprehensive, the Bank should release all previous ratings, component by component, for all previous years.

To conclude, let me say again that I welcome this report and I trust Bank management will respond to it positively.

Chapter 1

Evaluation Highlights

- This evaluation assesses the relevance of the CPIA criteria and the reliability of the ratings.
- The CPIA has evolved since its inception to cover 16 criteria in four clusters.
- Since IDA 12 the CPIA has been used to allocate IDA funds with a larger weight on the governance criteria—specifically, the governance cluster has 8.5 times the weight of each of the other three clusters.

Students in classroom, Turkey. Photo by Scott Wallace/World Bank

Introduction and Evolution of the CPIA

The Country Policy and Institutional Assessment (CPIA) assesses the quality of a country's present policy and institutional framework, with "quality" referring to the conduciveness of the framework to fostering poverty reduction, sustainable growth, and the effective use of development assistance (World Bank 2008b, p.1). It plays an important role in the country performance ratings (CPRs) that have been established annually since 1980 as a basis for the allocation of resources from the International Development Association (IDA) to eligible countries.

Although CPIA ratings were initiated and used for IDA allocation purposes, they can and are being used for wider purposes. For example, the Bank uses CPIA ratings for other corporate activities including the Global Monitoring Report. This evaluation takes the premise that beyond informing IDA allocations, the CPIA is useful as a broad indicator of development effectiveness.

Currently the CPIA consists of 16 criteria grouped into four clusters, with each cluster having equal weight in the overall CPIA rating. The four clusters are: economic management (cluster A); structural policies (cluster B); policies for social inclusion and equity (cluster C); and public sector management and institutions (cluster D) (see appendix A for a summary of the contents of each criterion).

This is the first self-standing evaluation of the CPIA by the Independent Evaluation Group (IEG). Prior to this, IEG had undertaken a review of the CPIA in the context of a "Review of the Performance-Based Allocation System" for its IDA 10–12 Review in 2001.[1]

Since the 2001 IEG review, there have been several developments and changes pertaining to the CPIA. These include two restructurings of the CPIA: in 2001 following the IEG[2] review, and in 2004 following an external panel review.[3] The external panel review of CPIA ratings and methodology was instituted by Bank management in the context of the discussions about broadening the disclosure of CPIA ratings for IDA-eligible countries. Other developments pertaining to the CPIA include IDA negotiations and the resulting changes in the country performance ratings used in the performance-based allocation (PBA) system for allocating IDA resources.

This evaluation will address the following questions:

1. What is the **relevance of the CPIA criteria** with respect to the policies and institutions that are important for sustained growth, poverty reduction, and the effective use of development assistance?

2. How **reliable are the CPIA ratings** (focusing on the most recently available ratings at the time of this writing, the 2007 ratings, in reflecting such policies and institutions in the countries concerned?

The evaluation assesses the relevance of CPIA criteria and the reliability of the CPIA ratings.

Chapter 2 of this report will evaluate the relevance of the CPIA criteria with respect to growth, poverty reduction, and the effective use of development assistance based on a review of the economics literature.

Changes to the CPIA in 1998 increased emphasis on institutions.

Chapter 3 will address the second question—the reliability of the CPIA ratings in two ways. First, it will compare the ratings of the various CPIA criteria with those of other indicators that measure similar criteria. Second, it will review the CPIA ratings generation process within the Bank.

Chapter 4 will summarize the findings presented in the previous chapters. Recommendations will be drawn aimed at strengthening the CPIA as an indicator that represents the factors in the country important for sustaining growth, fostering poverty reduction, and the effectiveness of development assistance.

The remainder of this chapter presents a brief discussion on the following: (i) the evolution in the content of the CPIA, including its relationship with the underlying development paradigm and IDA negotiations outcomes; (ii) other changes in the CPIA; and (iii) the role of the CPIA in the IDA allocation formula.

Evolution in the Content of the CPIA

The CPIA has been evolving since its introduction due either to changes in the Bank's thinking with respect to the development paradigm or to IDA negotiations, or to both. As stated by the Bank, "The [CPIA] methodology has evolved over time, reflecting lessons learned and mirroring the development paradigm"(World Bank 2004d).

Among the most prominent changes made to the CPIA were those introduced in 1998, the spirit of which has remained in place to date. The most important of the changes was the greater emphasis placed on institutions. Criteria were added to the CPIA on the capacity to manage and implement policies, and existing criteria were revised to include/emphasize institutional aspects (box 1.1). Greater weight was given to the public sector management cluster, which was raised from 14 percent of the CPIA in 1997 to 20 percent in 1998 (table 1.1).[4]

In addition, the Bank started emphasizing that the CPIA assess countries' policies and

---

Box 1.1: Changes to the CPIA Criteria in 1998 That Reflect the Emphasis on Institutions

Two criteria were added to the macroeconomic cluster, "macroeconomic management capacity" and "sustainability of structural reforms." The latter evaluates the commitment of the authorities to reforms and the support of such reforms from the society at large.

The criterion *legal and regulatory framework* was renamed *property rights and rule-based governance*, and specific references were added on contract enforcement, impartial judicial decisions, time spent by businessmen negotiating with bureaucrats, and theft and crime that raise the cost of doing business.

A specific reference to environmental regulations was added to the *environment* criterion.

The *civil administration* criterion was replaced by the criterion on *accountability of the public service*, with specific references added regarding accountability mechanisms, and the voice and participation of the general public in public activities.

Source: IEG, based on World Bank documents.

Table 1.1: CPIA Criteria 1998–2008

1998	2000	2004–08
Macroeconomic Management and Sustainability of Reforms (0.25)	**Economic Management (0.20)**	**Economic Management (0.25)**
General Macroeconomic Performance (0.05)	Management of Inflation and Current Account (0.05)	Macroeconomic Management (0.08) (q1)
Fiscal Policy (0.05)	Fiscal Policy (0.05)	Fiscal Policy (0.08) (q2)
Management of External Debt (0.05)	Management of External Debt (0.05)	Debt Policy (0.08) (q3)
Macroeconomic Management Capacity (0.05)	Management and Sustainability of the Development Program (0.05)	
Sustainability of Structural Reforms (0.05)		
Policies for Sustainable and Equitable Growth (0.40)	**Structural Policies (0.30)**	**Structural Policies (0.25)**
Trade Policy (0.05)	Trade Policy and Foreign Exchange Regime (0.05)	Trade (0.08) (q4)
Foreign Exchange Regime (0.05)		
Financial Stability and Depth (0.05)	Financial Stability and Depth (0.05)	Financial Sector (0.08) (q5)
Banking Sector Efficiency and Resource Mobilization (0.05)	Banking Sector Efficiency and Resource Mobilization (0.05)	
Competitive Environment for the Private Sector (0.05)	Competitive Environment for the Private Sector (0.05)	Business Regulatory Environment (0.08) (q6)
Property Rights and Rule-Based Governance (0.05)		
Factor and Product Markets (0.05)	Factor and Product Markets (0.05)	
Environmental Policies and Regulations (0.05)	Policies and Institutions for Environmental Sustainability (0.05)	

(continued on next page)

5

Table 1.1: CPIA Criteria 1998–2008

1998	2000	2004–08
Policies for Reducing Inequalities (0.15)	**Policies for Social Inclusion/ Equity (0.25)**	**Policies for Social Inclusion/ Equity (0.25)**
Pro-Poor Targeting of Programs (0.05)	Gender (0.05)	Gender Equality (0.05) (q7)
Safety Nets (0.05)	Equity of Public Resource Use (0.05)	Equity of Public Resource Use (0.05) (q8)
	Building Human Resources (0.05)	Building Human Resources (0.05) (q9)
	Social Protection and Labor (0.05)	Social Protection and Labor (0.05) (q10)
Poverty Monitoring and Analysis (0.05)	Poverty Monitoring and Analysis (0.05)	Policies and Institutions for Environmental Sustainability (0.05) (q11)
Public Sector Management (0.20)	**Public Sector Management and Institutions (0.25)**	**Public Sector Management and Institutions (0.25)**
Quality of Budget and Public Investment Process (0.05)	Property Rights and Rule-Based Governance (0.05)	Property Rights and Rule-Based Governance (0.05) (q12)
	Quality of Budgetary and Financial Management (0.05)	Quality of Budgetary and Financial Management (0.05) (q13)
Efficiency and Equity of Revenue Mobilization (0.05)	Efficiency of Revenue Mobilization (0.05)	Efficiency of Revenue Mobilization (0.05) (q14)
Efficiency and Equity of Public Expenditures (0.05)	Efficiency of Public Expenditures (0.05)	Quality of Public Administration (0.05) (q15)
Accountability of the Public Service (0.05)	Transparency, Accountability, and Corruption in the Public Sector (0.05)	Transparency, Accountability, and Corruption in the Public Sector (0.05) (q16)

Source: IEG, based on World Bank documents.
Note: Weight of the criterion in parenthesis.

the institutions that implement these policies, rather than development outcomes. Finally, the ratings were to be given based on the "level" of the countries' policies and institutions at the time, rather than the changes in these policies and institutions compared to the previous year, as had been done in the past. This in turn was predicated on the assumption that the levels of such policies and institutions were the main determinants of aid effectiveness.

The focus on the public sector continued in 1999. This reflected the interest of IDA deputies during the IDA 12 replenishment exercise. They noted that "accountability, transparency, the rule of law and participation represent four major pillars of governance that are critical to the development process and the effective use of IDA resources." This was also indicative of the new thinking by the Bank on public sector effectiveness. The weight of the public sector cluster was raised by another 5 percent to 25 percent with the transference of the criterion *property rights and rule-based governance* from the policies for sustainable and equitable growth cluster to the public sector cluster.

There was also a large increase in emphasis on social policies in 1999, reflecting the interest of IDA deputies during the IDA 12 Replenishment exercise. Two criteria were added to the social policy cluster: equality of economic opportunity and building human resources. The addition of these two criteria increased the weight of the social policy cluster from 15 percent in 1998 to 25 percent in 1999.

In sum, the changes in 1998 and 1999 resulted in much greater emphasis on social policies and on the public sector in the CPIA. The weights for these two clusters rose from 15 and 14 percent, respectively, to 25 percent each, and the weight for the economic management cluster fell from 25 to 20 percent, and that for the structural policies cluster fell similarly, from 40 to 30 percent.

Adjustments continued to be made to the CPIA after 1999 through 2003, although these were less extensive than those made in 1998 and 1999,

and the weights for the four clusters remained unchanged. The few prominent changes during this period included the replacement of the criterion on *equality of economic opportunity* by a criterion on *gender* in 2000. This effectively excluded discriminatory effects by socioeconomic group (for example, by race, caste, and ethnic group) from the assessment. Another change was the replacement of the criterion on *social safety net* by a criterion on *social protection and labor.* This broadened the assessment of the protection of the poor beyond safety nets, and reflected the new social protection strategy that was launched by the Bank at the time (World Bank 2000b).

In 1999, emphasis on social policies was increased in the CPIA.

The changes in 2001 included the addition of an explicit reference to economic growth in the assessment of fiscal policy. In 2002, domestic debt was included in the *public debt* criterion (formerly only external debt was covered), and other communicable diseases (in addition to human immunodeficiency virus/acquired immunodeficiency syndrome [HIV/AIDS], which was there already), was added to the *building human resources* criterion.

Finally, the most recent and major restructuring of the CPIA occurred in 2004. It was based on the recommendations of an external panel review of the CPIA noted above. Several changes were introduced. The number of criteria was reduced from 20 to 16. This entailed collapsing four criteria into two[5] and dropping two that were covered by other CPIA criteria.[6]

The content of virtually all the criteria was revised. For example, more detailed specification was provided on what was being assessed under each of the three criteria of the *economic management* cluster. Greater emphasis was also placed on customs and trade facilitation for the *trade* criterion. Assessment of gender disparities in political participation was added to the *gender* criterion. Tuberculosis and malaria were added to HIV/AIDS in the assessment of *building human resources* criterion, among other changes.

All the CPIA criteria were revised in 2004 and equal weights were given to each cluster.

7

Equal weights for each criterion were replaced by equal weights for each cluster. This raised the weight of the economic management cluster from 20 to 25 percent (bringing it back to the 1997–98 weight). The additional 5 percent weight given to the economic management cluster was effected by dropping the *monitoring and analysis of poverty outcomes and impacts* criterion from the social polices cluster. Although, ostensibly, the weight of the social policy cluster remained at 25 percent, it was only because the *environment* criterion was transferred to this cluster (from the structural policy cluster). In effect, therefore, the weight is lower for the non-environment social criteria. Between 2004 and 2008, the CPIA criteria and their weights remained unchanged.[7]

In 2004, the weight on the economic management cluster was raised from 20 to 25 percent, whereas the weight on the social policy cluster (excluding environment) was reduced from 25 to 20 percent.

In sum, over the past decade adjustments have been made to the CPIA with respect to the content, the number of criteria, and the weights of the criteria. Notwithstanding these adjustments, the coverage of the CPIA has remained largely unchanged since the changes in 1998–2000, which introduced the emphasis on the public sector and social policies (with the latter including the *gender* criterion) (table 1.1).

Although the CPIA is intended to assess policies and institutions, outcomes also affect ratings.

Other Changes in the CPIA

Many changes have been made over time in the preparation process of the CPIA ratings, some resulting from the findings of the IEG review of 2001 and the external panel review of 2004. The changes are as follows.

Benchmarking. Beginning in 1998, a benchmarking step has been introduced to the ratings process to strengthen the comparability of country scores. This entails the introduction of an initial phase in the CPIA preparation process of selecting and rating benchmark countries (IDA and IBRD), against which ratings for other countries would be compared during the CPIA preparation process.

The Bank's six regions, the networks, and the central departments are all involved in the selection of a representative sample of countries that cover all the regions and include IBRD- and IDA-eligible borrowers. Both good and poor performers are included in the sample, and the ratings of these countries have a similar distribution as the overall distribution of CPIA ratings. The set of benchmark countries is reviewed every year, taking into account the need to both maintain some continuity in the sample and to refresh it. The number of benchmark countries has increased from 11 in 1998 to 19 in 2008, with the inclusion of additional IDA countries comprising all of this increase. Over the same period, the share of IDA countries in the benchmarking group has risen from 45 to 68 percent.

Policies/institutions versus outcomes. As mentioned earlier regarding the evolution in the content of the CPIA, as part of the 1998 restructuring of the CPIA, the Bank emphasized that countries' policies and institutions are being assessed rather than outcomes. Nonetheless, in the instructions to staff (the CPIA questionnaire) with respect to preparing the ratings, it was clearly stated that Bank staff need to take into account country outcomes when assigning ratings, a statement that has remained in each of the CPIA questionnaires since then. Further, although most of the metrics and indicators specified for the assessment of various CPIA criteria are policies and institutions, for a few criteria outcome indicators were also included, in particular for the *financial sector* and for *gender.*

Rating scale and definition. In 1998, the rating scale was changed from five points to six points. In 2001, explicit definitions were provided for the rating levels of 2, 3, 4, and 5 for each of the CPIA criteria (previously only the 2 and 5 rating levels were defined). In 2004, the definition of rating levels was extended to rating levels 1 and 6. Prior to 2004, a "6" rating was given for criteria that had received a "5" rating for three or more years, and a "1" rating was given for criteria that had received a "2" rating for three or more years (World Bank 2003a).

Guideposts. These were introduced in 2001 and by 2005 were provided for each criterion. There have been both additions to and removal of guideposts since their introduction.

Country context. Since 2004, following the recommendations of the external panel review, a specific instruction has been added in the CPIA questionnaire that staff may need to take into account "the size of the economy and its degree of sophistication in implementing the guidelines." Specific references regarding this point have been added to the criteria on the *financial sector* and *social protection and labor*.

Written record. This requirement was introduced in 2001 for staff to provide written justification to accompany their rating proposals. The practice has been maintained since then.

Disclosure. At the start of IDA 12 in fiscal 2000, IDA initiated the disclosure, in quintile format, of the CPIA and IDA Country Performance (ICP) relative ratings for IDA eligible-countries. Management instructed country teams of IDA-eligible countries to discuss with each country's authorities their country's CPIA and ICP ratings and the resulting country IDA allocation. The quintile-based rating results for the CPIA, its four clusters, the country portfolio, and the quintile-based ICP rating were then posted on the external World Bank Web site.

On September 7, 2005, following the recommendation of the external review panel, the Board approved the disclosure of CPIA ratings for IDA eligible countries. For the first time in June 2006, IDA disclosed the numerical scores for all CPIA criteria and the overall score for all IDA-eligible countries as the "IDA Resource Allocation Index." This index is a misnomer, though, as IDA resources are actually not allocated according to this index, as will be discussed in the next section.

Role of the CPIA in IDA Allocation

The role of the CPIA in country performance assessments, and in turn in the allocation of IDA funds through the PBA formula, has evolved over time (see table 1.2). In particular, certain CPIA criteria—specifically those in the cluster on public

sector management and institutions (referred to as the *governance* criteria)—have played a greater role in IDA allocation than others, and their role in IDA allocation has received increased attention over the last decade.

Beginning in 1998 with IDA 12, and in response to IDA Deputies' suggestions, IDA allocations have been adjusted by the country's performance in the *governance*-related CPIA criteria and in procurement practices. According to IDA, "The stress on governance has evolved over the past decade and was put in place by donors because of its importance for improving the development performance of partner countries and for mitigating fiduciary risks to aid funds" (World Bank 2006b, p. i.).

Since 2004, the rating exercise is meant to take into account the size of the country and sophistication of its economy.

The governance adjustment was first introduced in 1998 for IDA allocations in the form of a governance discount. This was replaced by the governance factor in 2001 to address the problem of discontinuity in allocations under the governance discount. For both the governance discount and the governance factor, the adjustment took into account the ratings of the CPIA *governance* criteria and that of the procurement criterion of the Annual Review of Project Performance (ARPP).

Since IDA 12, greater weight has been given to the governance criteria for allocating IDA funds.

In 2004, the number of CPIA *governance* criteria included in the governance factor fell from six to five, as the 2004 restructuring of CPIA had removed one of the *governance* criteria. This reduced the effective weight of the *governance* criteria in the country performance rating from 68 to 66 percent. (See box 1.2 for a more detailed discussion of the evolution of the governance adjustment.)

Adjusting the country performance rating by the governance factor rendered the allocation formula more complex. The CPIA governance cluster and the procurement flag from the ARPP were double counted (see table 1.2). The exponential multiplier (of 1.5) on the governance rating (to arrive at the governance factor) made

Table 1.2: Evolution of IDA's Performance-Based Allocation Formula and the Adjustment for Governance

Period	Elements in the performance-based allocation formula (per capita)		Country Performance Rating CPIA	Portfolio performance rating	Governance adjustments in IDA allocation formula
1991–96	$GNPpc^{-0.25}$, $CPR^{1.8}$		100%[a]	0%	n.a.
1997	$GNPpc^{-0.125}$, $CPR^{0.5}$	CPR < 2	100%[b]	—	n.a.
	$GNPpc^{-0.125}$, $CPR^{1.6}$	2 < CPR < 2.9			
	$GNPpc^{-0.125}$, $CPR^{1.95}$	CPR >2.9			
1998–2000	$GNPpc^{-0.125}$, $(CPR/3)^{1.75}$	CPR < 3	80%	20%	Governance discount (introduced fiscal 2000): For countries with 3 or more ratings of 2 or below out of the 6 CPIA *governance* criteria, and over 30% of projects with deficient procurement practices (according to the ARPP rating), the CPR is cut by one-third.
	$GNPpc^{-0.125}$, CPR^2	CPR > 3			
2001–08	$GNPpc^{-0.125}$, CPR^2		CPR = (0.8*CPIA + 0.2*ARPP) * governance factor where governance factor = (governance rating/3.5)$^{1.5}$		2001–03: governance rating = average of 7 *governance* criteria (6 CPIA criteria plus procurement criterion of the ARPP portfolio rating). 2004–07: governance rating = average of 6 *governance* criteria (5 CPIA criteria plus a 3-year moving average of the procurement flag of the ARPP portfolio rating). Fiscal 2008: governance rating = average of 5 *governance* criteria
From fiscal 2009	$GNPpc^{-0.125}$, CPR^5		CPR = 0.24*$CPIA_{A-C}$ + 0.68*$CPIA_D$ + 0.08*Portfolio performance rating [c]		Governance rating = average of 5 *governance* criteria

Source: IEG, based on various IDA reports.

Note: ARPP = Annual Review of Project Performance; CPR = Country Performance Rating; GNPpc = Gross National Product Per Capita.

a. From 1998 through fiscal 2007, this was represented by the projects at risk rating in the ARPP. Projects at risk consist of actual and potential problem projects. Ratings of actual problem projects are done by task managers and reported in the implementation supervision reports. Ratings of potential problem projects are done by the Quality Assurance Group which looks at a number of criteria including the country's history of failure rate, defined as over 50 percent unsatisfactory outcome ratings by IEG. Beginning in 2001, the measurement of procurement enhancement was improved to capture not only the timeliness of the procurement process but also its quality. Beginning in fiscal 2008, only actual problem projects were included in the portfolio performance rating for the CPR. Hence, from then, the procurement flag has been dropped from the governance factor.

b. The CPIA included a portfolio performance element which made up 20 percent of the weight in 1994, 10 percent in 1995–96, and 7 percent in 1997.

c. CPIAA-C refers to CPIA clusters A (economic management), B (structural policies), and C (policies for social inclusion/equity), and CPIAD refers to CPIA cluster D (public sector management and institutions).

The formula used was very complex. the calculation and interpretation of the performance rating more complex.

The complexity of the allocation formula was especially problematic as IDA was taking steps to be transparent about how its resources were allocated, which led to the decision to disclose CPIA and country performance ratings beginning in June 2006 (see chapter 1, section on disclosure). In this light, at the Mid-Term Review of

Box 1.2: The Governance Adjustment in IDA's Country Performance Ratings, FY1998–2008

IDA introduced adjustments to the country performance ratings used in the performance-based allocation system in 1998, under IDA 12. These adjustments initially took the form of a governance discount. Specifically, IDA reduced the country performance rating in the allocation formula by one-third for those countries with three or more highly unsatisfactory ratings out of seven governance factors. Effectively, this reduced IDA allocations for those countries affected by the discount on average by half.

The 7 governance factors were 6 CPIA criteria plus the country's performance on procurement practices, according to the ARPP. The 6 CPIA criteria were: (i) *management and sustainability of structural reforms*; (ii) *property rights and rule-based governance;* (iii) *quality of budget and public investment process*; (iv) *efficiency and equity of revenue mobilization;* (v) *efficiency and equity of public expenditures*; and (vi) *accountability of the public service*. Ratings were considered to be highly unsatisfactory if they were "2" or below for the CPIA criteria and in the case of ARPP procurement criterion, if over 30 percent of projects had deficient procurement practices.

The governance discount produced a discontinuity effect at the point where the discount was triggered, with allocations dropping by one-half when only one criterion dropped from 2.5 to 2.0 (World Bank 2001b, p. 4). Perhaps because of this, there were upward pressures on the ratings at the cut-off point (World Bank 2002b, p. 4). IDA deputies were also concerned about the punitive bias of the governance discount, and the fact that it was not affecting all countries with weak governance (World Bank, 2002b, p. 4).

To address these drawbacks, the governance discount was replaced by a governance factor in 2001 (World Bank 2002b, p. 4),

which is equivalent to (governance rating/3.5).[1.5] The governance rating is derived from the country's average rating for the seven *governance* criteria mentioned above, with 3.5 being the mid-point of the rating. This governance factor is applied to the overall country performance rating. Under this new design, governance performance at all levels is taken into account in IDA allocations: countries that score above the mid-point on governance-related criteria receive a premium, and those that score below receive a discount.

There was still a discontinuity in allocation despite the replacement of the governance discount with the governance factor. Specifically, a one point drop in just one of the seven *governance* criteria results in a 7.5 percent drop in the overall IDA rating, and in turn a 15 percent drop in the country's allocation (World Bank 2003b, p. 2).

The seven *governance* criteria together had an effective weight of 68 percent in the IDA CPR. The effective weight fell slightly to 66 percent (World Bank 2004a, p. 3) in 2004 with the restructuring of the CPIA criteria that removed one of the *governance* criteria (the one on *management and sustainability of the development program*).

Adjusting the country performance ratings by the *governance* criteria raised the dispersion of these ratings, as was intended by IDA to better differentiate the allocated resources depending on the country's quality of governance. The governance adjustment also raised the volatility of the country performance ratings. The procurement ratings, in particular, were more volatile than ratings of the CPIA *governance* criteria. To address this issue, in 2004, IDA 14 introduced a three-year moving average for the procurement ratings (World Bank 2006a, p. 13).

Source: IEG, based on IDA documents.

IDA 14, IDA Deputies requested Bank management to "…simplify the allocation formula and reduce unwarranted ratings volatility" (World Bank 2006a).

IDA deputies decided that, beginning with IDA 15 (fiscal 2009), the country performance rating will be simplified to make the weights of the components more explicit. Specifically, the country performance rating (CPR) will be changed to:

$$CPR = (0.24 * CPIA_{A-C} + 0.68 * CPIA_D + 0.08 * \text{portfolio performance}),$$

where $CPIA_{A-C}$ refers to the average of the ratings of CPIA clusters A (economic management), B (structural policies) and C (policies for social inclusion/equity), and $CPIA_D$ refers to ratings of CPIA cluster D (public sector management and policies). Correspondingly, the PBA formula was changed from:

The formula has been simplified for IDA 15, making transparent the relative weights of the different CPIA clusters in the allocation formula—that is, that the governance cluster has 8.5 times the weight of each of the other clusters.

$$PBA = f(CPR^2, population, GNIpc^{-0.125})$$

to

$$PBA = f(CPR^5, population, GNIpc^{-0.125}),$$

where GNIpc is gross national income per capita. The exponent on the CPR was changed from 2 to 5 to maintain the same dispersion of ratings and therefore of allocations as before.[8]

These changes in the CPR (and associated change in the PBA) have made the IDA allocation formula more transparent—specifically that *CPIA cluster D has 8.5 times the weight of each of the clusters A–C in the CPR*. Yet, at the same time, by breaking up the CPIA into the different constituent parts that are used in the CPR, the changes have also made transparent the *weakness of the link between the overall CPIA index and IDA allocations*.

Chapter 2

Evaluation Highlights

- The CPIA covers the main determinants of sustained growth and poverty reduction, although some criteria can be usefully revised and streamlined and one added.
- The evidence is less clear regarding the relevance of the content of the CPIA for aid effectiveness broadly, that is, that it represents the policies and institutions important for aid to lead to growth.
- CPIA ratings are associated with a narrow definition of aid effectiveness, specifically the better performance of Bank loans.
- There is insufficient evidence to conclude that the governance cluster associates better with loan performance than the other clusters.
- The effects of a larger weight on governance in the IDA allocation formula (compared to equal weights on each cluster) are not due just to the governance rating but to how different that rating is compared to ratings on the other clusters.

Hong Kong, China

Relevance of the CPIA for Growth, Poverty Reduction, and Effective Use of Development Assistance

Accchording to the Bank, the CPIA assesses the quality of a country's present policy and institutional framework, where quality refers to how conducive that framework is to fostering poverty reduction, sustainable growth, and the effective use of development assistance (World Bank 2008b).

The review of economic literature (theoretical/conceptual as well as empirical) indicates that, by and large, the CPIA criteria pertain to policies and institutions that are found to be important for sustained growth and poverty reduction (and welfare more generally). The evidence is more mixed as to the criteria's importance for aid effectiveness.

The CPIA and Determinants of Sustained Growth

The literature on the determinants of sustained growth has undergone a significant evolution during the last 50 years. In the 1950s and 1960s, it was widely argued that long-run economic performance depends on capital investment and that raising savings through a "big push" (Rosenstein-Rodan 1943) would launch countries into self-sustaining growth or "take-off" (Rostow 1960). In the 1980s, the literature begins to emphasize the importance of a good economic policy environment (Williamson 1990; World Bank 1993) characterized by reduced tariffs, appropriate foreign exchange rates, and low inflation.[1] Then, in the 1990s, the literature emphasizes that these policies would have only limited impact in the absence of more fundamental institutional reforms (World Bank 1998).

Today, there is relative consensus in the literature around the idea that there is no single recipe for growth and that country specificities—including the country's stage of development—need to be taken into account.[2] Of course, countries can learn from each other, but no simple recipe can be pulled off the shelf to stimulate growth. Each country needs to learn through trial and error what works for it (World Bank 2004e). This does not mean, however, that there are no growth determinants. What it does point to is the need "...*to identify the exact set of policies and institutional changes needed to address binding constraints on growth, based on first principles in each instance*" (World Bank 2005).

By and large, this evaluation finds that the CPIA covers those growth determinants over which there is relative consensus in the literature. These are: institutions and governance; education; productivity and technological innovation; and equity and equality of opportunity (table 2.1).

The CPIA covers determinants of growth for which there is relative consensus.

Table 2.1: Mapping of the "Consensus" Determinants for Sustained Growth and the CPIA Criteria

Institutions and Governance	Security of Property rights	q12	Property Rights and Rule-Based Governance
	Rule of Law	q12	Property Rights and Rule-Based Governance
	Government Credibility, Corruption	q16	Transparency, Accountability, and Corruption in the Public Sector
	Quality of the Bureaucracy	q15	Quality of Public Administration
Human Capital	Education	q9	Building Human Resources
Investment, Productivity and Technological Innovation	Private investment		
	• Stable fiscal policy	q2	Fiscal policy
	• Stable monetary policy	q3	Debt policy
	• Sound financial systems	q13	Budgetary and financial management
	• Stable investment regimes	q14	Revenue mobilization
		q1	Macroeconomic management
	• Clear and transparent business environment	q5	Financial sector
		q6	Business regulatory environment
	• Labor mobility	q6	Business regulatory environment
	• Rule of law	q6	Business regulatory environment
	• Fighting corruption	q12	Property rights and rule-based governance
		q16	Transparency, accountability, and corruption in the public sector
	Public investment and infrastructure	q2	Fiscal policy
Equity and Equality of Opportunity	• Property rights	q12	Property rights and rule-based governance
	• Access to credit	q5	Financial sector
	• Access to education	q9	Building human resources
	• Gender equality	q7	Gender equality
	• Income transfers	q10	Social protection and labor

Sources: IEG, based on Cage (2009), background paper for this evaluation, and the CPIA 2008 questionnaire.

Three CPIA criteria do not appear in the above table: *trade* (q4), *equity of public resource use* (q8), and *environment* (q11). This does not mean, however, that they are not important for growth, only that there is less consensus in the literature on their impact on growth (specifically pertaining to *trade* and *environment)*, or what is important for the criteria already covered by other criteria in the CPIA (in the case of *equity of public*

The trade and environment criteria have less consensus in the literature. resource use). The evidence on the impact of *health* (part of q9) on growth is also inconclusive, although health is clearly important for welfare.

The rest of this section provides a brief summary of the literature on each of these determinants of growth—both those for which there is more consensus and those for which there is continuing controversy. The relationship between these

determinants and how they are treated in the CPIA will also be addressed.

Institutions and governance

Institutions and governance are among the main growth determinants around which there is relative consensus, and on which there is a sizeable literature (appendix B). In this literature, institutions refer to, variously, private property rights protection, contract enforceability, operation of the rule of law (including effectiveness and predictability of the judiciary, perception of the incidence of crime), the quality of the bureaucracy, accountability of the government (including independence of the media), and the extent of corruption.

The existing evidence on the impact of virtually all of these indicators on growth is positive. The one exception is corruption, where some earlier literature (from the mid-1960s to the mid-1990s) posits that corruption can have a positive impact on growth in instances where there are pre-existing policy distortions such as pervasive and cumbersome regulations, in which case corruption can help efficiency and growth. But all of the literature from the mid-1990s onward has found that corruption has a negative impact on growth (appendix B).

The institution and governance indicators identified in this literature are covered in three of the five governance indicators under the public sector management and institutions cluster of the CPIA. These are the criteria on *property rights and rule-based governance* (q12), the *quality of the bureaucracy* (q15), and *transparency, accountability, and corruption in the public sector* (q16).

The importance of institutions goes beyond these indicators. In particular, the institutional context within which policies are formulated is also important. For example, regarding macroeconomic policies, it is not just low and stable inflation that is important, but the conviction of the private sector that low and stable inflation is a permanent feature of the economic environment. The latter requires an appropriate institutional underpinning for price stability (World Bank 2005; Montiel and Servén 2006).

In the fiscal arena, an appropriate institutional setting needs to also ensure transparency, sustainable solvency, flexibility, and a pro-growth structure of the budget. The institutional aspects of macroeconomic (and fiscal) policy are covered in the *macroeconomic management* criterion (q1), the *fiscal policy* criterion (q2), the *quality of budgetary and financial management* criterion (q13), and the *efficiency of revenue mobilization* criterion (q14) of the CPIA.

Although there is adequate coverage of the policy (q2) and institutional (q13) aspects of fiscal management, an issue arises over the coordination of the assessment of these two criteria (in the Bank they are assessed by different groups).

This is particularly pertinent for low income countries which may perform well on the macro/fiscal stability front, yet have weak fiscal management capacity. In such cases, a good rating for q2 needs to be tempered by an appropriate rating for q13 in order that the fiscal aspect of the country in its entirety is realistically captured.

Similarly, finance depends on institutions, including informational and regulatory institutions, institutions that strengthen creditor rights, contract enforcement, and accounting practices and the legal and judicial framework (Levine, Loayza, and Beck 2000; World Bank 2005). These institutions are covered in the CPIA criteria on the *financial sector* (q5) and on *property rights and rule-based governance* (q12).

Human capital

Human capital—and in particular education—is one of the main determinants of sustained growth around which there is consensus in the literature. In particular, the link between primary enrollment and subsequent growth is well established in the literature (see appendix C). In addition, improvements in secondary and tertiary education systems are also important, depending on the stage of development of the country.[3] Education is adequately covered in the *building human resources* criterion (q9) of the CPIA, which includes assessment of both basic and post-basic education.

Although the importance of education on growth is clearly and strongly supported by evidence, the evidence on the impact of health on both the level of economic development (per capita incomes) and economic growth is less conclusive, mainly because population increases that result from better health have a negative effect on per capita income (see appendix C). Nonetheless, it is clear that health is important for welfare (the non-income dimension of poverty—see discussion later in this chapter).

The evidence on the impact of most institutional indicators on growth is positive.

The institutional context in which economic policies are formulated is important.

Although education is clearly important for economic growth, the evidence of health on economic growth is more mixed— although health is clearly important for welfare.

17

Investment, productivity, and technological innovation

It is widely acknowledged among economists that strong, enduring growth requires high rates of investment (World Bank 2008a; Aghion and Howitt 2009). All of the different growth theories have investment of one type or another driving growth.[4] Both private and public investments are important. Further, savings is equally important; indeed, the evidence shows that there is no case of a sustained high investment (and high growth) path that is not backed up by high savings (with the latter aided by fiscal prudence) (World Bank 2008a).

The CPIA covers the multiple elements necessary to foster private investment.

Private investment

Fostering private investment requires reducing risks for private investors, through stable fiscal and monetary policy, stable investment regimes, sound financial systems, and a clear and transparent business environment including flexibility of the labor market. It also requires ensuring the rule of law, and measures to fight corruption (World Bank 2001a).

The CPIA covers all these elements important for private investment in several of its criteria, including those on *macroeconomic management* (q1), *fiscal* (and *debt*) policies (q2 and q3), the *financial sector* (q5), *business regulatory environment* (q6), *property rights and rule-based governance* (q12), and *transparency, accountability, and corruption in the public sector* (q16).

Public investment, including for infrastructure, is covered in the criterion for fiscal policy.

All of the above criteria are conceptually distinct except for macroeconomic management, fiscal, and debt policies. Debt policies are clearly an intrinsic part of fiscal policies, and fiscal policies in turn are clearly also an intrinsic part of macroeconomic management. Indeed, the *macroeconomic management* criterion refers to public spending. It also refers to monetary/exchange rate policies aimed at price stability, which cannot be achieved without taking into account fiscal policies at the same time. Thus, it appears that the existing three macroeconomic criteria can be usefully assessed as one.

Public investment

Private investment needs to be complemented by public investment to enhance competitiveness and create new market opportunities. Complementary public investment in expanding infrastructure and communications and in upgrading the skills of the labor force is particularly important (Easterly and Rebelo 1993; World Bank 1994; Sachs 2005, 2008; Collier 2007; World Bank 2008a).

In fast-growing Asia, for example, public investment in infrastructure accounts for 5–7 percent of gross domestic product (GDP) or more. In China, Thailand and Vietnam, total infrastructure investment exceeds 7 percent of GDP. History suggests that this is the correct order of magnitude for high and sustained growth, although it is difficult to be precise (World Bank 2008a). Finally, public investment can be used as a tool to increase equality of opportunity, which is another determinant of sustained growth, discussed next. The CPIA covers public investment in it criterion on *fiscal policy* (q2), where there is an explicit reference to "*the provision of public goods, including infrastructure.... consistent with medium-term growth.*"

Equity and equality of opportunity

Development economics has seen a major shift in view regarding the role of inequality on growth, from one that initially saw increases in equality as a natural accompaniment to development (Kuznets 1955) or actually facilitating development (through the incentives it provides) (Lewis 1954) to the current view that inequality is detrimental to growth (Todaro 1997; Aghion, Caroli, and García-Peñalosa 1999; Bardhan 2000; Hoff and Stiglitz 2001). This view is supported by the results of several empirical (Alesina and Rodrick 1994; Perotti 1992, 1993, 1996; Persson and Tabellini 1994) and other studies (box 2.1).

Equality of opportunity is an important element, and indeed the starting point, of equity.[5] Systematic denial of opportunities to a group because of its ethnicity, religion, caste, or gender could

Box 2.1: Channels Through Which Inequality Affects Growth

Inequality can have adverse consequences on efficiency, and hence growth, through various channels. Inequality of wealth affects investment in physical and human capital. A better distribution of wealth reduces credit constraints; broader availability of credit has a significant and positive effect on growth (Perotti 1992; Bardhan 2000; World Bank 2005). Micropanel studies show that households with few physical and human assets are often caught in a poverty trap that sharply reduces their chance of economic advancement and thus harms the overall economic performance of the economy (Christiaensen, Demery, and Paternostro 2002; Woolard and Klasen 2005).

Inequality often induces more political instability, as well as crime and insecurity of property rights, all of which depress investment and productivity growth (Alesina and Perotti 1996; Bardhan 2000). Inequality (in the form of unequal access to investment opportunities) can lead to macroeconomic volatility (Aghion, Caroli, and Garcia-Penalosa 1999), which in turn has been found to reduce growth (Hausmann and Gavin 1996; Breen and Garcia-Penalosa 2005). Finally, too much inequality may also lead to social tension expressed through violent redistribution, which has a negative impact on growth (Bourguignon 2004).

Source: Cage (2009a)

undermine social peace and spark political unrest (World Bank 2008a). There is evidence that gender inequality—particularly in access to education—reduces economic growth as it fails to make adequate use of female resources (World Bank 2001a; Klasen 2002; Knowles, Lorgelly, and Owen 2002; Klasen and Lamanna 2003).

The literature has provided some measures that can improve equality and equality of opportunity. These include strengthening property rights over land (Besley and Burgess 2003), expanding access to education (Bardhan 2000; Dreze and Sen 2002; Chhibber and Nayyar 2007), and means-tested income transfers.[6] Strengthening property rights over rural land has resulted in higher agricultural productivity and output in China (Lin 1992) and India (Banerjee, Gertler, and Ghatak 2002); and strengthening land rights in urban areas can help poor households gain access to credit (De Soto 2000; Field 2002). Redistribution of land has played an important role in fostering economic growth;[7] today, such reforms would take the form of subsidized transactions in the land market (Bardhan 2000; Bourguignon 2004).

Access to credit is also important for reducing inequality (Aghion, Caroli, and Garcia-Penalosa 1999; Bardhan 2000; Besley and Burgess 2003; Beck, Demirguc-Kunt, and Levine 2004; Bourgui-

gnon 2004). There is a debate, however, as to how important microfinance is compared with overall financial development (as measured by private sector credit as a share of GDP intermediated through the formal banking sector). There are individual success stories of microfinance, including from impact assessments that show microfinance in general helps the poor, although all participants may not benefit equally.[8] However, other studies find that overall financial development (measured by financial depth) has had a larger and more certain impact on growth and poverty reduction than the expansion of microfinance (Honohan 2004b; Beck, Demirguc-Kunt, and Levine 2004).

Equality of opportunity is an important starting point for equity.

Although access to credit is clearly important, the importance of microfinance is less clear.

The CPIA covers the measures for equity (redistribution) and for equality of opportunity identified in the literature. These include *property rights* (q12); *access to credit* (q5); *access to education* (q9); *gender equality* (q7); and *income transfers* (q10) (table 2.1). The *financial sector* criterion covers both financial depth and microfinance. Thus, it covers all relevant ground irrespective of whether microfinance is important.

There are two issues related to the equity and equality aspect of growth that are important for the CPIA. The first is that only gender issues are included in the assessment. Concerns related to other socioeconomic groups that are discriminated against (due to race, caste, ethnic group) are not included. Yet evidence indicates that poverty can have a strong ethnic dimension in some countries (Bodewig and Sethi 2005). This implies that tackling social exclusion of such groups is important not only for reducing poverty, but also for raising growth for the country as a whole.

Although equity is important, it is already covered in other CPIA criteria and in ways more amenable to assessment than the criterion on equity of public resource use.

The second issue is whether a criterion on *equity of public resource use* is needed. The criterion has two subcomponents: public expenditures (66.6 percent weight) and revenue collection (33.3 percent weight) that affect the poor. According to the relevant network's review team, the assessment of public expenditures focuses on spending on education, health, rural infrastructure, and safety nets. Of these, education and safety nets have been identified in the literature as being important and, as mentioned in the previous paragraph, they are already covered by two other CPIA criteria, q9 (*education*) and q10 (*safety nets*). As for the other two items, spending on health is also covered in q9, and spending on rural infrastructure could be explicitly mentioned in the *fiscal policy* criterion (which already mentions public spending on infrastructure).

Integration into the global economy is important for growth, but the CPIA trade criterion does not allow for flexibility in the approach or give adequate attention to exports.

According to also to the network review team, the public revenue subcomponent, which focuses on whether taxes are progressive or regressive, is very difficult to assess. Such an assessment needs to be based on incidence analyses, which are typically not undertaken for many countries (or at best undertaken sporadically), so that results are generally outdated even if existent. In other words, Bank staff does not have enough information to meaningfully rate this subcomponent. The lack of information is even more acute for IBRD countries, as the issue is not as important for them.

In sum, the public expenditure subcomponent of the *equity of resource use* criterion is captured

by other CPIA criteria, although there is not enough information to meaningfully rate the public revenue subcomponent. At the same time, some socioeconomic groups that are discriminated against are not included in the assessment on equity and equality of opportunity. The recommendation is to replace the criterion on *equity of resource use* with a criterion on *equity and equality of opportunity for other socioeconomic groups*. Alternatively, there can be a reformulation of the criterion on *equity of resource use* by, among other things, incorporating an assessment of other socioeconomic groups.

Integration into the global economy

Integration into the global economy is a widely accepted determinant of growth although there is considerable debate in the literature on how this can be achieved. The experience of the 1990s demonstrates that there are many possible ways to integrate globally (World Bank 2005). The challenge is for policy makers to identify which best suits their country's political economy, institutional constraints, and initial conditions. Some analysts are in favor of granting temporary modest levels of import protection to emerging industries where there is a demonstrated need (Williamson 2004). Others have focused on choosing the right form of protection, advocating subsidies to initial entrants rather than the use of import duties. Indeed, when tariffs (the reduction of which is the most common policy prescription for trade openness) are tried as an explanatory variable for growth, they are not found to be statistically significant (Rodrik 2000).

The experience of the 1990s also indicates that trade reforms need to be part of a comprehensive growth strategy in order to be successful. Efforts to promote exports would need to be part of such a growth strategy, as the experience also shows that the successful liberalizers either explicitly or implicitly promote export growth (World Bank 2005). Many complementary factors are needed for export growth, the most important of which are macroeconomic stability and the building of trade-related infrastructure and institutions.

The CPIA criterion on *trade* (q4) covers trade policy restrictions (tariffs and non-tariff barriers) and custom and trade facilitation, with 75 and 25 percent weights, respectively. The CPIA guidelines provide instructions on the specific tariff rates for each of the ratings. This is problematic on at least two fronts. It does not allow for flexibility in trade reform approaches that have proven to work in different countries. Also, the implicit assumption behind the relative weights—that tariff reduction is much more important than complementary institutions for successful liberalization—is not supported by the evidence.[9] In particular, country experience in the 1990s indicates that at moderate levels of tariffs (which practically all countries currently have), further tariff reduction is not as important as complementary factors for successful integration into the global economy.

Further, the *trade* criterion in the CPIA does not give adequate attention to exports. Granted, a reduction in tariffs should promote exports,[10] and there is evidence that this was indeed the case in the 1990s (World Bank 2005). At the same time, however, tariff reduction by itself is not enough, especially in light of the possibility of different approaches to trade liberalization.

It would be useful if the CPIA *trade* criterion could add a subcomponent on exports (with equal weights, as for trade restrictions and trade facilitation) that assesses export performance, restrictions on exports (such as export taxes), and policies/institutions to reduce anti-export bias, such as having a functional export rebate or duty drawback system. The last is one of the indicators covered under the *efficiency of revenue mobilization* criterion, which could usefully be shifted to the *trade* criterion.

Environmental sustainability

A recent IEG evaluation (IEG 2008) on the environment finds that links among growth, poverty, and environment are complex and run in both directions. Many, if not all, environmental problems improve as output levels rise, but they may get worse before they get better.[11]

According to that IEG evaluation, the costs associated with environmental degradation—such as public health costs of pollution or soil nutrient loss from uncontrolled erosion—often reduce productivity, resulting in lower rates of economic growth than would otherwise be the case. Beyond this, people are frequently impoverished by a declining resource base and forced by their circumstances to further degrade the environment.

Hence, it seems reasonable that growth strategies in developing countries need to take into account environmental concerns from the outset, even if they do not immediately adopt the toughest environmental standards applied in developed countries (World Bank 2008a). The CPIA has a criterion that assesses environmental policy and regulations on pollution and natural resources.

The CPIA takes account of country specificity such as the size of the economy and stage of development.

Country specificity

The CPIA does take into account country specificity, and in particular the stage of development. Specifically, the CPIA guidelines indicate that "Staff may need to take into account the size of the economy and its degree of sophistication in implementing the guidelines." Specific references are added on this for the *financial sector* and *social protection and labor* criteria. Yet there are significant issues pertaining to the implementation of this in the CPIA exercise, which are discussed in chapter 3.

The application of equal weights to all four clusters does not allow for country specificity in the sense that different countries may face different policy and institutional priorities.

In addition to the stage of development, another important aspect of country specificity is the notion that different policies and/or institutions can produce similar outcomes. The CPIA instruction to staff to take into account outcomes when assessing policies and institutions could help to address this aspect of country specificity. Some criteria already assess outcomes, although outcome variables could be added to other criteria, in particular *trade*.

Links between growth, poverty, and the environment are complex and run in both directions.

Yet another aspect of country specificity is the fact that different countries may face different sets of

The four CPIA clusters are highly correlated, so the weighting scheme does not matter much for representing the overall policies and institutions of a country, but they do matter for the allocation of IDA funds.

institutional or policy priorities. Taking this into account would require larger weights to be applied to those criteria/clusters that are more important (or are the "binding constraints") to growth. The Global Competitiveness Index has, as of 2009, taken steps in this direction by applying different weights (derived based on econometric analysis) to different components of the index for countries at different stages of development (World Economic Forum 2008). Currently, the application of equal weights to each of the four CPIA clusters does not allow for this aspect of country specificity. Chapter 3 will discuss the ways in which the different aspects of country specificity are addressed in the CPIA rating exercise.

Weighting scheme of the CPIA

Country specificity aside, the question of how to weight the various criteria in the CPIA has also drawn a lot of attention because of the much greater weight given to cluster D (the governance cluster) in the formula for IDA allocation (see chapter 1). There are three main observations pertaining to weighting.

First, the CPIA ratings for the four clusters are relatively highly correlated (table 2.2), with the correlation coefficients ranging from 0.65 between clusters A and B to 0.88 between clusters C and D. This implies that countries that perform well on one cluster generally perform well on the other clusters.

Second, it follows from the relatively high correlations that the weighting scheme used for the CPIA does not matter very much in terms of representing the overall policies and institutions of a country. This can be seen from the relatively high correlations between an unequally weighted CPIA (no matter which cluster gets the greater weight) and a CPIA with equal weights on the four clusters (table 2.3).

Third, different weights on the CPIA clusters do, however, and very importantly, matter for the allocation of IDA funds, as discussed below.

As an illustration, this evaluation undertook simulations to compare the PBA under a weighting scheme of equal weights for each cluster (as is done for the CPIA overall country score) and a scheme of greater weight on governance (as is done in the PBA formula). The simulation replaced the country performance ratings (CPR) in the PBA formula with equal weights on the four clusters, holding all the other factors that affect the PBA constant.[12] The simulation was performed on "core" IDA countries—that is, those that are not subject to exceptions to the PBA due to post-conflict or re-engaging status or to caps on allocations.[13]

The simulation results indicate quite substantial changes to the PBA of countries (table 2.4). Although the simulations are based on data on

Table 2.2: Correlations between Ratings of CPIA Clusters, 2007

	CPIA$_A$	CPIA$_B$	CPIA$_C$	CPIA$_{overall}$
CPIA$_A$	1.00	0.65	0.71	0.87
CPIA$_B$	0.65	1.00	0.77	0.89
CPIA$_C$	0.71	0.77	1.00	0.91
CPIA$_D$	0.73	0.84	0.88	0.94

Source: IEG.

Table 2.3: Correlations between CPIA with Different Cluster Weights and CPIA with Equal Cluster Weights, 2007

Cluster that has the greater weight (as in PBA formula)	Correlation with overall CPIA (equal-weighted clusters)
Cluster A	0.93
Cluster B	0.95
Cluster C	0.96
Cluster D	0.97

Source: IEG.

Table 2.4: Simulation Results: Effects on Performance-Based Allocations for "Core IDA" Countries Arising from a Larger Weight on the "Governance" Cluster Compared to Equal Weights on All Clusters

	Change in performance-based allocation (%)	Rating of governance cluster (cluster D)	Average rating of clusters A to C	Rating of cluster D as a share of average rating of clusters A to C (%)
Country 1	31.4	3.4	3.4	99.7
Country 2	31.4	3.4	3.4	99.7
Country 3	27.4	3.9	4.0	98.3
Country 4	20.5	3.2	3.3	96.0
Country 5	19.5	3.3	3.5	95.5
Country 6	16.8	3.5	3.7	94.3
Country 7	15.3	3.7	3.9	94.1
Country 8	15.0	3.3	3.5	94.0
Country 9	14.3	3.5	3.7	93.7
Country 10	13.1	3.5	3.8	93.2
Country 11	11.4	3.5	3.8	92.6
Country 12	9.5	3.5	3.8	92.1
Country 13	6.2	3.2	3.5	90.9
Country 14	5.9	3.0	3.3	90.6
Country 15	4.6	3.3	3.7	90.3
Country 16	4.1	3.5	3.9	90.0
Country 17	2.8	3.2	3.6	89.4
Country 18	1.0	3.3	3.7	88.9
Country 19	0.3	3.3	3.7	88.4
Country 20	−0.2	3.5	4.0	88.5
Country 21	−1.5	2.8	3.2	87.8
Country 22	−1.6	3.4	3.9	87.9
Country 23	−1.9	3.4	3.9	86.9
Country 24	−2.1	2.9	3.3	87.0
Country 25	−4.1	2.7	3.1	86.8
Country 26	−4.2	3.3	3.8	86.6
Country 27	−6.2	3.0	3.5	85.7
Country 28	−8.3	2.9	3.5	83.9
Country 29	−8.7	3.3	3.9	85.1
Country 30	−12.7	3.7	4.4	83.3
Country 31	−13.0	2.7	3.3	82.1
Country 32	−15.2	3.0	3.6	82.3

(*continued on next page*)

Table 2.4: Simulation Results: Effects on Performance-Based Allocations for "Core IDA" Countries Arising from a Larger Weight on the "Governance" Cluster Compared to Equal Weights on All Clusters (*continued*)

	Change in performance-based allocation (%)	Rating of governance cluster (cluster D)	Average rating of clusters A to C	Rating of cluster D as a share of average rating of clusters A to C (%)
Country 33	−16.0	2.9	3.6	81.3
Country 34	−16.3	2.2	2.7	81.5
Country 35	−17.1	3.7	4.6	81.0
Country 36	−18.2	3.3	4.1	80.9
Country 37	−18.6	3.2	4.0	80.9
Country 38	−20.4	2.7	3.4	79.9
Country 39	−27.3	2.5	3.3	74.8
Country 40	−29.4	2.6	3.5	75.2
Country 41	−32.5	2.9	3.9	73.9

Source: IEG.

Note: "Core IDA" countries refer to those IDA countries that are not subject to exceptions to the PBA due to post-conflict or re-engaging status or to caps on allocations. Small states are also excluded because their base allocations exceed the PBA.

actual countries, the names of the countries are not presented in the table. It should be noted that the PBA constitutes only part of the overall IDA allocation, which also includes a base allocation of special drawing rights (SDR) 1.5 million per country per year. The simulation results demonstrate that, as intended by the PBA formula, a country that has a higher rating on the governance cluster but the same average ratings on the other three clusters compared to another country would gain (from the larger weight on governance compared to equal weights for all clusters), whereas the other country would lose. This can be seen from the simulation results for country 5 and country 27, both of which have the same average rating of 3.5 for clusters A–C, but country 5 has a higher rating of 3.3 for cluster D compared to country 27's rating of 3.0. Under the current PBA formula, country 5 would have a PBA nearly 20 percent higher than a formula for which all clusters have equal weights, whereas country 27 would have a PBA of 6 percent lower.

The effects of a larger weight on governance (compared to equal weights for each cluster) on the PBA are not due just to the governance rating, but also to how different that rating is compared to ratings on other clusters.

At the same time, however, the much larger weight on the governance cluster (compared to equal weights on each cluster) has also led to perhaps unexpected results. Specifically, the simulation results indicate that *the effects of the much larger weight on governance on the PBA are not due just to the governance rating, but to how different the governance rating is from ratings on other clusters.*

Two countries, country 4 and country 30, can be used as examples to illustrate this point. Country 30 has a better governance rating (3.7) than country 4 (3.2). Country 30 also performs better on all the other clusters compared to country 4, with the ratings for clusters A to C averaging 4.4 compared to country 4's average rating of 3.3. Yet, country 30 suffers a loss in PBA of 13 percent under the current PBA formula (compared to a formula with equal weights on all four clusters), whereas country 4 actually gains 20.5 percent. These results are attributable to the fact that country 30's governance rating is much worse than its ratings on other clusters, whereas country 4's ratings on governance are only slightly worse than its ratings on the other clusters. In other words, country 30 suffers a loss under the current PBA formula not because it has poor governance, but because its governance performance relative to performance on other fronts is worse than that of country 4, even though it performs better than country 4 on all fronts.

More generally, table 2.4 shows that all core IDA countries (excluding small states) have worse governance ratings than ratings on other clusters, yet some countries gain and other countries lose from the larger weight on governance. Whether they gain or lose depends on how much worse the ratio of their governance ratings to ratings on other clusters is than other countries (figure 2.1).

The CPIA and Determinants of Poverty Reduction

It is a straightforward supposition that growth will lead to poverty reduction— if it does not lead to greater inequality at the same time. A large empirical literature on the relationship between growth and changes in inequality finds no statistical correlation between the two.[14] This means that, on average, inequality does not

change with changes in per capita income, which in turn means that, on average, growth leads to reduction in poverty. Indeed, it is well-established in the literature that, again on average, economic growth is associated with a reduction in poverty (Ames and others 2001; Besley and Burgess 2000; Ravallion 2001; White and Anderson 2002; Christiaensen, Demergy, and Paternostro 2002; Dollar and Kraay 2002; Besley and Burgess 2003; Klasen 2002). Hence, the determinants of growth discussed in the preceding section are as important as the determinants of poverty reduction.

For countries that have worse governance ratings than ratings on other clusters, some gain and others lose from the larger weight on governance in the PBA formula depending on how much worse the ratio of their governance ratings to ratings on the other clusters is compared to other countries.

Although, on average, growth leads to poverty reduction, this is by no means the case for all countries or for everyone in a country. Actual data show considerable variation—there are cases where inequality goes up with growth, and cases where inequality goes down with growth (Kanbur 2004). One paper finds a huge range in the gains to the poor from a given rate of growth.[15] The reasons behind this wide range of

Figure 2.1: Relationship between Changes in PBA and the Ratio of Cluster D Ratings to Ratings on Other Clusters for "Core IDA" Countries

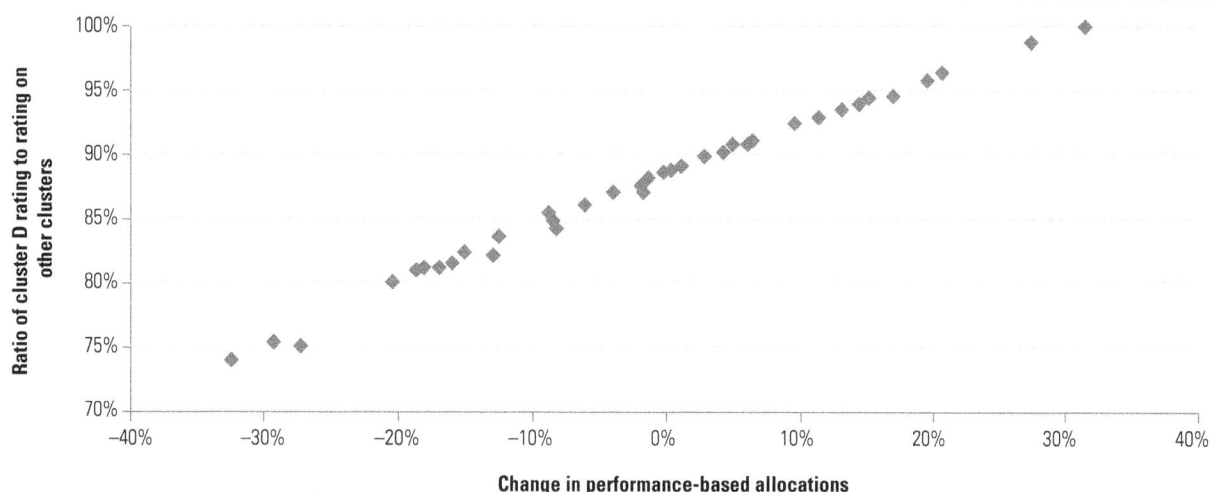

Source: IEG.

Note: "Core IDA" countries refer to those IDA countries that are not subject to exceptions to the PBA due to post-conflict or re-engaging status or to caps on allocations. Small states are also excluded because their base allocations exceed the PBA.

effects include differences in initial inequalities between countries and between regions within countries that create differences in how much the poor share in aggregate growth (or contraction). Another paper finds that the incomes of the poor do not grow one-for-one with increases in average income (Foster and Svékely 2008).

Growth that reduces inequality will have a larger impact on poverty. This evidence implies that growth that reduces inequality will have a larger impact on poverty. Therefore, policies need to take into account the distributional impact of economic growth (the so-called "pro-poor growth" policies) (Ghura, Leite, and Tsangarides 2002; Besley and Burgess 2003). In addition, there are also policies that can have a direct impact on poverty independent of the growth channel (the so-called "super pro-poor" policies).[16]

The rest of this section will discuss the determinants of pro-poor growth and super pro-poor *Financial depth, human capital, equality, and institutions and governance directly affect poverty reduction.* policies. This will be followed by a discussion on two controversial determinants of poverty reduction— trade and the environment. Finally, other non-income dimensions of poverty will be addressed.

Pro-poor growth and super pro-poor policies

There is a significant overlap between the determinants of pro-poor growth and of super pro-poor policies identified in the literature. Financial depth, human capital, equality, and institutions and governance are found to be important for poverty reduction directly as well as through the growth channel. They are also important for reducing inequality and hence enhancing the poverty reduction effects of economic growth.

Quite apart from reducing poverty through growth, *financial sector development* may benefit the poor directly by facilitating access to credit and improving risk sharing.[17] Empirically, there is evidence that financial (banking) depth is negatively associated with headcount poverty, even after taking into account mean income and inequality.[18] Further, financial development has also been found to reduce income inequality by disproportionately boosting the incomes of the poor (Beck, Demirguc-Kunt, and Levine 2004). Financial depth is addressed in the CPIA criterion for the *financial sector.*

As discussed earlier, *education* improves the equality of opportunity for the poor and other disadvantaged groups (including women). An empirical study on Brazil finds that investments in human capital are very important to make growth more pro-poor (Menezes-Filho and Vasconcellos 2004). Education is covered in the CPIA criterion on *building human resources.*

Not only does *inequality* have a negative impact on growth, but higher initial levels of inequality also lower the poverty reduction impact of growth (Ravallion 2001; Bourguignon 2004; Chhibber and Nayyar 2007). Hence, changing the initial level of inequality enhances pro-poor growth. This requires measures to redistribute wealth as well as to improve equality of opportunity. (Such measures and how they are addressed in the CPIA are discussed earlier in this chapter.)

Regarding *institutions and governance,* establishing property rights can help the poor access credit (Fleisig 1995; de Soto 2000; Field 2002) and enhance their ability to utilize and invest in land they cultivate (Deolalikar and others 2002). It has been empirically found that increased protection of property rights has strong effects in reducing poverty (Acemoglu, Johnson, and Robinson 2001). One estimate finds that increasing the protection of property rights across the globe by half of one standard deviation would halve global poverty (Besley and Burgess 2003).

Protection of property rights requires the presence of rule of law, specifically controls over crime and violence. Studies also find that the victims of crimes are more likely to come from the poorer part of the population (Bourguignon 1999; Deolalikar and others 2002; Heinemann and Verner 2006). One study finds that police corruption, especially in slum areas of poorer countries, may increase the uncertainty of property rights of the very poor (Andvig and Fjeldstad 2008).

Corruption also directly affects poverty by increasing income inequality. One possible reason could be that the benefits of corruption are likely to accrue to the better-connected individuals in the society, who belong mostly to high-income groups (Gupta, Davoodi, and Terme 1998). It is also possible that corruption distorts government allocations of goods and services (Tanzi 1998). One study finds that an increase in the corruption index of a country by one standard deviation (2.52 points on a scale of 1–10) increases the Gini coefficient by 5.4 points (Gupta, Davoodi, and Terme 1998, 2002). Another study finds that corruption decreases the share of government expenditures on health and education (Gupta, Davoodi, and Terme 2002).

Finally, government accountability can have a direct impact on poverty. It has been argued that no country with a free press has ever had a major famine (Dreze and Sen 1989), and that a free flow of information pressures (even non-democratic) governments into public action (Dreze and Sen 1995).

All of these different elements of institutions and governance that have been identified in the literature as being important determinants of pro-poor growth or super pro-poor policies are covered in various criteria under the CPIA cluster on *public sector management and institutions*.

Aside from these four determinants of pro-poor growth, which are also determinants of growth, *agriculture* has been identified in the literature as being important for pro-poor growth. Pro-poor growth needs to take place in sectors where the poor are active and draw on the factors of production that the poor possess. The vast majority of the poor live in rural areas, and a majority of them depend directly or indirectly on agriculture for their livelihood. The factor of production that the poor possess and use most is labor, and sometimes land as well (World Bank 2000c; Ames and others 2000; World Bank 2000a; Ravallion and Datt 2002; Eastwood and Lipton 2001). Therefore, pro-poor growth must focus on rural areas, improve incomes in agriculture, and make intensive use of labor (Klasen 2002).

Indeed, a review of the East Asian experience indicates that "the countries that have been most successful in attacking poverty have achieved rapid agricultural growth and broader economic growth that makes efficient use of labor and have invested in the human capital of the poor"(Rosegrant and Hazell 2000). Another paper finds that rural growth reduced poverty in both rural and urban areas, although urban growth had only some impact on urban poverty (Ravallion and Datt 2002).

Agriculture is important for pro-poor growth; it would be useful to add a reference on the provision of public goods in agriculture to the fiscal policy criterion of the CPIA.

Improvements in labor productivity in agriculture are found (in both cross-country analyses and country case studies) to have been more pro-poor than such improvements in non-agricultural sectors (Eastwood and Lipton 2001). Increases in agricultural yields by 20 percent are found to reduce the numbers of the poor by 18 percent in a cross-country empirical investigation (Irz and others 2001). Agricultural research, in particular, is important in this respect, as it has led to crop yield gains in the past. Some researchers conclude from this that "it is unlikely that there are many other development interventions capable of reducing the numbers in poverty so effectively" (Irz and others 2001; Hazell and Haddad 2001). The CPIA does not explicitly cover agriculture—nor does it cover any other economic sectors. It does, however, allow for the provision of public goods in the *fiscal policy* criterion. This is pertinent for agriculture, in view of its importance identified in the literature. Hence, the CPIA instructions may usefully include a specific reference to public goods in agriculture (in addition to the current mention of infrastructure) for the *fiscal policy* criterion.

Trade and poverty

From an analytical point of view, the relationship between trade and poverty is ambiguous—that is, trade can have a positive or a negative impact on poverty, as it does on growth (Agenor 2004; World Bank 2005). Indeed, there are several channels through which trade can affect poverty, and they can have opposite effects. These channels are household production, household

Assessment of the trade criterion needs to take into account the extent of intersectoral labor mobility.

consumption, participation in the labor markets, government revenues, and social expenditures.[19] Given that theory is ambiguous with respect to the impact of trade on poverty, the issue becomes an empirical one. Alas, the empirical literature—both cross-country and case studies—is equally inconclusive (Winters, McCulloch, and McKay 2004; Ravallion 2004; Harrison 2006).

What seems to be clear, though, is that impediments to exports exacerbate poverty (although it is less definitive as to what the effects of import liberalization are). One study finds that informal export barriers to trade (such as transport costs, cumbersome customs practices, and costly regulations and bribes) have significant adverse effects on poverty in Moldova.[20] Another study (Balat, Brambilla, and Porto 2007) finds that lower export marketing costs encourage agricultural exports and lower the poverty levels of those engaged in export cropping compared to others in the rural areas. Export marketing costs could be reduced by investments in infrastructure such as roads, provision of marketing information, provision of credit and technical assistance to farmers, and promotion of out-grower schemes among others (Balat, Brambilla, and Porto 2007; Otsuka 2002; Anderson 2003; Harrison 2006).

Linkages between the environment and poverty are complex.

Labor mobility is another important complementary factor. The negative impact of trade reforms on poverty in India is found to be related to the extremely limited mobility of labor across regions and industries in the country (Topalova 2004, 2005). Similarly, labor market reforms are found to be important for minimizing the adverse effects of trade reform on the poor in Colombia (Goldberg and Pavcnik 2005).

The CPIA does not adequately take into account the importance of complementary factors in the *trade* criterion to avert the potential negative impacts of trade liberalization on poverty. Specifically, this relates to the complementary factor of labor mobility. The CPIA does address labor mobility

(specifically flexibility in hiring and firing) in its criterion on *business regulatory environment* (q6). However, it is important that such mobility be ensured before trade liberalization proceeds, lest liberalization exacerbate poverty. Therefore, assessment of the *trade* criterion needs to take into account the extent of labor mobility.

Environment and poverty

As in the case of linkages between the environment and growth, the linkages between the environment and poverty are similarly complex. On the one hand, there is evidence that environmental regulations have a negative impact on poverty. One paper finds that although, in general, low-income households appear to bear a disproportionate share of existing environmental risks, policies that reduce environmental risks are not necessarily progressive (Parry and others 2005). Another paper studying the distributional effects of environmental policy finds that many effects of such policies are likely regressive (Fullerton 2008). On the other hand, there is also evidence that resource degradation has a negative impact on the poor (World Bank 2008f).

Nonetheless, the impact of the environment on welfare is clear—environmental pollution is clearly detrimental to health (World Bank 2008d). Given that poverty needs to be viewed as a multidimensional concept that includes welfare, environmental sustainability should clearly be taken into account as an important factor in poverty reduction.

Multidimensional poverty

Over the last decade or so, there has been increasing recognition that the notion of poverty encompasses more than just income poverty. Indeed, poverty includes a host of other dimensions that are central to the Millennium Development Goals (MDGs). These other dimensions are education, health, gender equality, and environmental sustainability, all of which are covered by the CPIA.

The notion has also been advanced that poverty goes beyond these income and non-income measures of physiological deprivation (inability to meet basic material needs) to incorporate measures of social deprivation (for example, access to the components of power such as decision making).[21] The World Bank has indicated that "poverty is more than inadequate income or human development—it is also vulnerability and a lack of voice, power, and representation" (World Bank 2000c).

It is in this context that the concept of empowerment of the poor has emerged. Specifically, it is thought that because the poor are the main actors in the fight against poverty, they must be brought to center stage in designing, implementing, and monitoring anti-poverty strategies. This requires, among other things, empowering "pro-poor" coalitions, which can involve parts of governments, non-governmental organizations, donors, and civil society (World Bank 2000a). Such coalitions can be helped by a free press, democratic institutions, and accountable governments— particularly in countries where the poor are the majority. The CPIA covers media freedom and accountability in its criterion on *transparency, accountability, and corruption in the public sector.*

The CPIA and the Effective Use of Development Assistance

The notion of using the CPIA as an indicator in the allocation of IDA resources is based on two premises. The first premise is that IDA resources are important for supporting "…the world's poorest countries in their efforts to boost economic growth, lower poverty and improve the living conditions of people" (World Bank 2008e). The second premise is that such resources could only be used effectively in the presence of sound policies and institutions that are assessed under the CPIA. This section reviews the theoretical and empirical bases for these two notions.

The theoretical foundation of the effect of aid on growth[22] is the neoclassical growth model.[23] Under this model, aid fills the gap in domestic savings or foreign savings to finance investment, leading to growth. This theoretical foundation underpins a sizeable empirical literature (of well over 100 papers) on the impact of aid on growth from the 1960s through the mid-1990s.

This theoretical foundation has been questioned by several researchers, dating back to the 1960s. Their main criticism is the key assumption of the theory that foreign aid finances investment instead of financing consumption. Perhaps partly reflecting this less than robust theoretical foundation, no consensus in the empirical literature can be found through the mid-1990s of the impact of aid on growth. The various reviewers of this literature come to differing conclusions. One review (Hansen and Tarp 2000) concludes that a majority of the literature up to the mid-1990s finds that aid has a positive impact on growth. Two other reviews (Clemens, Radelet, and Bhavnani 2004; McGillivray and others 2005) find no consensus.

The notion of poverty encompasses both income and non-income dimensions as well as social deprivation.

A watershed in the empirical literature was reached in the mid-1990s with the publication of a seminal paper in 1994 that empirically tested the assumption that aid financed investment (Boone 1994).[24] The paper finds that aid did not finance investment but financed public and private consumption instead. Furthermore, the higher consumption did not benefit the poor, as reflected in the absence of a significant impact of aid on improvements in infant mortality, primary schooling ratios, and life expectancy.[25] This paper demarcates the earlier generation of aid impact literature based on the financing gap models from the latest generation, that is, underpinned by the new growth theory. The latter generation of literature specifically takes into account the effect of economic policies and institutions on growth.[26]

For many researchers, the Boone 1994 paper confirms the "macro-micro paradox": that many aid-funded projects report positive microlevel economic returns which are somehow undetectable at the macrolevel. The literature that emerges after this paper can be classified into three strands: those that deny the existence of the macro-micro paradox; those that try to explain it; and those that, like the 1994 paper, do not find any impact of aid at all (see appendix D for the list of papers).

Those that belong to the first strand find that aid works on average, without conditions (the "unconditional" strand). Then there are those that accept the contention that aid does not work on average but seek to identify conditions under which it could be effective (the "conditional" strand). Foremost among the conditional strand is the 1997 World Bank working paper (Burnside and Dollar 2000) that spearheads this strand of literature with the finding that aid is effective (that is, has a positive impact on growth) only in the presence of good policies (specifically fiscal, monetary, and trade policies[27]), which are themselves important for growth. Further, the paper finds that *aid does not lead to good policies*, but that having the right policies in place matters for aid to be effective in terms of higher growth.

Among those researchers who find that aid has an impact on growth, one group finds that it works unconditionally and the other group finds that it only works under specific conditions.

A number of other empirical papers that followed find other conditions to be important for aid effectiveness. These conditions range from countries emerging from civil war and have good policies, to countries prone to external shocks such as climatic and trade shocks (or terms of trade shocks), to countries outside of the tropics.

Different analyses find that different conditions matter for aid to have an impact on growth.

The third strand of literature finds that aid has no impact on growth at all. In addition to the seminal paper of 1994 mentioned above, two others find that by and large aid did not increase investment and that investment did not raise growth (Easterly 2001, 2003). A recent paper that takes into account the motivations of donors in granting aid[28] also finds it "… difficult to discern any systematic effect of aid on growth" (Rajan and Subramaniam 2008).

Some analyses find that aid has no impact on growth.

Not only are the findings of this latest generation of literature diverse, they are also not robust. A paper that tested many of these studies (belonging to both the "conditional" and the "unconditional" strands) for robustness finds that none of the results of these studies withstood the tests.[29] Perhaps the most striking outcome of the tests is that modification of the sample period affects the regression results the most, thereby highlight-ing the fragility of the empirical results of these papers.

Yet none of the researchers who find no impact of aid on growth, or who overturn the findings of aid having an impact on growth, conclude definitively that aid is not effective, or that policies, governance, or exogenous conditions do not matter for aid to be effective. What they do conclude is that cross-country empirics may not be very useful for analyzing whether and when aid works, fraught as they are with data problems.[30]

In the midst of this ongoing controversy, some researchers have forged new ground by analyz-ing the impact of different types of aid on growth. One type of disaggregation is by donor objectives, based on the rationale that donors have strategic as well as developmental objectives for giving aid; hence, not all aid will lead to higher growth. In general, bilateral aid has strategic/geopoliti-cal objectives (although bilateral aid from some countries has developmental goals), whereas multilateral aid has developmental objectives. By and large, the emerging literature on this finds that multilateral aid leads to higher growth, but not bilateral aid.[31]

Another type of disaggregation focuses on aid that could have an impact in the short run. One analysis finds that such "short-impact aid" (that includes budget and balance of payments support, investments in infrastructure, and aid for productive sectors such as agriculture and industry) causes growth, on average, regard-less of the recipient's quality of institutions and policies.[32]

Hence, a decade after the publication of the World Bank working paper that put the conditional aid effectiveness literature on the map, there is no consensus in the cross-country literature on the impact of aid on growth.

Findings of this literature range from (i) aid having no impact on growth to (ii) aid having a positive impact on growth conditional on policies or exogenous factors (but with no consensus on which policies and institutions matter) to (iii) aid having a positive impact on growth regardless of policies and institutions.

Yet, despite the ambiguity of the impact of aid from the cross-country empirical literature, there are many specific examples of aid being effective. These examples range from the eradication of certain diseases (for example, smallpox globally and polio in the western hemisphere) or the Green Revolution in India in the 1960s, to improvements in school attendance and health indicators resulting from conditional cash transfer programs more recently.

Yet another strand of aid effectiveness literature has emerged, whereby efforts are focused on narrower evaluations of the impact of specific aid project interventions. Such evaluations have been conducted in the context of so-called impact evaluations—or randomized evaluations—that evaluate the impact of specific interventions by comparing the effects on those who received the intervention with a comparable group who did not.[33]

Randomized evaluations over the last 10 years or so have found positive benefits of aid projects in education, health, physical infrastructure, and agriculture, among others (see appendix E). This has led some researchers to propose that development assistance should be mainly devoted to such project-specific efforts.

Empirical analysis of CPIA and loan performance

The preceding discussion indicates that the evidence is mixed regarding the relevance of the content of the CPIA on aid effectiveness in the broad sense—that is, whether the CPIA represents the policies and institutions important for aid to lead to growth. An empirical analysis of the association between CPIA ratings and aid effectiveness is fraught with data difficulties (see chapter 2, section on findings and recommendations). Therefore, this evaluation takes a different approach and examines the relevance of the CPIA in a narrower sense—that is, whether it is associated with the performance of Bank loans.

Econometric analysis finds that the policies and institutions that are assessed by the CPIA matter for loan performance (see appendix G). Specifically, overall CPIA ratings are found to be negatively associated with the share of problem projects as assessed by Bank staff in loan implementation status reports. (The share of problem projects is also found to be positively associated with loan outcomes with a correlation coefficient of 0.63).

Empirical analysis finds that policies and institutions assessed by the CPIA matter for loan performance, although there is insufficient evidence to conclude that the governance cluster matters more than the others.

Further, ratings of each of the four CPIA clusters are also found to be negatively associated with loan performance. It is not possible, however, to discern the relative importance of the four CPIA clusters on loan performance because the ratings of the four clusters are highly correlated with each other. Hence, there is not sufficient evidence to conclude that the governance cluster associates better with loan performance than the other clusters.

Findings and Recommendations

By and large, the CPIA criteria cover the main determinants of sustained growth and poverty reduction identified in the literature. The CPIA covers important determinants for both income and non-income poverty, with the latter including many of the MDGs (specifically, education, health, gender equality, and environmental sustainability). It also covers some of the key aspects of another important notion of poverty—empowerment.

The CPIA covers the main determinants of sustained growth and poverty reduction.

It would have been useful to analyze empirically the impact of CPIA ratings including when present together with IDA assistance, on the actual growth performances of the countries rated. However, this was not possible because of the major restructuring of the CPIA content as well as the 2004 rating scale. The discontinuity in the CPIA ratings implied by the restructuring would invalidate any analysis using data that spans 2004. Using only data from 2004 onward would not allow for a long enough time period for such analysis.

Data constraints limit the use of econometric analysis to establish a link between CPIA ratings and growth outcomes.

Although data limitations make it difficult to establish an empirical link between the CPIA and growth outcomes and hence aid effectiveness broadly, the CPIA is found to be associated with aid effectiveness in a narrower sense—specifically in the performance of Bank loans. However, there is insufficient evidence to conclude that any one of the four CPIA clusters is more important for loan performance than the others.

Based on the findings in this chapter, the evaluation derives recommendations regarding the following broad issues.

Tax policy could reasonably be combined with the fiscal policy criterion.

Weighting of the CPIA

The findings indicate that when the CPIA is considered broadly as an index of a country's policies and institutions, the weighting scheme is not so important because the various CPIA clusters are highly correlated. However, the weighting of the different clusters in the PBA formula does matter for a country's allocations of IDA funds.

The utility of aggregating the CPIA clusters into an overall index is questionable.

These findings raise the question of the usefulness of aggregating the various CPIA clusters into an overall index according to any predetermined weighting scheme. In the case of the broad use of the CPIA, it does not allow for country specificity which could imply different weights on the different clusters, depending on the initial conditions and stage of development of the country. In the case of IDA allocation, the overall index is already not used as such (see chapter 1). The recommendation, then, is for Bank management to consider not producing an overall CPIA index, although continuing to produce and publish the separate components of the CPIA.

Streamlining CPIA criteria

The CPIA is quite exhaustive in its coverage of the main determinants of growth and poverty reduction. Indeed, consideration needs to be given to streamlining it.

Equity of public resource use is covered in other criteria and could be dropped or reformulated.

First, the criterion regarding the *equity of public resource use* (q8) is largely covered by other criteria; consideration needs to be given to dropping or reformulating it. This criterion has two subcomponents. The first subcomponent on public expenditures is by and large covered by other CPIA criteria, though Bank staff do not have enough information to meaningfully rate the second one on tax revenues. Dropping q8 would lead to only minor changes in the relative rankings of countries—the rank correlation between the CPIA with q8 and one without is 0.999—as well as only small changes to the PBA (table 2.5). A few more countries would gain than would lose. However, the changes on both the upside and downside would be rather small, with the largest loser experiencing a 1.7 percent drop in PBA and the largest winner a 2.5 percent gain.

Second, currently tax policy is assessed in the criterion on *efficiency of revenue mobilization* (q14a). Yet tax policy is an intrinsic part of fiscal policy, and it would be reasonable to combine the assessment of the two in the *fiscal policy* (q2) criterion. Further, the part of the tax policy subcriterion that deals with trade—specifically import taxes and export rebate or duty drawback—really belongs to the *trade* criterion (q4). In fact, q4 already deals with import taxes, so there is an overlap that needs to be removed. Export rebate or duty drawback needs to be incorporated into the *trade* criterion, given the importance of promoting exports for integration into the global economy.

Third, there are some overlaps in content between various criteria in the public sector management and institutions cluster that could be usefully streamlined. Judicial independence is covered in both the criterion on *property rights and governance* (q12) and the criterion on *transparency, accountability, and corruption in the public sector* (q16). Administrative corruption is assessed in the criteria on *efficiency of revenue mobilization* (q14) (in the subcomponent on tax administration), *quality of public administration* (q15) (in the subcomponent on merit and ethics), and *transparency, accountability, and corruption in the public sector* (q16).

Fourth, interviews with Bank staff conducted for this evaluation suggest that it is onerous for country teams to have to answer 85 questions to arrive at one rating for the *environment* criterion.[34] This is particularly the case in light of the mixed evidence of the environment on growth, as well as the mixed evidence of the environment on poverty. IEG recommends that Bank management drastically simplify the assessment of this criterion.

Fifth, the three *economic management* criteria are not conceptually distinct from each other, unlike the rest of the CPIA criteria. Discussions with the relevant network reviewer indicate that the three criteria are indeed assessed as an integral whole. Yet separate scores are prepared and reported for each of the three criteria, which could lead to double (or triple) counting or confusion. For example, a country that has suffered deterioration in *fiscal policy* would experience a reduction in both the *fiscal policy* and the *macroeconomic management* ratings, which means that such deterioration would be double counted. Yet if Bank staff tries to avoid double counting by downgrading only the *fiscal policy* but not the *macroeconomic management* rating, the resulting ratings would appear contradictory. Although there may be merit in preparing three separate scores, Bank management needs to consider publishing only the consolidated *economic management* rating to avoid the impression of contradictory scores when staff are avoiding double (or triple) counting.

Omissions to the CPIA criteria

Notwithstanding the exhaustiveness of the CPIA coverage, there are a few omissions. First, there is the exclusion of socioeconomic groups other than gender (such as by race, caste, and ethnicity). IEG recommends that assessment of the treatment of such socioeconomic groups be included in the CPIA.

Second is the absence of any reference at all to agriculture. As mentioned, this can be remedied by adding a reference to agriculture in the criterion on *fiscal policy* with reference to public goods.

Table 2.5: Simulation Results: Changes in PBA from Dropping q8

Countries that would lose PBA		Countries that would gain PBA	
Country	Percentage lost	Country	Percentage gained
Armenia	−0.04	Mozambique	0.12
Honduras	−0.13	Bolivia	0.13
Madagascar	−0.13	Tanzania	0.18
Azerbaijan	−0.18	Sierra Leone	0.37
Nigeria	−0.23	Nepal	0.41
Lao PDR	−0.27	Zambia	0.42
Tajikistan	−0.32	Senegal	0.43
Burkina Faso	−0.39	Malawi	0.44
Nicaragua	−0.44	Mongolia	0.44
Georgia	−0.57	Ghana	0.46
Vietnam	−0.69	Mali	0.72
Niger	−0.85	Mauritania	0.72
Yemen, Rep.	−0.88	Guinea	0.72
Chad	−0.98	Kyrgyz Republic	1.04
Uganda	−1.01	Bangladesh	1.05
Rwanda	−1.14	Cameroon	1.05
Ethiopia	−1.63	Kenya	1.31
Papua New Guinea	−1.71	Sri Lanka	1.33
		Uzbekistan	1.40
		Benin	1.64
		Cambodia	1.79
		Moldova	1.81
		Bosnia and Herzegovina	2.49

Source: IEG.
Note: PBA=performance-based allocation.

Coordinating assessment of CPIA criteria

The reviews of a few criteria need to be coordinated. This has emerged in the context of the *trade* criterion, which needs to be evaluated in connection with the assessment of the *labor* criterion. Similarly, *fiscal policy* (q2) needs to be evaluated in conjunction with the *quality of budgetary and financial management* (q13).

Overlaps could be reduced between the criteria in the public sector management and institutions cluster.

Assessment of the environment criterion needs to be simplified.

The absence of agriculture and socioeconomic groups other than gender needs to be addressed.

Content of the CPIA criteria

The 2004 restructuring of the CPIA was the last time its criteria were reviewed and revised. Bank management also agreed with the external panel recommendation at the time that, for the sake of continuity and comparability, the CPIA criteria will not be revised too frequently (World Bank 2004d). Bank management further indicated that periodic reviews (for example, every three years) of the CPIA will be undertaken by an external technical advisory committee charged with reviewing the CPIA methodology, procedure, and ratings quality.

This evaluation has found that the time has come for Bank management to undertake a thorough review and revision of the CPIA. The general growth literature review conducted for this evaluation derives findings and recommendations for restructuring the *trade* criterion; likewise, an in-depth literature review undertaken for the *financial sector*

Add a subcomponent on exports to the trade criterion; assign equal weights to exports, trade restrictiveness, and trade facilitation.

criterion derives findings and recommendations for revising that criterion.

Revise trade *criterion*

The importance of complementary institutions for global integration is not adequately reflected in the weighting scheme for the *trade* criterion, nor is adequate attention given to exports. IEG recommends that trade restrictiveness and trade facilitation be given equal weights (replacing the current weighting scheme of 75 and 25 percent, respectively, on these two subcomponents).

In addition, a subcomponent on exports needs to be added (with the same weight as the other two) to assess export performance and policies and institutions to reduce anti-export bias. The subcomponent on exports needs to include the assessment of export rebate and duty drawback that should be transferred from the criterion on *efficiency of revenue mobilization* (q14) as suggested in chapter 2 (in the section pertaining to streamlining CPIA criteria). All three trade subcomponents—trade restrictiveness, trade facilitation, and exports—need to be given equal weights.

Simulations of equal weights for the trade subcomponents on restrictiveness and facilitation indicate that there will be no change in ratings on trade for half of the countries (70 of 140 countries), with slightly more than half of the IBRD countries (52 percent) and slightly less than half of the IDA countries (48 percent) experiencing no rating changes (table 2.6).

About equal numbers of IBRD countries will gain and lose ratings on trade (16 and 15 countries, respectively), although many more IDA countries would lose (27 countries) than would gain (12 countries). This implies that IDA countries have worse ratings for trade facilitation than for trade restrictiveness compared with IBRD countries. For all but one country, the change in ratings (whether up or down) is 0.5 points; the exception is Tunisia, which would gain 1 point (table 2.7).

The proposed change would increase the comparability of the CPIA trade rating with that

Table 2.6: Simulation Results: Changes in Trade Ratings Arising from Changes in Weights of Trade Subcriteria by Numbers and Shares of IBRD and IDA Countries

	No change in ratings on trade	Rise in ratings on trade	Fall in ratings on trade	Total
	Number of countries			
IBRD	34	16	15	65
IDA	36	12	27	75
Total	70	28	42	140
	Share of countries (%)			
IBRD	52	25	23	100
IDA	48	16	36	100
Total	50	20	30	100

Source: IEG.

Note: IBRD= International Bank for Reconstruction and Development; IDA= International Development Association.

Table 2.7: Simulation Results: IBRD and IDA Countries That Would Experience Changes in Trade Ratings Due to Changes in Weights for Trade Subcriteria

Fall in ratings on trade		Rise in ratings on trade	
IDA	**IBRD**	**IDA**	**IBRD**
Malawi	Trinidad and Tobago	Cape Verde	Morocco
Burkina Faso	Colombia	Uganda	Iran, Islamic Rep.
São Tomé and Principe	Montenegro	Senegal	Malaysia
Niger	Micronesia, Fed. Sts.	Nigeria	Guatemala
Tajikistan	Thailand	Ethiopia	Uruguay
Guyana	Ukraine	Rwanda	Swaziland
Azerbaijan	Chile	Bosnia and Herzegovina	Algeria
Lao PDR	Albania	Bangladesh	Namibia
Moldova	Croatia	Lesotho	St. Kitts and Nevis
Mauritania	Bulgaria	Sri Lanka	Estonia
Yemen, Rep.	Lebanon	Eritrea	Botswana
Mongolia	Kazakhstan	Pakistan	South Africa
Armenia	Dominican Republic		Korea, Rep.
Papau New Guinea	Paraguay		Belize
Chad	Costa Rica		Latvia
Comoros			Tunisia
Bolivia			
Honduras			
Kyrgyz Republic			
Georgia			
Congo, Dem. Rep.			
Togo			
Timor-Leste			
Côte d'Ivoire			
Haiti			
Angola			
Congo, Rep.			

Source: IEG.
Note: All changes are 0.5 points, with the exception of Tunisia which would experience a 1-point gain.
IBRD= International Bank for Reconstruction and Development; IDA= International Development Association.

of a comparator—the Enabling Trade Index (ETI). Specifically, the rank correlation coefficient between the proposed CPIA trade rating and one based on the ETI[35] will rise from 0.70 to 0.75.[36] This in turn reflects the greater comparability of the ratings on customs/border administration than on trade restrictiveness (tariffs and nontariff barriers) between the CPIA and the ETI.

The financial sector *criterion focuses more on intermediate outcomes. It would be useful to include in the assessment those policies and institutions that foster an enabling environment for the financial sector.*

Indeed, the rank correlation for customs/border administration between those two indexes is 0.77, compared with a rank correlation of 0.59 for trade restrictiveness.

The proposed change would alter the PBA, although not very significantly.[37] Many more countries would lose than would gain, reflecting the larger number of countries that have worse ratings on trade facilitation than on trade restrictiveness. The magnitudes of the changes would be small, however. Bangladesh would gain the most (by 1.6 percent), whereas Chad would lose the most (3.4 percent) (table 2.8).

Financial sector *criterion*

A review of the literature indicates that the *financial sector* criterion does cover the dimensions along which finance is currently thought to be important: stability; depth and efficiency; and access. However, the way in which some of the dimensions are currently being assessed can be strengthened.

Some of the indicators of the financial sector *criterion need to be strengthened.*

First, the application of equal weights to the three financial sector dimensions can be revisited, particularly in light of the ongoing global financial crisis, as well as the considerable evidence of a large impact of banking crises on output losses (Hoggarth, Reis, and Saporta 2002)[38] and on the national budget (Laeven and Valenciana 2008; Honohan 2008b).[39] Further, it is also widely accepted that financial stability is a prerequisite for the effective deployment of many types of development assistance (although there is less systematic evidence on this front (Honohan 2009). Hence, it would be useful for Bank management to consider giving financial stability a larger weight than the other two dimensions in the CPIA criterion.

Second, compared to almost every other CPIA criteria, there is a greater focus in this criterion on assessing intermediate outcomes rather than policies and institutions. This is particularly the case in the assessment of financial depth, which focuses almost entirely on intermediate outcomes, such as size of financial markets, interest rate spreads, and so on. It would be useful to include in the assessment policies and institutions that foster an enabling environment for the financial sector such as the legal, contractual, informational, and governance framework.

Third, some of the indicators used in the assessment of the *financial sector* criterion can be strengthened. One example is the indicator on banking system soundness, which specifies two alternative intermediate outcome measures related to non-performing loans (NPLs).[40] Although NPLs may predict crises to some extent, they are typically a lagging indicator, with high values suggestive of a problem that has already crystallized. Hence these NPL measures are crude and inadequate even as indicators of current or imminent problems. This is clearly reflected in the fact that NPLs for residential mortgages did not provide a sensitive early warning system in the recent crisis in advanced economies. There are other good or even better flags for systemic risk, for example, indicators of foreign exchange risk in finance such as the dollarization of banking deposits or assets (De Nicoló, Honohan, and Ize 2005; Cashin and Duttagupta 2008). Rapid growth of credit also needs to be monitored as a possible warning sign. The assessment of this dimension would be strengthened by taking into account such indicators.

Appendix F presents a more detailed discussion of the indicators in the CPIA *financial sector* criterion based on a review of the literature. It also offers recommendations for restructuring and strengthening the criterion.

Table 2.8: Simulation Results: Changes in PBA Arising from Changes in Weights for Trade Subcriteria

Countries that will lose PBA (%)		Countries that will gain PBA (%)	
Country	Percentage lost	Country	Percentage gained
Mali	−0.6	Rwanda	1.2
Zambia	−0.6	Senegal	1.3
Benin	−0.6	Uganda	1.4
Cambodia	−0.6	Bosnia and Herzegovina	1.4
Cameroon	−0.6	Ethiopia	1.4
Ghana	−0.6	Sri Lanka	1.4
Guinea	−0.6	Nigeria	1.5
Kenya	−0.6	Bangladesh	1.6
Madagascar	−0.6		
Mozambique	−0.6		
Nepal	−0.6		
Nicaragua	−0.6		
Sierra Leone	−0.6		
Tanzania	−0.6		
Uzbekistan	−0.6		
Vietnam	−0.6		
Armenia	−2.2		
Georgia	−2.3		
Moldova	−2.3		
Burkina Faso	−2.4		
Malawi	−2.4		
Mongolia	−2.4		
Honduras	−2.4		
Bolivia	−2.5		
Azerbaijan	−2.6		
Papau New Guinea	−2.6		
Kyrgyz Republic	−2.6		
Niger	−2.6		
Mauritania	−2.7		
Yemen, Rep.	−2.7		
Lao PDR	−2.8		
Tajikistan	−2.9		
Chad	−3.4		

Source: IEG.
Note: PBA= Performance-based allocation. Ranking changes based on equal weights for all CPIA criteria.

Women weaving on loom, China. Photo by Curt Carnemark/World Bank

Chapter 3

Evaluation Highlights

- The CPIA correlates well with similar indicators in terms of both the relative rankings of countries and the direction of change.
- CPIA ratings correlate better for IBRD than for IDA countries with ratings of similar indicators—this could be because ratings for IDA countries take into account the stage of development.
- Accounting for the stage of development is problematic because of the judgment involved and because of uneven practice across the Bank.
- Having network reviewers validate ratings helps minimize potential bias in the ratings.

Morocco. Photo by Curt Carnemark/World Bank.

Reliability of the CPIA Ratings

Assessing the reliability of the CPIA ratings is an intrinsically difficult if not impossible task, given that a benchmark (that is, the "true" rating) does not exist. Recognizing this major limitation, this evaluation assesses reliability in two ways: it compares the CPIA ratings with those of similar indicators, and it reviews the Bank's CPIA ratings generation process.

With respect to the former, CPIA ratings are found to correlate well with similar indicators in terms of the rankings of countries and in terms of direction of change. This means that the CPIA ratings are not out of line with other indicators that measure similar policies and institutions. With respect to the latter, the Bank's review processes are found to guard against potential biases in ratings.

CPIA ratings are found to correlate better for IBRD than for IDA countries. One reason for this could be that more information is available on IBRD than on IDA countries, which increases the likelihood of different institutions having similar assessments on IBRD countries. Another reason for this could be the need to take into account the stage of development in the CPIA ratings. This means that more judgment is involved in rating IDA countries, because accounting for the stage of development is more important for IDA than for IBRD countries. This introduces additional subjectivity into the rating exercise, which is already centered on the expert judgment of staff. The issue is further complicated by the fact that different networks treat the issue of the stage of

development differently, which means that even more unevenness is introduced into the CPIA ratings exercise.

The quality of CPIA ratings could be enhanced by minimizing the amount of subjectivity involved in the rating exercise. This could be done by excluding accounting for the stage of development from the ratings exercise.

Comparability with Other Indicators

Fourteen indicators are identified that could be compared with the CPIA (table 3.1). Two of the 14 are strictly comparable with the CPIA—these are the CPIA ratings by the Asian Development Bank (ADB) and the African Development Bank (AfDB) (appendix H). The ADB uses exactly the same questionnaire as the Bank. For the AfDB, all the questions are either exactly the same or very close to those of the Bank with the exception of the question on *trade* (q4), for which the AfDB includes an assessment on economic cooperation and regional integration.[1] The rest of the indicators are selected to match as closely as possible with relevant CPIA criteria, some of

Table 3.1: Rank Correlation Coefficients between CPIA Ratings and Comparator Ratings for 2007

CPIA	ADB	AfDB	ICRG	GCI	ETI	DB	Bertelsmann Transformation Index	Index of Economic Freedom	WGI	Corruption Perception Index	Ibrahim Index of African Governance	ESI	Gender Gap Index	Gender Empowerment Measure	Average
q1	0.74	0.82													0.78
	(26)	(50)													
q2	0.61	0.82													0.72
	(26)	(50)													
q3	0.67	0.91													0.79
	(26)	(50)													
q4	0.67			0.72	0.71										0.70
	(26)			(91)	(85)										
q5	0.62	0.75		0.71		0.67									0.69
	(26)	(50)		(91)		(139)									
q6	0.80	0.84		0.62	0.55	0.57	0.79	0.67	0.89						0.72
	(26)	(50)		(90)	(85)	(139)	(111)	(114)	(140)						
q7	0.78	0.66											0.67	0.61	0.68
	(26)	(50)											(93)	(60)	
q8	0.58	0.80													0.69
	(26)	(50)													
q9	0.80	0.68		0.69											0.72
	(26)	(50)		(91)											
q10	0.72	0.77					0.72								0.74
	(26)	(50)					(111)								

(continued on next page)

Table 3.1: Rank Correlation Coefficients between CPIA Ratings and Comparator Ratings for 2007 (continued)

CPIA	ADB	AfDB	ICRG	GCI	ETI	DB	Bertelsmann Transformation Index	Index of Economic Freedom	WGI	Corruption Perception Index	Ibrahim Index of African Governance	ESI	Gender Gap Index	Gender Empowerment Measure	Average
q11	0.71	0.77										0.59			0.69
	(26)	(50)										(110)			
q12	0.75	0.82	0.73	0.69			0.74	0.69	0.88						0.76
	(26)	(50)	(95)	(92)			(111)	(114)	(140)						
q13	0.54	0.89													0.72
	(26)	(50)													
q14	0.61	0.72													0.67
	(26)	(50)													
q15	0.68	0.80	0.66						0.83						0.74
	(26)	(50)	(95)						(140)						
q16	0.72	0.79	0.51				0.82	0.75	0.86	0.86	0.77				0.76
	(26)	(50)	(95)				(111)	(114)	(140)	(135)	(46)				
Average	0.69	0.79	0.63	0.69	0.63	0.62	0.77	0.70	0.87	0.86	0.77	0.59	0.67	0.61	0.72

Source: IEG.

Note: The number of observations is presented in parenthesis below the correlation coefficients. All correlations are for 2007 ratings except for the Ibrahim Index of African Governance (2006 ratings) and Environmental Sustainability Index (ESI) (2005 ratings). ADB = Asian Development Bank; AfDB = African Development Bank; DB = Doing Business; ETI = Enabling Trade Index; GCI = Global Competitiveness Index; ICRG = International Country Risk Guide; WGI = Worldwide Governance Indicators. All coefficients are significant at the 1 percent level.

Box 3.1: Comparator Indicators

This evaluation selected 12 other indicators, in addition to the CPIA ratings produced by the AfDB and the ADB, to compare with the Bank's CPIA:

- Three are produced by the Bank—the Logistics Performance Index, Doing Business, and the Worldwide Governance Indicators.
- Four are produced by the World Economic Forum—the Enabling Trade Index, the Environmental Sustainability Index, the Global Gender Gap Index, and the Global Competitiveness Index.

- The rest are produced by the Bertelsmann Foundation (Bertelsmann Transformation Index), Heritage Foundation (Index of Economic Freedom), the Political Risk Services Group (the International Country Risk Guide), Transparency International (Corruption Perception Index), the United Nations Development Programme (the Gender Empowerment Measure), and the Mo Ibrahim Foundation (Ibrahim Index of African Governance).

Appendix I provides details on the specific subindicators used for comparison.

Source: IEG.

which are guideposts for certain CPIA criteria (box 3.1).

For certain CPIA criteria, very few comparators can be identified. In particular, it is difficult to identify comparators other than those by the ADB and AfDB for the three *economic management* criteria (q1, q2, and q3),[2] and the criteria on *equity of public resource use* (q8), the *quality of budgetary and financial management* (q13),[3] and *efficiency of revenue mobilization* (q14). Hence, for those criteria, only comparisons with ratings by ADB and AfDB are made.

In contrast, quite a few more comparators are found for the criteria on *business regulatory environment* (q6) and *transparency, accountability, and corruption in the public sector* (q16). For both these criteria, six other indicators in addition to the ones from ADB and AfDB are found.

Rank correlations

Interpretation of the correlation coefficients[4] of the CPIA ratings with other indicators is complicated by the fact that the content of the indicators, other than those of the other development banks, is not exactly the same as the CPIA. The overlap between these other indicators and

the CPIA criteria varies. Some overlap much better with the content of certain CPIA criteria than others. Nonetheless, for each criterion the correlation coefficients with both the development and nondevelopment bank comparators are similar and relatively high, averaging between 0.7 and 0.8 (see last column of table 3.1). This provides some assurance that the CPIA ratings are not out of line with those of other indicators that assess similar policies and institutions. The correlation coefficients presented in table 3.1 also indicate that there is not much difference between all 16 CPIA criteria in terms of their comparability with other indicators.

Although on average the CPIA ratings correlate well with other indicators, there is a dispersion to the correlation coefficients that range from a low of 0.54 (for q13 with ADB) to a high of 0.89 (for q13 with AfDB and q6 with the World Governance Indicators). Several possible reasons may account for this dispersion. First, as mentioned, except for the AfDB and the ADB, the other indicators are not assessing the exact same criteria as the CPIA. Second, judgment is involved in the rating exercise (by the Bank and by virtually all the other institutions; see table 3.2), which is exacerbated when there is not enough information available on the criteria.

Table 3.2: Other Indicators—Expert Judgment or Hard Data?

External data source	CPIA Criterion	Expert Judgment/ Survey	Hard data	Expert Judgment/Survey and Hard Data
ADB	q1 to q16			
AfDB	q1 to q16			✓
Global Competitiveness Index	q4			✓
	q5			✓
	q6			✓
	q9			✓
	q12	✓		
International Country Risk Guide	q12	✓		
	q15	✓		
	q16	✓		
Enabling Trade Index	q4			✓
	q6			✓
Doing Business	q5			✓
	q6			✓
Bertelsmann Transformation Index	q6	✓		
	q10	✓		
	q12	✓		
	q16	✓		
Index of Economic Freedom	q6			✓
	q12	✓		
	q16	✓		
Worldwide Governance Indicators	q6	✓		
	q12	✓		
	q15	✓		
	q16	✓		
Corruption Perception Index	q16	✓		
Ibrahim Index of African Governance	q16			✓
Environmental Sustainability Index	q11			✓
Gender Gap Index	q7			✓
Gender Empowerment Measure	q7		✓	

Source: IEG.
Note: ADB= Asian Development Bank; AfDB= African Development Bank.

For example, even though the ADB uses the same CPIA questionnaire as the Bank, the correlation coefficients for two criteria, q8 and q13, are relatively low (the respective correlation coefficients are 0.58 and 0.54). Very different rankings for two to three countries (of 26 countries) are responsible for the relatively low correlations overall. In the case of q8, these are Micronesia, Cambodia, and Timor-Leste, and for q13, these are Azerbaijan and Tonga. Two of these countries are Pacific Islands, for which the Bank has little up-to-date or firsthand information (according to region and network reviewers who were interviewed for this evaluation).

For all of the criteria for which there are comparable indicators other than those from ADB and AfDB (that is, all criteria except for q1, q2, q3, q8, q13, and q14 as discussed above), comparisons of rank correlations were undertaken to assess whether these other indicators correlate better[5] with the Bank's CPIA or with those of the other two development banks. (The ratings by the AfDB and the ADB are the points of reference here because they are the most comparable with the Bank's ratings both because of their content, and because all three institutions take into account country context in the ratings whereas the other indicators do not.) *The comparisons indicate that, overwhelmingly, these other indicators correlate better with the Bank's ratings than with ratings by AfDB and ADB* (table 3.3).

Other comparator indicators correlate better with the Bank's CPIA ratings than with the ratings by the AfDB and the ADB.

Comparing changes in ratings

The two previous sections indicate that the *level* of the CPIA ratings (and implied rankings) compare relatively well with other indicators. This section examines how well the changes in ratings compare with *changes* in the comparator indicators between 2006 and 2007.

Strictly speaking, a similar assessment of a particular criterion by different institutions would imply that a change or no change in ratings by one institution would be associated with similar movements in ratings by the other institutions. Because the timing of the CPIA assessment exercise varies across these institutions, a

Table 3.3: Are Other Comparator Indicators Closer to the Bank or to AfDB and ADB?

CPIA criterion	Majority of other indicators correlates better with		Majority of other indicators correlates better with	
	Bank	AfDB	Bank	ADB
q4	n.a.	n.a.	✓	
q5	✓			✓
q6	✓		No difference	
q7	✓		✓	
q9	No difference		No difference	
q10	No difference		✓	
q11	✓			
q12	✓		✓	
q15	✓		✓	
q16	✓		✓	

Source: IEG.

Note: The comparison for q4 is not valid with AfDB because AfDB defines q4 differently from the Bank. ADB= Asian Development Bank; AfDB= African Development Bank; n.a.= not applicable.

change in the assessment by one institution may not always be associated with a similar change in assessment by the other institution. However, at the very least, these assessments—if they are similar—would not contradict each other or, in other words, the ratings would not move in opposite directions.

The comparisons of changes in ratings indicate that the Bank's assessments are very similar to those of the AfDB and the ADB. Only for a few criteria and a very small share of countries do the ratings of the Bank and AfDB/ADB move in opposite directions (table 3.4).

In the comparison with the AfDB, for 10 of the 15 criteria (q4 is excluded from the analysis for reasons stated earlier), none of the countries has ratings that move in the opposite direction. For four criteria—q2 *(fiscal policy)*, q7 *(gender)*, q8 *(equity of public resource use)* and q13 *(quality of budgetary and financial management)*—the ratings move in the opposite direction for only 2 percent of the countries (one out of 50 countries). For q1 *(macroeconomic management)*, a slightly higher 4 percent of the countries (2 out of 50 countries) have ratings that move in the

The Bank's CPIA ratings and those of AfDB and ADB correlate well in terms of direction of change.

Table 3.4. Comparison of Changes in CPIA Ratings 2006–07 between the Bank, AfDB, and ADB

Criterion	Comparison with AfDB			Comparison with ADB		
	Change in the same direction(%)	Change in the opposite direction (%)	Change for one institution but no change in the other (%)	Change in the same direction (%)	Change in the opposite direction (%)	Change for one institution but no change in the other (%)
q1	60.0	4.0	36.0	50.0	4.2	45.8
q2	42.0	2.0	56.0	41.7	0.0	58.3
q3	64.0	0.0	36.0	33.3	0.0	66.7
q4	n.a.	n.a.	n.a.	58.3	0.0	41.7
q5	72.0	0.0	28.0	54.2	4.2	41.7
q6	66.0	0.0	34.0	75.0	0.0	25.0
q7	58.0	2.0	40.0	62.5	0.0	37.5
q8	52.0	2.0	46.0	54.2	0.0	45.8
q9	66.0	0.0	34.0	66.7	0.0	33.3
q10	74.0	0.0	26.0	50.0	0.0	50.0
q11	64.0	0.0	36.0	66.7	4.2	29.2
q12	80.0	0.0	20.0	50.0	0.0	50.0
q13	56.0	2.0	42.0	33.3	0.0	66.7
q14	72.0	0.0	28.0	54.2	0.0	45.8
q15	70.0	0.0	30.0	70.8	0.0	29.2
q16	56.0	0.0	44.0	54.2	0.0	45.8

Source: IEG.

Note: q4 is excluded from this analysis because of the additional dimension of regional integration that is included in q4 by AfDB but not the Bank. ADB= Asian Development Bank; AfDB= African Development Bank.

opposite direction. In the comparison with ADB, for 13 of 16 criteria, none of the countries have ratings move in the opposite direction. For the remaining 3 criteria—q1 (*macroeconomic management*), q5 (*financial sector*), and q11 (*environmental sustainability*), 4 percent of the countries (1 of 26 countries) have ratings move in the opposite direction.

The same comparison with the other indicators is not reported here because the CPIA ratings (by the Bank and the other two development banks) are more discrete (with intervals of 0.5) than the other indicators. This implies that changes in the ratings of the other indicators may not correspond to changes in CPIA ratings, even if the assessments are similar to those of the Bank. In other words, small changes in policies and institutions may lead to a change in a rating that is on a more continuous scale (such as the Global Competitiveness Index), whereas the same small change would not be reflected in changes in the CPIA rating because it takes a relatively significant change in policies and institutions for the CPIA rating to change by 0.5.

Therefore, comparisons of changes in CPIA ratings with changes in the ratings of other indicators could only be made for instances where the CPIA ratings change. They cannot be made in cases when CPIA ratings do not change. This restricts the number of observations significantly, because CPIA ratings do not change very much over time. The restricted number of observations per criterion (these are at most slightly above 20, and in many instances well below 20) weakens the confidence in the analysis; hence the results are not reported here.

IBRD versus IDA ratings

The Bank's CPIA ratings correlate better with ratings from AfDB and other institutions for IBRD countries than for IDA countries[6] (table 3.5). AfDB ratings are closer to those of the Bank for twice as many criteria for IBRD than for IDA countries (6 versus 3 criteria). Ratings of *other indicators* are overwhelmingly closer to Bank ratings for IBRD than for IDA countries. They are closer to Bank ratings for 8 criteria for IBRD countries and for no criteria for IDA countries.

CPIA ratings correlate better with other comparator indicators for IBRD than for IDA countries.

Two possible reasons may account for these findings. First, in general, more information is available on IBRD countries than on IDA countries (see appendix J) which increases the likelihood of different institutions (AfDB as well as other institutions) having similar assessments on IBRD countries as the Bank. Second, the stage of development (taken into account by the Bank and the AfDB) is more pertinent for IDA than for IBRD countries, and the additional judgment involved in accounting for the stage of development would likely make ratings for IDA countries less comparable. Regardless of whether one or both reasons are valid here, *CPIA ratings correlate better with those of other indicators for IBRD than for IDA countries.*

Conclusions on comparability of CPIA with other indicators

The findings indicate that CPIA ratings for all 16 criteria correlate relatively well with those of similar indicators in terms of both the relative rankings of countries as well as the direction of change. The rank correlations of CPIA ratings with ratings of other indicators average between 0.7 and 0.8 for each of the 16 CPIA criteria. Ratings of other indicators correlate better with CPIA ratings by the Bank than those by the AfDB and the ADB. Finally, CPIA ratings correlate better for IBRD than for IDA countries with ratings of other indicators.

CPIA Ratings Generation Process

The central determinant of CPIA ratings is the professional judgment of Bank staff, who can also draw on other indicators (including outcome indicators/hard data) provided as guideposts in the CPIA Questionnaire. The ratings are produced in a multistep process, which entails two levels of review—first at the regional level, and then at the network level (see box 3.2). In cases where the regions and the networks disagree over the final ratings, the networks have the final say unless the regions have supporting evidence.

Regional review

Interviews with regional reviewers indicate that there is no one standard review practice across

Table 3.5: Rank Correlations between the CPIA and Other Indicators: IBRD versus IDA Countries

CPIA Criterion	Bank ratings correlate better with AfDB ratings for		Bank ratings correlate better with other Indicators for	
	IBRD countries	IDA countries	IBRD countries	IDA countries
q1		✓	n.a.	n.a.
q2	No difference		n.a.	n.a.
q3		✓	n.a.	n.a.
q4	n.a.	n.a.	✓	
q5	✓		✓	
q6	No difference		✓	
q7	✓		No difference	
q8	No difference		n.a.	n.a.
q9	No difference		✓	
q10	✓		No difference	
q11	No difference		✓	
q12		✓	✓	
q13	✓		n.a.	n.a.
q14	✓		n.a.	n.a.
q15	No difference		✓	
q16	✓		✓	

Source: IEG.

Notes: a. A better correlation is defined here as a correlation coefficient that is higher by at least 0.05.

b. q4 is excluded from the comparison with AfDB because AfDB defines q4 differently from the Bank.

c. For q1, q2, q3, q8, q13, and q14, no other indicators except for AfDB (and ADB) can be identified as comparators, as mentioned.

ADB= Asian Development Bank; AfDB= African Development Bank; IBRD= International Bank for Reconstruction and Development; IDA= International Development Association; n. a. = not applicable.

regions. One factor that influences the regional review practices is the size of the region.

For regions with numerous countries, such as the Africa and the Europe and Central Asia Regions, reviewers undertake statistical exercises using external indicators to review country team rating proposals. In the Africa Region, sector specialists undertake such exercises, which are used as inputs in the regionwide review process before the first round of rating proposals are submitted to Operations Policy and Country Studies (OPCS).

In smaller regions, such as the Middle East and North Africa and South Asia, sectoral staff are generally knowledgeable about their sectors for many countries in the region, whereas staff in the Chief Economist's office are knowledgeable about all the countries in the region. Hence these regional reviews do not entail cross-country statistical exercises.

Further, though a regional review is meant to ensure intraregional rating comparability prior to submitting the first round of rating proposals to OPCS, interviews with regional reviewers indicate that not all regions do that. The varying extents to which regions undertake this review may account for the varying extents to which

There is no one standard CPIA review practice across regions.

Box 3.2: The Process of Preparing CPIA Ratings

The process begins with a *benchmarking* phase, which entails rating a small representative sample of countries drawn from all the regions (see chapter 1, "Other Changes in the CPIA"). This is followed by a *roll-out* phase, during which the rest of the countries are rated. Both phases entail a multistep procedure.

In the *first* step, the country teams generate a set of proposed ratings for their respective countries. This step is usually led by country economists with participation from sector specialists and country management.

In the *second* step, the Regional Chief Economist offices review and revise (as necessary) the ratings for the countries within the respective regions to ensure cross-country comparability within each region.

In the *third* step, the network anchors and other central units review the ratings at the Bank-wide (global) level to ensure cross-regional comparability of ratings.

The *fourth* step is somewhat different for the benchmarking versus the roll-out phase. For the benchmarking phase, the fourth step entails a meeting of representatives from Operations Policy and Country Services (OPCS), the regions, networks, and central departments to review the proposed ratings for all of the criteria and for all of the benchmark countries, after which the ratings are "frozen" and the roll-out phase proceeds. For the fourth step of the roll-out phase, most of the ratings are finalized through virtual communication because of the large number of countries involved. Meetings are only held to discuss the few cases that have not been resolved by virtual communication.

Source: IEG, based on interview with OPCS.

---

networks disagree with the regions over the initial rating proposals (table 3.7).

All regional reviewers were asked the open-ended question of which criteria are difficult to assess. Reviewers found that the criteria in the public sector management and institutions cluster were the most difficult, pointing to the lack of data and the judgment involved. One of the network reviewers for this cluster indicated that a lot of judgment is involved in most of the criteria in that cluster and pointed out the criterion on *transparency, accountability, and corruption* as an example.

Network review practices also vary.

Network review

The review practices of the networks vary depending on various factors, including: (i) the extent to which other quantitative indicators are available for cross-checking the CPIA ratings; (ii) the extent to which any other information is available on the criteria at all; (iii) the importance the particular network accords to the exercise (and hence the amount of resources devoted to it); and (iv) the clarity of the criteria content and associated ease of assessment. These factors affect the extent of

the review, which varies quite significantly across criteria (box 3.3).

Expert judgment and potential conflict of interest

As indicated by the external panel in the 2004 review of the CPIA (World Bank 2004a), the depth of country knowledge by Bank staff is a major strength of the exercise. The practice of relying on expert judgment for ratings is also used by virtually all of the other indicators against which the CPIA was compared in the previous section (table 3.2).

Although the expert judgment of Bank staff is clearly an asset in the CPIA exercise, at the same time there is a potential conflict of interest in having staff provide ratings, particularly for IDA countries. This potential for conflict of interest arises from the fact that ratings produced by staff are in turn used for allocating IDA resources for the same countries on which the work programs of those staff depend. Therefore, staff may potentially be upwardly biased in assigning ratings for their countries. The regional review is meant to adjust for such potential biases at the regional level, although there could still be issues

Box 3.3: The Network Reviews of CPIA Ratings

For the *economic management* cluster (criteria q1 to q3), the reviewers read every write-up submitted by the region, as well as reports from the International Monetary Fund, Debt Sustainability Assessments, and private sector reports for the country being reviewed. Many reviewers in the Economic Policy and Debt Department (PRMED) are involved in this exercise, with each reviewer assigned about six countries. A coordinator then reviews about 60 percent of all the reviewers' comments to ensure consistency of ratings across countries.

Perhaps because of the resource-intensiveness of the review, these were also the criteria on which there were the most comments. In 2007, for each of the criteria q1, q2, and q3, the network commented on 86 percent of the countries, compared with comments on an average of 38 percent of the countries for all 16 CPIA criteria (appendix K). Further, these were also the criteria for which the network disagreed with the regional proposals for a higher share of countries than for most other criteria (see table 3.7).

For the criteria on *trade* (q4), *business regulatory environment* (q5), *financial sector* (q6) up to last year, *gender* (q7), *property rights and rule-based governance* (q12), *quality of budgetary and financial management* (q13), parts (c) and (d) of *quality of public*

administration (q15), and *transparency, accountability, and corruption in the public sector* (q16), the networks use other quantitative indicators to cross-check the ratings.

For the *gender* criterion (q7), the network actually first generate the ratings based on quantitative indicators which are passed onto the region for review. These initial gender ratings are then adjusted if country teams provide additional country-specific information that is not captured by the ratings. Some networks supplement assessments based on quantitative indicators with the write-ups submitted by the regions.

For the *financial sector* (q5) for fiscal 2009, *building human resources* (q9), and *efficiency of revenue mobilization* (q14), the networks review all of the write-ups that were submitted. The network reviewer for q14 supplements these with quantitative indicators from various other sources.

For the *equity of public resource use* (q8) and *social protection and labor* (q10), the networks' review focuses only on countries for which the proposed ratings are different from the previous years. For the *environment* (q11), the network relies more on the region's judgment because it has little other information on the criterion.

Source: IEG, based on interviews with network reviewers.

with the *levels* of the ratings even if the relative rankings of countries are adjusted at the regional level.

The network review—among other functions—is meant to adjust potential biases in the levels of ratings across regions (box 3.3). The evidence from the 2007 review process indicates that there was not much difference between IBRD and IDA countries in terms of the extent of network disagreement with the regions' initial rating proposals. For all countries, the networks disagreed with about 12.5 percent of the initial regional ratings proposed for IDA countries, compared with only a slightly lower share of 11.8 percent of the ratings for IBRD countries (table 3.6).

The differences were much more significant when the comparison was made at the regional level. For every region except Latin America

and the Caribbean, the networks challenged initial regional proposals for a larger share of IDA than IBRD countries. For both IBRD and IDA countries, there was greater disagreement between network and regions for Europe and Central Asia than for all the other regions (for 16 and 20 percent of Europe and Central Asia countries, respectively). For 7 of the 16 criteria, the networks disagreed more often with regional proposals of ratings for IBRD countries, whereas for 9 of the 16 criteria, they disagreed more often with ratings for IDA countries (table 3.7).

The networks challenged the regional proposals more often for IDA than for IBRD countries for all regions except Latin America and the Caribbean.

Ratings were more likely to be challenged by the networks when the regions proposed an increase from 2006, and much more so for IDA than for IBRD countries. Specifically, when the networks challenged regional proposals, it was

Table 3.6: Numbers and Shares of Initial Regional Rating Proposals on Which the Networks Disagreed with the Regions, by Criteria, for 2007

CPIA criterion	Total		For IBRD countries		For IDA countries	
	No. of times networks differed	Share of all ratings (%)	No. of times networks differed	Share of all ratings (%)	No. of times networks differed	Share of all ratings (%)
q1	24	17.1	12	18.5	12	16.0
q2	28	20.0	12	18.5	16	21.3
q3	27	19.3	12	18.5	15	20.0
q4	12	8.6	6	9.2	6	8.0
q5	15	10.7	9	13.8	6	8.0
q6	11	7.9	6	9.2	5	6.7
q7	28	20.0	11	16.9	17	22.7
q8	8	5.7	3	4.6	5	6.7
q9	22	15.7	10	15.4	12	16.0
q10	6	4.3	2	3.1	4	5.3
q11	10	7.1	4	6.2	6	8.0
q12	10	7.1	5	7.7	5	6.7
q13	17	12.1	4	6.2	13	17.3
q14	22	15.7	12	18.5	10	13.3
q15	13	9.3	7	10.8	6	8.0
q16	20	14.3	8	12.3	12	16.0
Total	273	12.2	123	11.8	150	12.5

Source: IEG, based on World Bank data.

Note: IBRD= International Bank for Reconstruction and Development; IDA= International Development Association.

Networks challenged regional proposals more often for Europe and Central Asia—for 18 percent of the ratings compared to 12 percent for all regions.

found that in 59 percent of the time the regions had proposed an increase. This ratio was 66 percent for IDA countries compared to a much lower 50 percent for IBRD countries (table 3.8). *This indicates that the networks perceived more of an upward bias in the ratings for IDA countries than for IBRD countries.*

higher for IBRD countries (86 percent) than for IDA countries (73 percent) (table 3.9). Thus, the conclusion can be drawn that for those 73 and 86 percent of instances, there was indeed an upward bias in ratings. However, these instances made up *only 6 percent of the ratings for IDA countries and about 5 percent of the ratings for IBRD countries, which implies that there was not a severe upward bias in ratings for either group of countries.*

The role of the networks in validating the ratings helps to minimize the potential for bias in the ratings.

Regarding the instances in which the networks challenged a rating increase from the regions, the networks prevailed in an overwhelming majority of 77 percent of the time. The share was

Taking into account all disagreements—that is, including also instances where regions proposed no change or a decrease in ratings in addition to an increase in ratings—the 73 percent in which network views prevailed dropped somewhat to

Table 3.7: Number and Share of Initial Regional Rating Proposals on Which the Networks Disagreed with the Regions, by Region and IBRD and IDA Countries for 2007

Region	Number of rating proposals on which networks disagreed with regions			Share of rating proposals on which networks disagreed with regions (%)		
	Total	IBRD	IDA	Total	IBRD	IDA
Africa	82	10	72	11.4	7.8	12.2
East Asia and Pacific	28	6	22	8.8	4.2	12.5
Europe and Central Asia	81	55	26	17.5	16.4	20.3
Latin America and Caribbean	55	40	15	12.3	13.2	10.4
Middle East and North Africa	16	12	4	10.0	9.4	12.5
South Asia	11	n.a.	11	8.6	n.a.	8.6
Total	273	123	150	12.2	11.8	12.5

Source: IEG, based on data from OPCS.

Note: IBRD= International Bank for Reconstruction and Development; IDA= International Development Association.

68 percent, which is still high (table 3.10). In sum, the evidence reflects *the central role of the networks in the review process, which helps to minimize potential biases in ratings*.

The networks prevailed in the majority of the cases for all regions except South Asia and prevailed most often for Latin America and the Caribbean. *The networks also prevailed more often for IBRD than for IDA countries overall* (77 versus 61 percent of the time). This could either mean that the regions have more supporting evidence for the ratings they proposed for IDA than for IBRD countries, or that the regions make a bigger effort for IDA countries because IDA funds are involved (this evaluation has obtained anecdotal evidence from interviews with World Bank staff on this).

The nature of the network review (that is, the resource-intensiveness of the review) appears to have an effect on the extent of the review, and hence possibly on the quality of the ratings. The evidence from the 2007 review process indicated that four criteria stood out as having been more rigorously reviewed than other criteria, including the three *economic management* criteria and

the criterion on *building human resources*. For these four criteria, the networks commented on the initial regional rating proposals even when the regions did not propose a change in ratings from the previous year (table 3.11). As discussed in box 3.3, these were also the criteria on which the networks had invested the most time. For the four criteria the reviewer read all of the write-ups. Additionally, for the three criteria on *economic management*, each reviewer was responsible for

Table 3.8: Network Disagreements with Initial Regional Rating Proposals

Regional proposals	All countries (%)	IBRD countries (%)	IDA countries (%)
Lower rating than 2006	1.9	2.7	1.3
Same rating as 2006	39.2	47.8	32.7
Higher rating than 2006	58.9	49.6	66.0

Source: IEG based on World Bank data.

Note: IBRD= International Bank for Reconstruction and Development; IDA= International Development Association.

Table 3.9: Share of Instances Where Networks Prevailed When Networks Disagreed with Regions over Proposed Increases in Ratings from 2006

Region	All countries (%)	IBRD countries (%)	IDA countries (%)
Africa	74.5	83.3	73.5
East Asia and Pacific	80.0	100.0	78.6
Europe and Central Asia	69.8	82.6	55.0
Latin America and Caribbean	92.6	89.5	100.0
Middle East and North Africa	81.8	85.7	75.0
South Asia	75.0	n.a.	75.0
Total	77.4	85.7	72.7

Source: IEG, based on OPCS data.

Note: IBRD= International Bank for Reconstruction and Development; IDA= International Development Association.

about six countries for which he or she also read reports from the International Monetary Fund (IMF), Debt Sustainability Assessments, and the private sector reports.

Conclusions

Analysis of the 2007 review process indicates that the networks perceived more of an upward bias in ratings for IDA than for IBRD countries. This upward bias did not seem very severe, as it could only be detected in about 6 percent of the ratings for IDA countries and about 5 percent of the ratings for IBRD countries. Analysis of the 2007 review process also indicates that the networks did have a central role in the ratings review process, as they prevailed in the majority—although not all—of the cases when there were initial disagreements between them and the regions. This helps to minimize potential biases in the ratings. Finally, the quality of the ratings is likely to be enhanced by greater intensiveness in the network review, which would entail more resources than have been provided for the exercise.

Country context

The greater comparability of the ratings on IBRD than IDA countries with other indicators highlights one issue with respect to the CPIA ratings generation process—that aspect of country context that refers to the stage of development. Specifically, the questionnaire stated, "The criteria were developed to ensure that, to the extent possible, their contents are developmental neutral; that the higher scores do not set unduly demanding standards, and can be attained by a country that,

Table 3.10: Share of Instances Where Networks Prevailed When Networks Disagreed with Regions, 2007

Region	All countries (%)	IBRD countries (%)	IDA countries (%)
Africa	68.3	90.0	65.3
East Asia and Pacific	60.7	66.7	59.1
Europe and Central Asia	63.0	70.9	46.2
Latin America and Caribbean	87.3	87.5	86.7
Middle East and North Africa	68.8	66.7	75.0
South Asia	27.3	n.a.	27.3
Total	68.1	77.2	60.7

Source: IEG, based on OPCS data.

Note: IBRD= International Bank for Reconstruction and Development; IDA= International Development Association.

Table 3.11: Shares of Countries on Which Networks Commented in 2007 When Regions Proposed the Same Ratings as in 2006

CPIA criterion	All countries (%)	IBRD countries (%)	IDA countries (%)
q1	89.2	88.9	89.6
q2	84.5	89.6	80.0
q3	85.3	88.6	82.4
q4	50.8	58.5	44.8
q5	3.4	5.9	1.5
q6	3.6	5.7	1.7
q7	28.8	28.8	28.8
q8	9.2	9.3	9.2
q9	83.8	88.5	80.0
q10	44.6	44.6	44.6
q11	0.0	0.0	0.0
q12	13.7	16.7	11.4
q13	1.0	0.0	1.9
q14	14.0	18.0	10.9
q15	5.0	7.4	3.1
q16	8.4	8.0	8.8
Total	31.5	33.7	29.6

Source: IEG, based on data from OPCS.

Note: IBRD= International Bank for Reconstruction and Development; IDA= International Development Association.

given its *stage of development* [italics by IEG], has a policy and institutional framework that strongly fosters growth and poverty reduction." (CPIA Questionnaires 2004–08). (The most recent CPIA Questionnaire available at the time of this writing was for 2008).

Different practices are adopted by the regions and networks with respect to country context. Discussions with regional reviewers indicate that none of the regions take country context into account in the rating exercise. Discussions with network reviewers indicate that "country context" is interpreted quite differently by different network reviewers. Some interpret it to mean that the country-specific information provided by the country teams needs to be taken into account in the assessment. Some interpret it to mean that different policies and institutions can

achieve similar results. Still others interpret it to mean the stage of development, but account for it in different ways, with some ways being more subjective than others. Those who account for the stage of development objectively adjust the indicators they are assessing by per capita incomes (for the *gender* criterion, and for the *finance* criterion until two years ago). Regardless of how country context is interpreted, many network reviewers find the concept difficult to implement, and had comments such as "...this is the single toughest thing."

The greater comparability of the ratings for IBRD than for IDA countries with other indicators highlights the problem with accounting for the stage of development in the CPIA ratings.

Aside from the mixed interpretation of "country context"—which can distort the quality of the ratings—the fact that judgment is involved in accounting for "country context" introduces

Regardless of how it is interpreted, network reviewers find the concept of country context difficult to implement.

further subjectivity to an exercise that already relies centrally on judgment. Minimizing the amount of subjectivity involved in the rating exercise would help to enhance the quality of the ratings.

The first interpretation of country context by network reviewers—taking into account country-specific information—is reasonable. After all, the deep country knowledge of Bank staff is the major value added that the Bank brings to the CPIA rating exercise.

Accounting for the stage of development is problematic because of the judgment involved and the uneven practice across the Bank.

An example can be found in the *gender* criterion, which assesses, among other things, the share and growth rate of parliamentary seats occupied by women. However, a straightforward use of these indicators could be misleading. For example, a recent study on Bangladesh revealed that although gender quotas increased the total number of women in political arenas, their representation in the decision-making process is still not ensured as elected female representatives in Bangladesh face social, cultural, and religious challenges which hinder their participation (Panday 2008). This is the very kind of useful qualitative information that the country team could potentially provide in terms of "country context."

Regarding the second interpretation that different policies and institutions can lead to similar results, the literature review conducted for this evaluation indicates that, by and large, the CPIA criteria overlap with what are considered as the consensus determinants of growth and poverty reduction by the wider research community, and not just by the Bank (chapter 2). However, the *trade* criterion is problematic and needs to be revised, as discussed in chapter 2.

Implementation of the third interpretation of country context—the stage of development—is also problematic. The simplest way would be to adjust the ratings quantitatively, using per capita incomes. The issue then arises as to which criteria or subcriteria to adjust, because the stage of development is only pertinent for some (sub) criteria but not others. For example, the development of the financial sector clearly depends on the stage of development of the country. Therefore, it is reasonable to adjust the indicator being assessed (for example, private sector credit as a GDP) by per capita incomes, which had previously been, but is no longer, done by the network reviewer. It is not clear how much the stage of development matters for other criteria. Thus, deciding which criteria or subcriteria to adjust for the stage of development would itself be controversial.

In addition to which (sub)criteria to adjust for stage of development, how to adjust such (sub)criteria is also an issue. Although it is more straightforward to adjust quantitative indicators (although the methodology can be subject to debate), when it comes to qualitative indicators (and many CPIA criteria are assessed on such indicators), it is very difficult to adjust and the process could be open to a lot of arbitrariness.

The adjustment of CPIA ratings by the stage of development has affected the quality of these ratings, to the extent that some network reviewers indicated to the IEG team that they do not use the ratings for their own analytical work. In contrast, network reviewers who do not adjust the CPIA ratings for the stage of development indicated to the IEG team that they do use the ratings for their own analytical work, reflecting the confidence they have in the ratings.

IEG recommends excluding accounting for the stage of development from the CPIA exercise. If this cannot be done, at the very least it is important to clarify and justify in the CPIA guidelines which criteria need to take into account the stage of development and how such adjustments need to be made.

Chapter 4

Quay crane on docks, Sri Lanka. Photo by Dominic Sansoni, World Bank

Findings and Recommendations

The CPIA criteria are largely relevant for sustaining growth and improving welfare. By and large, the CPIA covers the determinants—policies and institutions—of growth and poverty reduction identified in the literature. However, some criteria can be streamlined and one needs to be added. The assessment of certain criteria needs to be coordinated, and the content of all criteria reviewed (see recommendations later in this chapter).

Overview

This evaluation takes the premise that beyond informing IDA allocation, the CPIA is useful as a broad indicator of development effectiveness. It reviews the appropriateness of the CPIA as an indicator that assesses the conduciveness of a country's policies and institutions to fostering poverty reduction, sustainable growth, and the effective use of development assistance. It assesses the relevance of the content of the CPIA through a review of the economics literature. It also assesses the reliability of CPIA ratings in two ways—through comparing CPIA ratings with similar indicators, and through reviewing the CPIA ratings generation process. Based on these assessments, the main findings and recommendations are as follows.

Main Findings
CPIA content

The evidence is mixed as to whether the CPIA criteria are relevant for aid effectiveness as defined in the literature—that is, *whether the criteria represent the policies and institutions that are important for aid to lead to growth.* Much of the literature on aid effectiveness uses cross-country empirics to estimate the impact of aid on growth, with growth representing aid effectiveness. The review of the literature indicates that there is limited consensus on the impact of aid on growth itself, and on the conditions under which aid can have a positive impact on growth. Also, this evaluation could not estimate the impact of IDA assistance and CPIA ratings on growth because the restructuring of the CPIA in 2004 has resulted in a discontinuity in the CPIA series.

However, CPIA ratings are found to be positively associated with Bank loan performance. Specifically, empirical analysis conducted for this evaluation finds that the ratings of the overall CPIA as well as those for each of the CPIA clusters are negatively associated with the share of problem loans (that are in turn correlated with loan performance).

Empirical analysis also indicates that there is insufficient evidence from the data to conclude that cluster D associates better with loan performance than the other three clusters. The new country performance rating that is used for IDA allocations has made explicit the relative weights applied to the different clusters of the CPIA, that is, 8 percent on each of CPIA clusters A, B, and C, and 68 percent on CPIA cluster D. Neither the literature review on the determinants of growth, poverty reduction and development effectiveness, nor the empirical analysis conducted by IEG, has provided evidence to justify these (or any other) specific weights. It can therefore be surmised that *the way the CPIA is currently being used for IDA allocation—that is, with a large emphasis on cluster D—seems to be driven much more by fiduciary and possibly other concerns of donors than by the objectives of achieving sustained growth and poverty reduction.*

The CPIA strives to allow for country specificity, although there are some potential pitfalls. An important aspect of country specificity is that different policies and institutions can produce similar outcomes. The CPIA strives to provide for this aspect of country specificity in its instruction to staff: when assessing policies and institutions, outcomes need to be taken into account. Indeed, outcome indicators are included in the assessment of certain CPIA criteria (for example, *finance* and *gender*), but they could be added to other criteria, in particular *trade*.

The CPIA does not adequately allow for country specificity in its trade criterion. The way in which the *trade* criterion is specified does not allow for different approaches to trade liberalization that have proven successful in country experiences. The specification of particular tariff rates for different ratings reflects a one-size-fit-all approach to trade liberalization that is not supported by country experience. Revising this criterion by changing the way trade restrictiveness is assessed, and including an assessment of export performance as the outcome variable, would allow for more country specificity to be incorporated into the criterion.

The trade criterion does not reflect the importance of complementary institutions for improving trade performance. Incorporating export performance in the assessment of the *trade* criterion would also reflect the evidence that integrating into the global economy—an important determinant of growth—requires integration on both the export and import fronts. Country experience further indicates that complementary factors—including trade facilitation—are also important for export growth and, in fact, more important than further tariff reduction once countries reach moderate tariff levels (which practically all countries currently have). Yet not only does the *trade* criterion of the CPIA focus mostly on the import side, but the much larger weight accorded to trade restrictiveness (two-thirds) than to trade facilitation (one-third) also does not give enough importance to complementary factors.

Accounting for country specificity requires substantial judgment. Incorporating outcome variables in the assessment of CPIA criteria allows for country specificity, although it needs to be recognized that this entails substantial judgment. On the one hand, the reason the CPIA focuses on assessing policies and institutions is to avoid penalizing countries for not achieving certain outcomes because of exogenous factors. On the other hand, assessing outcomes could penalize countries at a lower stage of development for not achieving those outcomes (such as the share of private sector credit as a share of GDP). Thus, substantial judgment is needed to take these two aspects into account in a balanced fashion.

The debate over the weighting scheme is not very relevant for the use of the CPIA as a broad index, although it is very relevant in its use in the PBA formula. With respect to the use of the CPIA as a broad index of policies and institutions, the debate over the weighting scheme is not very relevant given the high correlation between the ratings of the CPIA clusters. However, the weights applied to the different CPIA clusters do matter for the allocation of IDA funds.

These findings raise the question of the usefulness of aggregating the different CPIA clusters into an overall index according to any predetermined weighting scheme. In the case of the CPIA as a broad index of development effectiveness, it does not allow for country specificity which would imply different weights on the clusters depending on the initial conditions and the countries' stage of development. In the case of the CPIA as an indicator for the allocation of IDA funds, the *overall* CPIA index is no longer used as such.

The CPIA is missing an assessment on other disadvantaged socioeconomic groups aside from gender. Currently, only gender is being assessed with respect to equality. Yet country evidence indicates that social exclusion of other groups could have severe poverty and growth implications.

Important interlinkages between certain criteria are not reflected in the CPIA. Country evidence indicates that intersectoral labor mobility needs to be ensured before trade liberalization proceeds. Otherwise, trade liberalization could exacerbate poverty. Similarly, the assessment of *fiscal policy* (q2) and the *quality of budgetary and financial management* (q13) needs to go hand-in-hand so that the fiscal aspect of the country in its entirety is realistically captured.

Assessment or reporting of certain CPIA criteria can be streamlined or restructured. The current content of the criterion on *equity of public resource use* is redundant. This does not mean that equity is not important. In fact, equity has been identified in the literature as one of the determinants of growth on which there is consensus. However, the measures identified in the literature as being important for equity—property rights, access to credit, access to education, gender equality, and income transfers—are already covered by other CPIA criteria. The criterion is currently assessed on two fronts—the public expenditure and public revenues sides. The former is covered by other CPIA criteria, whereas the assessment of the latter requires incidence analysis of taxes, which is rarely done. As a result, Bank staff does not

have enough information to meaningfully rate this subcomponent.

There are overlaps in the assessment of some criteria. Tax policy is an intrinsic part of fiscal policy and can be assessed as part of it rather than separately, as is the case now. Judicial independence is assessed in two different criteria and corruption in three different criteria of cluster D, all of which can be streamlined.

The assessment of the *environment* criterion is onerous. It requires country teams to answer 85 questions to arrive at one rating.

The three *economic management* criteria—*macroeconomic management, fiscal policy,* and *debt policy*—are conceptually not distinct from each other, and hence need to be, and indeed are assessed together. Yet separate scores are prepared and published for each of the three criteria (for IDA countries), which could lead to confusion.

The in-depth literature review of the financial sector criterion reveals room for improvement. Although the criterion covers the dimensions along which finance is currently thought to be important—stability, depth and efficiency, and access—the relative weights of the three dimensions (which are currently equally weighted) need to be revisited. This follows from the considerable evidence of a large impact of banking crises on output losses and on the national budget. At the same time, the evidence on microfinance is mixed. Further, there is a greater focus in this criterion on assessing intermediate outcomes rather than policies and institutions, in particular regarding the financial depth dimension. It would be useful to include policies and institutions for fostering an enabling environment for the financial sector here, namely the legal, contractual, informational, and governance framework. Also, the indicators for assessing financial stability can be strengthened.

CPIA ratings
The CPIA ratings correlate relatively well with similar indicators in terms of relative

rankings of countries and direction of change. For each of the 16 CPIA criteria, the rank correlations of CPIA ratings with similar indicators average between 0.7 and 0.8. Other indicators are found to correlate better with the CPIA ratings by the Bank than by the AfDB and the ADB, which are the closest comparators to the Bank, as they use almost exactly the same CPIA guidelines as the Bank.

CPIA ratings correlate better with other indicators for IBRD than for IDA countries. This could be because more information is available on IBRD countries than on IDA countries, which increases the likelihood of different institutions having similar assessments on IBRD countries. This could also be because the Bank takes into account the stage of development when rating countries. This is more pertinent for IDA countries and entails judgment, which would likely make ratings for IDA countries less comparable with those by other institutions.

Accounting for the stage of development in the CPIA ratings is problematic. As noted, accounting for the stage of development could have affected the quality of the CPIA ratings, not only because of the judgment involved, but also because of the different practices employed across the Bank. None of the regional reviewers and only some of the network reviewers take the stage of development into account in their ratings. The network reviewers who take stage of development into account do it in a variety of ways—some by adjusting quantitative indicators with per capita incomes, and some by their own judgment. Further, accounting for the stage of development means that the CPIA is no longer an index in the true sense of the word.

The strength of the CPIA ratings is Bank staff's professional judgment. The central determinant of the ratings is the expert judgment of Bank staff (with deep country knowledge), which is clearly the major asset of this exercise. At the same time, however, there is a potential conflict of interest in having Bank staff provide ratings that are used for allocating IDA resources to those countries on which the work programs

of Bank staff depend. However, analysis of the 2007 review process indicates that there did not seem to be much of an upward bias in ratings for either IDA or IBRD countries. Such an upward bias could be detected in only 6 percent of the ratings for IDA countries, and a slightly lower 5 percent of the ratings for IBRD countries.

The multistep review process of the CPIA, with the networks having the central role in the validation of the ratings, helps guard against the potential biases in ratings. Specifically, the networks were found to prevail for a large majority of the time when they disagreed with the regions over the latter's initial rating proposals in 2007. Interestingly, the networks prevailed more often for IBRD countries than for IDA countries. This could either mean that the regions have more supporting evidence for the ratings they proposed for IDA than for IBRD countries, or that the regions put up a greater effort for IDA countries because IDA funds are involved (this evaluation has obtained anecdotal evidence on that front).

Both the regional and network reviewers pointed out the high degree of judgment involved in rating the criteria in the public sector management and institutions cluster (D). This calls into further question the large weight this cluster has in the IDA allocation formula. All of the regional reviewers who were asked the open-ended question of which criteria they found particularly difficult to rate gave cluster D as their response. One of the network reviewers for cluster D indicated that a lot of judgment was involved in most of the criteria in that cluster and pointed to the criterion on *transparency, accountability, and corruption* as an example.

Recommendations

Based on the above findings, IEG has several recommendations to Bank management for improving the CPIA as an indicator that represents the policies and institutions that are important for sustaining growth, fostering poverty reduction (or enhancing welfare more broadly), and the effective use of development assistance.

These recommendations are aimed at enhancing the CPIA as a broad indicator of policies and institutions, more than just as an indicator for the allocation of IDA funds. If the CPIA were viewed only in the latter context, then the question could be raised as to the necessity of rating IBRD countries.

Adoption of these recommendations could result in a discontinuity in the CPIA ratings, which Bank management has been trying to avoid. However, it is important that the CPIA reflect the latest thinking in development paradigm and lessons learned (both of which are stated intentions of the Bank regarding the CPIA). It would also provide the opportunity to address an issue that some network reviewers have raised regarding the quality of the ratings for some criteria because of what they perceive as inflated baseline ratings from a few years ago. The proposed recommendations are as follows:

Disclose ratings for IBRD countries. Disclosure is important for accountability and transparency and would further enhance the quality of the ratings.

Remove accounting for the stage of development in the CPIA rating exercise. If this cannot be done, at the very least the CPIA guidelines need to specify and justify which criteria should take into account the stage of development and how the adjustments should be made.

Undertake a thorough review of each CPIA criterion and revise as necessary. It is recommended that the review entail an in-depth literature review for each criterion and reflect the latest thinking on development and lessons learned. The review needs to take into account the balance between liberalization and regulation. It also needs to examine the clustering of the criteria, in particular having social sectors and the environment in one cluster. Guideposts for assessing the criteria need to be reviewed at the same time. It is also recommended that the following be taken into account in the review and revisions:

- Revision of the *trade* criterion (q4). A subcomponent on exports needs to be added that assesses export performance and policies and institutions to reduce anti-export bias (such as export rebate and duty drawback). This new subcomponent, and the existing subcomponents on trade restrictiveness and trade facilitation, need to all receive equal weights (that is, one-third weight each). The tariff rates in the trade restrictiveness subcomponent need to be revised to reflect country experience that at moderate tariff levels (which almost all countries have), further tariff reduction is less important than complementary factors (such as macroeconomic stability and trade facilitation) for global integration.

- Dropping or reformulating the criterion on *equity of public resource use* (q8), as the current content is already covered by other criteria.

- Addition of an assessment of other marginalized socioeconomic groups to the CPIA. The assessment of other marginalized socioeconomic groups could either be added as a new criterion (in place of the criterion on *equity of public resource use,* which IEG recommends dropping) or added to a reformulated criterion on *equity of public resource use.*

- Revision of the *financial sector* criterion (q5). The weights on the three subcomponents—stability, depth and efficiency, access—need to be revisited in light of the importance of stability and the mixed evidence on microfinance. Policies, regulations, and institutions for fostering an enabling environment for the financial sector need to be added. The indicators used in the assessment of financial stability need to be strengthened.

- Combining the assessment of *tax policy* (q14a) with the assessment of *fiscal policy.* That part of tax policy that assesses import tariffs is already being assessed in the *trade* criterion, whereas the part on export rebate and duty drawback need to be incorporated into the revised *trade* criterion as suggested above.

- Streamlining the assessment of judicial independence in the public sector management and institutions cluster. Currently, judicial independence is assessed in both the criterion on *property rights and governance* (q12) and the criterion on *transparency, accountability, and corruption in the public sector* (q16).

- Streamlining the assessment of corruption in the public sector management and institutions cluster. Currently corruption is assessed in the criteria on *efficiency of revenue mobilization* (q14), the *quality of public administration* (q15), and *transparency, accountability, and corruption in the public sector* (q16).
- Strengthening the assessment of the *environment* criterion (q11) and make the process more efficient. Currently, staff need to answer 85 questions to arrive at one rating.
- Reporting only the consolidated score for the *economic management* cluster.

Consider not producing an overall CPIA index although continue to produce and publish the separate CPIA components. IDA is already using the components separately in the PBA formula. With respect to the use of the CPIA as a broad index of policies and institutions, this would allow for country specificity, as different weights could be assigned to the different clusters depending on the country's initial conditions and stage of development. Producing the different components of the CPIA without assigning weights to them to arrive at an aggregate index would allow for different weights to be applied according to country contexts and use.

Appendixes

Landscape view of water, glaciers and mountains, Chile. Photo by Curt Carnemark/World Bank.

CLUSTER (weight in index)		CRITERIA (weight in index)	INDICATORS (weight in index)
Economic management (0.25)	q1	Macroeconomic management (0.083)	• Monetary/exchange rate policy with clearly defined price stability objectives • Aggregate demand policies focus on maintaining short- and medium-term external balance. • Avoid crowding out private investment
	q2	Fiscal policy (0.083)	• Primary balance managed to ensure sustainability of public finances • Public expenditure/revenue can be adjusted to absorb shocks • Provision of public goods including infrastructure consistent with medium-term growth
	q3	Debt policy (0.083)	• Debt burden indicators do not signal debt servicing difficulties • External and internal debt contracted with view to achieving/maintaining debt sustainability • Coordination between debt management and other macroeconomic policies • Debt management unit well established, has adequate system for recording and monitoring debt, and good analytical capacity as indicated by regular analytical work on debt • Accurate, timely, and publicly available debt data • Government has clear financing strategy and the legal framework for borrowing is clearly defined.
Structural policies (0.25)	q4	Trade (0.083)	• 75 percent weight for *trade restrictiveness*: (0.063) • Average tariff rates, number of tariff bands, maximum tariff band • Internal taxes do not discriminate between imported and local products • Transparency and predictability of trade regime including in the use of non-tariff barriers • 25 percent weight for *customs/trade facilitation*: (0.02) • Reputation of customs with respect to professionalism and corruption • Use of risk management, information technology (IT), physical examination • Processing of collections and refunds • Documentation of customs procedures • Resolutions of appeals of customs decisions.
	q5	Financial Sector (0.083)	*Financial stability* • Banking sector's vulnerability to shocks • Banking system soundness (share of non-performing loans [NPLs] and level of capital at risk) • Adherence to Basel Core Principles • Quality of risk management in financial institutions • Quality of supervision. *Financial sector efficiency, depth, and resource mobilization* • Size and reach of financial markets • Development of capital markets • Interest rate spreads • Private sector credit/GDP • Efficiency of microfinance.

(*continued on next page*)

CLUSTER (weight in index)		CRITERIA (weight in index)	INDICATORS (weight in index)
Structural policies (0.25) (cont.)			*Access to financial services* • Development of payment, clearance, and credit reporting systems • Share of population with access to formal sector financial services • Access of small and medium enterprises (SMEs) to finance • Legal and regulatory framework supporting access to finance.
	q6	Business Regulatory Environment (0.083)	*Regulations affecting entry, exit, and competition* (0.028) • Bans on, or, investment licensing requirements • Entry and exit procedures • Legal framework (and implementation thereof) to address anti-competitive conduct by firms • Procurement by public sector firms. *Regulations of ongoing business operations* (0.028) • Operational licensing, permits, compliance and inspection requirements including taxes and customs • State intervention in goods markets (state ownership in competitive sectors, price controls, state making administrative allocation/decisions about production) • Corporate governance laws (and enforcement thereof) to encourage disclosure and protect shareholders rights. *Regulations of goods and factor markets* (0.028) • Employment law provides for flexibility in hiring and firing • State intervention in labor and land markets limited to regulation and/or legislation to smooth out market imperfections • Procedures to register property are simple and low-cost.
Policies for Social Inclusion/ Equity (0.25)	q7	Gender Equality (0.05)	*Human capital development* (0.017) • Differences (between male and female) in primary completion rates, and access to secondary education (female to male enrollment) • Access to delivery care and family planning services • Adolescent fertility rate. *Access to economic and productive resources* (0.017) • Gender disparities in labor force participation, land tenure, property ownership, and inheritance practices. *Status and protection under the law* (0.017) • The law gives men and women equal individual and family rights • Violence against women considered a crime • Gender disparities in political participation at the national level.
	q8	Equity of Public Resource Use (0.05)	*Government spending* (0.033) • Identification of individuals, groups, or localities that are poor, vulnerable, or have unequal access to services and opportunities • Adoption of national development strategy with explicit interventions to assist groups identified above • Systematic tracking of composition and incidence of public expenditures and their results feedback into subsequent allocations. *Revenue collection* (0.017) • Incidence of major taxes (progressive or regressive) and their alignment with poverty reduction priorities.
	q9	Building Human Resources (0.05)	*Health and nutrition including reproductive health* (0.017) • Equitable access to basic health services • Prevention of malnutrition.

CLUSTER (weight in index)		CRITERIA (weight in index)	INDICATORS (weight in index)
Policies for Social Inclusion/ Equity (0.25) (cont.)	q9 (cont.)	Building Human Resources (0.05)	*Education* (0.017) • Sustained progress toward universal basic education, literacy, and more equitable access to early child development program services • Standards for teacher preparation, student learning, and oversight of private/non-governmental organization (NGO) providers • Systematic tracking of school performance and student learning outcomes and feedback to schools and parents • Policies for post-basic education and training services • Quality, equity of access, and efficiency of resource use. *Human immunodeficiency virus/Acquired immunodeficiency syndrome (HIV/AIDS), tuberculosis, malaria* • Prevention, treatment, care and support of HIV/AIDS, tuberculosis, and malaria • Track disease prevalence, resources, and program implementation. • Quality and timeliness of services • Focus on the poor • Cost-effective use of public resources
	q10	Social Protection and Labor (0.05)	*Social safety net programs* (0.01) • Social protection programs provide income support to poor and vulnerable groups. *Protection of basic labor standards* (0.01) • Ratification and implementation of international core labor standards. *Labor market regulations* (0.01) • Labor market regulations on health and safety, working conditions, and hiring and firing. *Community-driven initiatives* (0.01) • Encourage and support communities' own development initiatives or local accountability mechanisms. *Pension and old-age savings programs* (0.01) • Pension and savings programs provide income security to most potentially vulnerable groups.
	q11	Policies and Institutions for Environmental Sustainability (0.05)	• Regulations and policies (and implementation thereof) for pollution and natural resource • Information widely available • Priority setting • Sector ministries incorporate environmental concerns.
Public Sector Management and Institutions (0.25)	q12	Property Rights and Rule-Based Governance (0.05)	*Legal basis for secure property and contract rights* (0.017) • Transparent and well-protected property rights • Current and non-corrupt property registries • Enforced contracts. *Predictability, transparency, and impartiality of laws and regulations affecting economic activity* (0.017) • Transparent and predictable laws and regulations affecting businesses and individuals • Low-cost means for pursuing small claims • Impartial and predictable applications of laws and regulations. *Crime and violence as impediment to economic activity* (0.017) • Well-functioning and accountable police force protects citizens and their property from crime and violence.

(*continued on next page*)

CLUSTER (weight in index)	CRITERIA (weight in index)		INDICATORS (weight in index)
Public Sector Management and Institutions (0.25) (cont.)	q13	Quality of Budgetary and Financial Management (0.05)	*Comprehensive and credible budget linked to policy priorities* (0.017) • Multiyear expenditure projections integrated into budget formulation process • Spending ministries and the legislature consulted in budget formulation, adhering to fixed budget calendar • Budget classification system comprehensive and consistent with international standards • Minimal and transparent off-budget items. *Financial management* (0.017) • Budget implemented as planned • Budget monitoring based on management information systems • Negligible payment arrears. *Fiscal reporting* (0.017) • Reconciliation of banking and fiscal records • Regular in-year fiscal reporting • Timely preparation of public accounts • Timely auditing of accounts and appropriate action taken on budget reports and audit findings.
	q14	Efficiency of Revenue Mobilization (0.05)	*Tax policy* (0.025) • Bulk of revenues from low-distortion taxes such as sales/value-added tax (VAT), property, and so forth • Low and relatively uniform import taxes • Functional export rebate or duty drawback • Broad tax base • Few arbitrary exemptions. *Tax administration* (0.025) • Rule-based tax administration • Low administrative and compliance costs • Taxpayer service and information program • Efficient and effective appeals mechanism.
	q15	Quality of Public Administration (0.05)	*Policy coordination and responsiveness* (0.0125) • Effective coordination mechanism to ensure high degree of policy consistency. *Service delivery and operational efficiency* (0.0125) • Organizational structures along functional lines with little duplication; regular review of business processes to ensure efficient decision making. *Merit and ethics* (0.0125) • Hiring and promotion based on merit and performance; ethics prevail. *Pay adequacy and management of the wage bill* (0.0125) • Sustainable wage bill that does not crowd out public services spending • Pay and benefit levels adequate • Flexibility in paying higher wages for hard-to-fill positions.
	q16	Transparency, Accountability, and Corruption in the Public Sector (0.05)	*Accountability of the executive to oversight institutions and of public employees for their performance* (0.017) • Strong public service ethic reinforced by audits, inspections, and adverse publicity for performance failures • Independent and impartial judiciary • Corruption monitored and sanctions implemented. *Access of civil society to information on public affairs* (0.017) • Results and costs of government decisions clear and communicated to public • Citizens can access government documents at nominal cost • Media independent of government and can fulfill critical oversight roles. *State capture by narrow vested interests* (0.017) • Conflict of interest and ethics rules for public servants observed and enforced • Top government officials required to disclose income and assets and can be prosecuted for malfeasance.

Country Policy and Institutional Assessment (CPIA) Criteria/Indicators	Literature on:		
	Sustained growth	Poverty reduction	Development effectiveness
Property Rights and Rule-Based Governance			
Legal basis for secure property and contract rights			
Transparent and well-protected property rights	• Property rights associated with per capita incomes (Besley 1995). • Property rights associated with investments (Acemoglu, Johnson, and Robinson 2005; Bardhan 2006b). • Existence of market exchange presupposes property rights (Rodrik 2003). • Positive correlation between property rights and growth—cross-country studies (Knack and Keefer 1995; Mauro 1995; Hall and Jones 1999; Rodrik 1999; De Soto 2000; Rodrik, Subramanian, and Trebbi 2002; Summers 2003; Kerekes and Williamson 2008). • Positive correlation between property rights and growth—micro studies (Mazingo 1999; Johnson, McMillan, and Woodruff 2002).	• Governments can help the poor with access to credit by establishing functioning property rights (Fleisig 1995). • Obtaining property rights over land in urban areas helps poor households gain access to credit (De Soto 2000; Fields and others 2002). • Giving the poor land rights enhances their ability to utilize and invest in land they cultivate (Deolalikar and others 2002). • Increase in protection of property rights across the globe of half of one standard deviation would halve global poverty (Besley and Burgess 2003). • Increased protection of property rights has strong effects in reducing poverty (Acemoglu, Johnson, and Robinson 2001).	
Current and non-corrupt registries	• Use of registration system to establish identity of property owners (Shavell 2003). • De Soto (2000) used counter-examples from Malawi and Peru to underline the importance of a current and non-corrupt registry system.		
Enforced contracts	• Contract enforcement and growth (North 1990; Knack and Keefer 1995; Levine 1998; Hall and Jones 1999; Kaufmann, Kraay, and Mastruzzi 1999; Hellman, Jones, and Kaufmann 2003; Summers 2003).		

(continued on next page)

Country Policy and Institutional Assessment (CPIA) Criteria/Indicators	Literature on:		
	Sustained growth	Poverty reduction	Development effectiveness
Predictability, transparency, and impartiality of laws and regulations affecting economic activity			
Transparent and predictable laws and regulations affecting businesses and individuals	• Laws and regulations should be transparent to enable very imperfect courts to verify violations and correct wrongs (Hay, Shleifer, and Vishny 1996). • Unpredictable regulations are a disincentive to investment and hence lower growth: example (Gyimah-Brempong and Munoz de Camacho 2006). • Growth depends positively on the rule of law (Barro 2003).		
Low-cost means for pursuing small claims	• La Porta, Lopez-de-Silanes, and Shleifer (2008) emphasize that costly contract claims do not protect investors [and hence would be a disincentive to investment].		
Impartial and predictable applications of laws and regulations	• Predictability and impartiality characterizes the quality of the law enforcement, and richer countries have higher quality law enforcement (La Porta and others 1998).		
Crime and violence as impediment to economic activity			
Well-functioning and accountable police force to protect citizens and their property from crime and violence	• The police (and the courts) are most directly involved in determining and defending property rights (Andvig and Fjeldstad 2008). • High crime rates may have devastating impacts on investments and economic growth (Andvig and Fjeldstad 2008). • Crime has direct costs on firms through theft losses and security-related expenses, which reduce competitiveness and lower investment (Bourguignon 1998). • Security issues must be addressed to fully comprehend the nature and possibilities for socioeconomic development (Londono 1996; Moser 1996; Moser and Holland 1997; Inter-American Development Bank 1997; Ayers 1997; Buvinic, Morrison, and Shifter 1998; Call 2000). • Crime and violence are major obstacles to development objectives including lost growth in Latin America and the Caribbean (Schneidman 1996; Ayers 1997; Buvinic and Morrison 2000) and through losses in human capital (Heinemann and Verner 2006).	• Police corruption especially in slum areas of poorer countries may increase uncertainty of property rights of the very poor (Andvig and Fjeldstad 2008). • Violence disproportionately affects the poor in Latin America, eroding their assets and livelihoods (Heinemann and Verner 2006). • Victims of crimes are more likely to be the poorer part of the population (Bourguignon 1999; Deolalikar and others 2002).	
Quality of budgetary and financial management			

Good budgetary and financial management is of particular importance in developing countries because the absence of aggregate fiscal discipline could result in large unsustainable deficits that translate into an unstable macroeconomic environment (high inflation, high interest rates, burgeoning current account deficits) that ultimately retard growth (Fischer 1991; Easterly, Rodriguez and Schmidt-Hebbel, 1995; Gupta and others 2005). More effective public expenditure management and macroeconomic and budget stability are important for public expenditures to better serve the poor (Foster and others 2002).

Country Policy and Institutional Assessment (CPIA) Criteria/Indicators	Literature on:		
	Sustained growth	Poverty reduction	Development effectiveness
Comprehensive and credible budget linked to policy priorities			
Multiyear expenditure projections integrated into budget formulation process	• Aggregate fiscal discipline depends on the existence of a medium-term expenditure framework (Campos and Pradhan 1996). • Rationale for multiyear budget approach based on several potential benefits (Boex, Martinez-Vasquez, and McNab 2000).	Evidence is mixed: • Serving the poor more effectively through public expenditure requires a medium–term process for budget allocation (Foster and others 2002). • Changes in budgeting and expenditure planning unlikely to generate significantly improved performance where core functions continue to operate inadequately (Fozzard and Foster 2001).	
Spending ministries and the legislature consulted in budget formulation, adhering to fixed budget calendar	• Consulting spending ministries is important for them to have the correct perception of their budget constraints, which in turn reduces the possibility of excess spending (resulting from "aid illusion") (McGillivray and Morrissey 2001a, 2001b). • Explicit rules that put specific limits on spending and borrowing and that impose penalties on overspending by line ministries give central ministries more leverage over claimants (Campos and Pradhan1996).		
Budget classification system comprehensive and consistent with international standards	• No evidence available	• No evidence available	• No evidence available
Minimal and transparent off-budget items	• Integration of all expenditures in budget can help improve accountability and transparency by imposing political costs on politicians and bureaucrats for violating rules, and raise quality of budgetary and financial management (Campos and Pradhan 1996).		
Financial management			
Budget implemented as planned	• No evidence available	• No evidence available	• No evidence available
Budget monitoring based on management information systems	• No evidence available	• No evidence available	• No evidence available
Negligible payments arrears	• No evidence available	• No evidence available	• No evidence available

(*continued on next page*)

73

Country Policy and Institutional Assessment (CPIA) Criteria/Indicators	Literature on:		
	Sustained growth	Poverty reduction	Development effectiveness
Fiscal Reporting. This seems to be important for economic growth. In Latin America, countries with better fiscal transparency and additional spending controls have average fiscal *surpluses* of 1.7 percent of gross domestic product (GDP), whereas those with fewer spending controls and lowest levels of transparency have average *deficits* of 1.8 percent of GDP (Alesina 1997). Fiscal transparency—and transparency of the banking sector—is crucial in reducing vulnerability to economic shocks, particularly following the Asian Economic Crisis (International Monetary Fund 2000). The latter stemmed from inadequate disclosure of risks by government and banks (Fozzard and Foster 2001). Fiscal reporting is a core element of transparency, empowerment, and accountability (World Bank 2004g).			
Reconciliation of banking and fiscal records	• No evidence available	• No evidence available	• No evidence available
Regular in-year fiscal reporting	• No evidence available	• No evidence available	• No evidence available
Timely preparation of public accounts	• No evidence available	• No evidence available	• No evidence available
Timely auditing of accounts and appropriate action taken on budget reports and audit findings	• No evidence available	• No evidence available	• No evidence available
Efficiency of revenue mobilization			
Tax policy			
Bulk of revenues from low-distortion taxes (sales/VAT, property, and so on)	Value-Added Tax (VAT) • VAT is central to a good tax system in most countries (Bird 2005; Bahl and Bird 2008). • It is a low distortionary manner to raise taxes, non-cascading, and does not interfere with production efficiency (Burgess and Stern 1993). • It is also a good instrument to reduce potential for corruption as it minimizes contact between taxpayers and tax administrators and moves toward self-assessment (Bahl and Bird 2008). • It is a broad-based tax which is an important part of tax policy (Ames and others 2001). Land (Property) Tax • If well designed and political opposition is well handled, property taxes and especially land taxes can raise substantial revenues (Heady 2001). • Property taxation is a potential source of significant income for many municipal and metropolitan authorities to whom central governments have devolved increasing responsibilities without commensurate increases in fiscal transfers (Bird and Slack 2002; Dillinger 1992; Mikesell 2003). • Taxing property is much easier now because of digital databases of modern property registries (Fjeldstad and Moore 2007).	VAT • Although VAT has long been known to be likely regressive (Ahmad and Stern 1987; Cnossen 2004; Bird 2005), a recent survey of studies of consumption tax incidence have shown significantly less regressive results than those reported for similar taxes in earlier surveys (Bird and Gendron 2006). • VATs in developing countries are not always, or not necessarily, regressive (Bird and Gendron 2007). • Even when VAT is regressive, it is found to be more progressive than the import and excise taxes that it replaced (Gemmell and Morrissey 2003).	

Country Policy and Institutional Assessment (CPIA) Criteria/Indicators	Literature on:		
	Sustained growth	Poverty reduction	Development effectiveness
Tax policy (cont.)		• To the extent that the poorest sectors of the society remain outside of the market economy, a VAT may be broadly progressive (Bird and Gendron 2007; Bird and Zolt 2007). Property Tax • Property incomes and property wealth are significantly undertaxed and an important source of inequity (Fjeldstad and Moore 2007).	
Broad tax base and few arbitrary exemptions	• Exemptions in many developing countries generally protect the interest of powerful groups, so reducing exemptions not only raises revenues, but also improves economic efficiency and income distribution (Heady 2001). • Most developing countries do not have the right conditions (macroeconomic stability and a stable political and administrative system) under which exemptions work, with the result that exemptions reduce revenues and complicate the fiscal system without achieving their stated objectives (Bird and Zolt 2007). • Tax incentives (through exemptions) are often distortive and inefficient and divert scarce resources into less than optimal use (McLure 1999). • There may be a limited role for simple incentives, for example as part of a growth-oriented fiscal strategy as the East Asian experience suggests (Bird and Chen 1998).	• Exemptions in many developing countries generally protect the interest of powerful groups, so reducing exemptions not only raises revenues, but also improves economic efficiency and income distribution (Heady 2001). • Exempting only five narrowly defined items in Jamaica cut the VAT burden on the lowest 40 percent of the income distribution in half (Bird and Miller1989).	

Tax administration. Reforms to tax administration are just as important as tax policy reforms for overall fiscal reform (Mookherjee and Das-Gupta 1995; Devas, Delay, and Hubbard 2001). It is estimated that two-thirds of the rapid increase in Argentina's tax revenues (from 13 to 23 percent of GDP) over the 1989–92 period was attributable to improved administration effort.

Rule-based tax administration	• An efficient tax administration has to be rule based—the legal environment is important (Bird 2003). • A stable transparent tax system inspires more confidence in its fairness and will result in greater compliance (Boskin 2006). • A less discretionary tax administration is likely to encourage political mobilization of taxpayers around taxation issues, and reduce temptations to pursue corrupt deals (Moore 2004).		

(*continued on next page*)

Country Policy and Institutional Assessment (CPIA) Criteria/Indicators	Literature on:		
	Sustained growth	Poverty reduction	Development effectiveness
Low administrative and compliance costs	• One of the most efficient ways to facilitate tax compliance is to decrease compliance costs (Bird 2003). • Low compliance costs also lower the potential of corruption as they lower the amount of a bribe a taxpayer might be willing to pay to avoid taxes (Bahl and Bird 2008). • It lowers the costs of operating in the formal sector and hence facilitates growth (Bird 2008). • It has a direct effect on economic growth since high compliance costs divert resources toward administering and complying with taxes (Bird 2008).		
Tax payer service and information program	• Provision of extensive information for taxpayers reduces compliance costs (Bird 2003; Braithwaite 2003; Fjeldstad and Moore 2007). • Taxpayer information programs reduce the potential of corruption, and of non-compliance (Bahl and Bird 2008).		
Efficient and effective appeals mechanism	• A time-bound appeal procedure reduces delays in payments (Mexico versus India) (Mookherjee and Das-Gupta 1995).		
Quality of public administration			
This is a very important element in the literature on sustained growth. The literature finds that administrative reforms can foster faster economic growth and sustain poverty reduction by removing the obstacles to private sector development that a poorly performing public sector creates. Reforms can also: increase public resources for priority spending; reduce corruption; and increase accountability of the public sector. A seminal paper (Mauro 1995) finds that the efficiency of the bureaucracy is associated with better rates of investment and growth. Deolalikar and others (2002) underline that administrative reforms, including reform of the bureaucracy and civil service, are one of the major areas of reform involving public institutions for poverty reduction.			
Policy coordination and responsiveness; service delivery and operational efficiency			
Effective coordination and organizational structures along functional lines	• Improving the quality of the bureaucracy requires improving coordination among agencies with overlapping functions; organizational structures should be formed along functional lines (Deolalikar and others 2002).		
Merit and ethics			
Hiring and promotion based on merit and performance; ethics prevail	• Inefficiency of public administration stems from constraints imposed by the civil service system on human resource management, especially hiring, firing, promotion, and rewards (Devas, Delay, and Hubbard 2001).		

Country Policy and Institutional Assessment (CPIA) Criteria/Indicators	Literature on:		
	Sustained growth	Poverty reduction	Development effectiveness
Quality of public administration (cont.)	• Using a "Weberianness Scale" that measures meritocratic recruitment and long-term, predictable, rewarding careers, Evans and Rauch (1999) found that these characteristics significantly enhance prospects for economic growth even after taking into account initial levels of per capita GDP and human capital. This is because longer–term horizons associated with predictable, rewarding careers will increase the bureaucracy's propensity to advocate public sector infrastructure rather than consumption expenditures. Meritocratic recruitment also increases competence. • Effective bureaucracy is important, or even essential, for implementing or maintaining a policy environment conducive to economic growth (Rauch and Evans 2000).		
Pay adequacy and management of wage bill			
Sustainable wage bill does not crowd out public services spending	• Containing salary expenditures (through downsizing) will help increase public resources for priority spending (Deolalikar and others 2002; Bardhan 2006b).		
Pay adequacy and management of the wage bill	Mixed evidence: • Seminal paper (Becker and Stigler 1974) shows that high wages paired with non-zero audit probability could be used to deter misbehavior and corruption. • Empirically, no evidence that wages deter corruption (Van Rijckeghem and Weder 1997; Rauch and Evans 2000; Treisman 2000). • Higher wages are correlated with higher corruption (La Porta and others 1999). • Di Tella and Schargrodsky (2003) explain the apparent empirical failure of the Becker-Stigler hypothesis because the empirical studies include observations from environments with no active audits where the probability of being punished for corruption is near zero, or very high auditing levels where the probability of being punished is near one. • Incentive pay structure is one of the most effective ways of fighting corruption (Bardhan 1997, 2006a; Chand and Moene 1999; Van Rijckeghem and Weder 2001; Di Tella and Schargrodsky 2003; Andvig and Fjeldstad 2008).		

(*continued on next page*)

Country Policy and Institutional Assessment (CPIA) Criteria/Indicators	Literature on:		
	Sustained growth	Poverty reduction	Development effectiveness
Pay adequacy and management of wage bill (cont.)	• Consensus among international organizations and leaders of African states that one of the causes of poor tax administration is low wages of officials (Werlin 1979; Due 1988; Kiser and Sacks 2007; Jenkins 1994; Devas, Delay, and Hubbard 2001). • Adequate pay needed to attract competent individuals for budgetary institutions (Campos and Pradhan 1996) and for the judiciary (Posner 1998).		
Flexibility in paying higher wages	• Adequate compensation is particularly important for tax officials in developing countries (with large informal sectors, low levels of literacy and public morality, poor salary structure for public servants, poor communications, malfunctioning judicial systems, and entrenched interests against radical reforms) (Bird 2003). • Reforms in tax enforcement in many countries which include a bonus to the tax officer based on tax collection have often been associated with greater tax compliance, higher revenues, and lower corruption (Mookherjee 1995; Mookherjee and Das-Gupta 1995).		

Transparency, accountability, and corruption in the public sector

Accountability of the executive to oversight institutions and of public employees for their performance.
Accountability is very important in the literature on sustained growth, poverty reduction and the effective use of development assistance. A number of empirical studies show the benefits of accountability for the quality of government (Besley and Case 1995; La Porta and others 1999; Adsera, Boix, and Payne 2003; Eijffinger and Geraats 2005; Olken 2007; Dyck, Moss, and Zingales 2008; Ferraz and Finan 2008; Bjorkman and Svensson 2009; Djankov and others 2009). Accountability of elected officials is also found to be directly important for economic growth (Kaufmann, Kraay, and Zoido-Lobaton 1999; Besley and Burgess 2003).

Strong public service ethic reinforced by audits, inspections, and adverse publicity for performance failures	• A randomized field experiment using over 600 village road projects in Indonesia finds that the probability of external audits substantially reduces missing funds in the project, and the benefits of the audits exceeded their costs (Olken 2007). • Monitoring policies (together with doubling of wages) results in a large decline in prices paid by all public hospitals in Buenos Aires for a number of very basic supplies (Di Tella and Schargrodsky 2003). • Increased government monitoring and media campaign informing local communities of their entitlement to school funds from the central government of Uganda reduced diversion of funds by intermediating provincial governments from 80 to 20 percent (Reinikka and Svensson 2004).		• For development assistance to be used more effectively, donors should reinforce or support audit findings of Auditor Generals of the countries (Stevens 1999).
Independent and impartial judiciary	• Discussed in the property rights and rule-based governance section.		

Country Policy and Institutional Assessment (CPIA) Criteria/Indicators	Literature on:		
	Sustained growth	Poverty reduction	Development effectiveness
Transparency, accountability, and corruption in the public sector (cont.) Corruption monitored and sanctions implemented	There are two strands of literature, with the strand that finds corruption having a negative impact on growth dominating. Corruption has a positive impact on growth: • Where there are pre-existing policy distortions including pervasive and cumbersome regulations, corruption may help efficiency and growth (Leff 1964; Huntington 1968; Lui 1985; Beck and Maher 1986; Lien 1986; Bardhan 1997). Corruption has a negative impact on growth when: • Corruption is directly related to variations in the growth of per capita income (Knack and Keefer 1995). • Corruption and red tape are significantly associated with increased levels of investment, which is shown empirically to be one of the most powerful predictors of growth (Mauro 1995). • Corruption has adverse effects on investment and growth (Bardhan 1997, 2006a). • Corruption is associated with higher military spending as a share of GDP, hence reduction in corruption will improve composition of government spending toward more productive, non-military outlays (Gupta, de Mello, and Sharan 2000). • Higher bribes imply lower profitability of productive relative to rent-seeking investments (Kaufmann, Kraay, and Zoido-Lobaton 1999; Tanzi 1998; Acemoglu and Verdier 2000). • Corruption increases uncertainty, hence reducing investment in physical and human capital (Wei 2000; Alesina and Weder 2002). • Societies' willingness to tax themselves depends on perception that government institutions are honest; hence corruption, VAT evasion, and size of underground economy are found to be closely linked (Bird and Gendron 2006). • Corrupt police may have a negative impact on growth by taxing businesses through predation, or by supplying protection in competition or in cooperation with organized crime units (Andvig and Fjeldstad 2008); police corruption is shown to have significant negative impacts on business activities (Wei 2000).	Corruption increases income inequality: a worsening in the corruption index by one standard deviation increases the Gini coefficient by 5.4 points (Gupta and others 1998). Corruption increases income inequality in a sample of developing countries and decreases the share of government expenditures on education and health (Gupta, Davoodi, and Terme 2002).	Aid has a larger effect in displacing domestic revenues in countries with higher levels of corruption—doubling of grants as a share of GDP is associated with a 1.3 percentage point decline in revenues as a share of GDP in relatively corrupt countries, and as much as 3.8 percentage point decrease in the most corrupt countries (Gupta and others 2003).

(*continued on next page*)

Country Policy and Institutional Assessment (CPIA) Criteria/Indicators	Literature on:		
	Sustained growth	Poverty reduction	Development effectiveness
Access of civil society to information on public affairs			
Media independent of government and fulfill critical oversight roles	• Free flow of information pressures (even nondemocratic) governments to public action (Dreze and Sen 1995). • Local newspapers increase responsiveness of Indian state governments to natural disasters (Besley and Burgess 2002). • Media campaign via radio and newspapers informing local communities of their entitlement to school funds from the central government of Uganda (along with increased government monitoring) reduced diversion of funds by intermediating provincial governments from 80 to 20 percent (Reinikka and Svensson 2004). • Negative correlation between press freedom and corruption (Ahrend 2001; Brunetti and Weder 1999). • Mass media makes governments more accountable (Besley, Burgess, and Prat 2002). • Media can provide a counterbalance to the power of vested interests especially by informing voters (Dyck, Moss, and Zingales 2008).	• No country with a free press has ever had a major famine (Dreze and Sen 1989).	• Provision of more information (for example through the use of local newspapers) increases aid efficiency and reduces the negative impact of aid volatility on aid efficiency (Cagé 2009b).
State capture by narrow vested interests. Vested interests are a restraint for economic growth (Mokyr 1990; Maine 1980; and Landes 1983). Vested interests (such as those arising from import substitution policies or capital taxes) can be detrimental to economic growth (Krusell and Rios-Rull 1996; Acemoglu and Robinson 2000).			
Top government officials required to disclose income and assets and can be prosecuted for malfeasance	• Disclosure is correlated with lower corruption when it is public, identifies sources of income and conflicts of interest, and when a country is a democracy; but there is no significant evidence of benefits from disclosure of values of income, consumption, and wealth (Djankov and others 2009).		

APPENDIX C: 2007 CPIA CRITERIA ON ECONOMIC MANAGEMENT, STRUCTURAL POLICIES, AND POLICIES FOR SOCIAL INCLUSION/EQUITY AND EVIDENCE IN THE LITERATURE

CPIA criteria/indicators		Sustained growth	Poverty reduction	Development effectiveness
Macroeconomic Management (0.083)	• Monetary/exchange rate policy with clearly defined price stability objectives. • Aggregate demand policies focus on maintaining short- and medium-term external balance. • Avoid crowding out private investment.	• Sound money and fiscal solvency (Rodrik 2003). • Keep inflation low and stable; monetary policy stance consistent with low and stable inflation (World Bank 2005).	• Adverse impact of inflation on the poor (Easterly and Fisher 2001). • Inflation hurts the poor (Dollar and Kraay 2002; Ravallion and Datt 2002). • Potential effect of inflation on poverty, once controlled for direct effect of growth on poverty, is mixed (Epaulard 2003).	
Fiscal Policy (0.083)	• Primary balance managed to ensure sustainability of public finances. • Public expenditure/revenue can be adjusted to absorb shocks. • Provision of public goods including infrastructure consistent with medium-term growth.	• Transparency, sustainable solvency, flexibility, pro-growth structure of budgets (World Bank 2005). • Infrastructure (Easterly 2001; World Bank 1994; Sachs 2005, 2008; Collier 2007).	• Public investment in basic infrastructure facilitates access of the poor to markets or to basic social services (Loayza 1996; Calderon and Serven 2003, 2004).	• Randomized literature on infrastructure: water and sanitation infrastructure (Ashraf, Berry, and Shapiro 2007; Kremer and others 2008).
Debt Policy (0.083)	• Debt burden indicators do not signal debt servicing difficulties. • External and internal debt contracted with view to achieving/maintaining debt sustainability. • Coordination between debt management and other macroeconomic policies.	• Reduce recourse to external debt (World Bank 2005).		

(*continued on next page*)

CPIA criteria/indicators		Sustained growth	Poverty reduction	Development effectiveness
Debt Policy (0.083) (cont.)	• Debt management unit well established, has adequate system for recording and monitoring debt, and good analytical capacity as indicated by regular analytical work on debt. • Accurate, timely, and publicly available debt data. • Government has clear financing strategy and the legal framework for borrowing is clearly defined.			
Trade (0.083)	75 percent weight for *trade restrictiveness*: (0.063) • Average tariff rates, number of tariff bands, maximum tariff band. • Internal taxes do not discriminate between imported and local products. • Transparency and predictability of trade regime including in the use of non-tariff barriers. 25 percent weight for *customs/trade facilitation*: (0.02) • Reputation of customs with respect to professionalism and corruption. • Use of risk management, information technology, physical examination. • Processing of collections and refunds.	• Need to take into account promotion of export growth (World Bank 2005, 2008a). • Need to have complementary policies (World Bank 2005).	• No conclusive evidence in the relationship between trade liberalization and poverty (Winters, McCulloch, and McKay 2004; Harrison 2006; Ravallion 2004). • For trade liberalization to have positive impact on poverty reduction, needs to be accompanied by improved infrastructure, adequate competition policies, enhanced access to credit, better education and health, and low marketing or intermediation costs (Balat, Brambilla, and Porto 2007; Harrison 2006). • When trade reforms are accompanied by labor market reforms (hire and fire, relocation), the adverse impact of trade liberalization on poverty disappears (Goldberg and Pavcnik 2005).	

CPIA criteria/indicators		Sustained growth	Poverty reduction	Development effectiveness
Trade (0.083) (cont.)	• Documentation of customs procedures. • Resolutions of appeals of customs decisions.		• Negative impact of trade reforms on poverty is due to limited labor mobility (Topalova 2004, 2005).	
Financial Sector (0.083)	*Financial stability* • Banking sector vulnerability to shocks • Banking system soundness (share of non-performing loans and level of capital at risk). • Adherence to Basel Core Principles. • Quality of risk management in financial institutions. • Quality of supervision.	• Considerable evidence of large impact of banking crises on output losses (Hoggarth, Reis, and Saporta 2002).	• Crises do not systematically worsen the Gini coefficient although the poor are likely less able to absorb adverse shocks (Honohan 2004a).	
	Financial sector efficiency, depth, and resource mobilization • Size and reach of financial markets. • Development of capital markets. • Interest rate spreads • Private sector credit/gross domestic product (GDP). • Efficiency of microfinance. *Access to financial services* • Development of payment, clearance, and credit reporting systems. • Share of population with access to formal sector financial services. • Access of small and medium enterprises (SMEs) to finance. • Legal and regulatory framework supporting access to finance.	• Finance is a determinant of sustained growth (Aghion, Howitt, and Mayer-Foulkes 2005; Krebs 2003; Levine 1997, 2003, 2005; Levine, Loayza, and Beck 2000). • Efficient domestic financial system is important for growth (World Bank 2005). • Cross-country regressions do not suggest any strong influence of household financial access on growth or poverty reduction (Honohan 2008a). • Access of SMEs to finance promotes firm entry, firm growth, innovation, and size distribution of firms (Beck, Demirguc-Kunt, and Levine 2005; Ayyagari, Demirguc-Kunt, and Maksimovic 2007; Klapper, Laeven, and Rajan 2006).	• Financial (banking) depth is negatively associated with headcount poverty (Honohan 2004b). • Impact of national income volatility on child labor is insignificant for countries with deep financial systems (Dehejia and Gatti 2002). • Financial development reduces income inequality by disproportionately boosting the incomes of the poor (Beck, Demirguc-Kunt, and Levine 2004). • Emergence of microfinance as a source of credit is both efficient and equitable as it has enabled the poor to invest, thereby promoting growth and reducing poverty (Khandeker 2005).	

(*continued on next page*)

CPIA criteria/indicators	Sustained growth	Poverty reduction	Development effectiveness
Financial Sector (0.083) (cont.)	• Informational, regulatory, legal, and judicial framework (World Bank 2005).	• Massive social banking experiment in India has led to significant falls in rural poverty (Burgess and Pande 2005). • Impact assessments show microfinance in general helps the poor (Hossain 1988; Hashemi, Schuler, and Riley 1996; Khandker 1998, 2005; Khandker and Pitt 2003).	
Business Regulatory Environment (0.083)	*Regulations affecting entry, exit, and competition (0.028)* • Bans on or investment licensing requirements. • Procedures to enter or exit. • Legal framework (and implementation thereof) to address anti-competitive conduct by firms. • Procurement by public sector firms. *Regulations of ongoing business operations (0.028)* • Operational licensing, permits, compliance and inspection requirements including taxes and customs. • State intervention in goods markets (state ownership in competitive sectors, price controls, state making administrative allocation/decisions about production). • Corporate governance laws (and enforcement thereof) to encourage disclosure and protect shareholders rights. *Regulations of goods and factor markets (0.028)* • Employment law provides for flexibility in hiring and firing.	• Red tape (Mauro 1995). • Reducing risks for private investors (World Bank 2000c). • Clear and transparent business environment (World Bank 2000c). • Importance of investor protection (La Porta and others 2000). • Importance of labor market reforms for minimizing adverse effects of trade reform on the poor (Goldberg and Pavcnik 2005; Topalova 2004, 2005; Welch, MacMillan, and Rodrik 2004). • Getting the labor market right (World Bank 2008a; Ocampo 2003; Cardenas, Ocampo, and Thorp 2000).	• Improve climate for doing business (Besley and Burgess 2003).	

CPIA criteria/indicators		Sustained growth	Poverty reduction	Development effectiveness
Business Regulatory Environment (0.083) (cont.)	• State intervention in labor and land markets limited to regulation and/or legislation to smooth out market imperfections. • Procedures to register property are simple and low cost.			
Gender Equality (0.05)	*Human capital development* (0.017) • Differences (between male and female) in primary completion rates, and access to secondary education (female to male enrollment). • Access to delivery care and family planning services. • Adolescent fertility rate. *Access to economic and productive resources* (0.017) • Gender disparities in labor force participation, land tenure, property ownership and inheritance practices. *Status and protection under the law* (0.017) • The law gives men and women equal individual and family rights. • Violence against women considered a crime. • Gender disparities in political participation at national level.	• Education for girls (World Bank 2006b, 2008a). • Fertility (Easterly 2001).	• Higher gender inequality increases poverty, and female literacy is one of the most important determinants of the effects of growth on income poverty (World Bank 2001a; Ravallion and Datt 2002). • Educating girls and integrating them into the workforce is one way to break the intergenerational cycle of poverty (World Bank 2008a).	
Equity of Public Resource Use (0.05)	*Government spending* (0.033) • Identification of individuals, groups or localities that are poor, vulnerable, or have unequal access to services and opportunities. • Adoption of national development strategy with explicit interventions to assist groups identified above. • Systematic tracking of composition and incidence of public expenditures and their results feed back into subsequent allocations.	• Inequality is negatively related to growth: conceptual papers (Todaro 1997; Aghion, Caroli, and Garcia-Penalosa 1999; Bardhan 2000; Hoff and Stiglitz 2001). • Inequality is negatively related to growth: empirical evidence (Alesina and Rodrick 1994; Perotti 1992, 1993, 1996; Persson and Tabellini 1994).	• Inequality reduces the poverty reduction impact on growth (Ravallion 2001).	

(*continued on next page*)

CPIA criteria/indicators		Sustained growth	Poverty reduction	Development effectiveness
Equity of Public Resource Use (0.05) (cont.)	*Revenue collection* (0.017) • Incidence of major taxes (progressive or regressive) and their alignment with poverty reduction priorities.	• Channels through which inequality affects growth: credit constraints (Perotti 1992; Bardhan 2000; the World Bank 2005); political instability, crime, insecurity of property rights (Alesina and Perotti 1996; Bardhan 2000); volatility (Aghion, Caroli, and Garcia-Penalosa 1999); social tension and violent redistribution (Bourguignon 2004). • Micropanel studies show households with few physical and human assets caught in poverty trap reducing chance of economic advancement and lowering overall growth (Christiaensen, Demery, and Paternostro 2002; Woolard and Klasen 2005). • Redistribution measures—income transfers (Skoufias, Davis, and de la Vega 2001; Bourguignon Ferreira, and Leite 2003).		
Building Human Resources (0.05)	*Health and nutrition including reproductive health* (0.017) • Equitable access to basic health services. • Prevention of malnutrition.	Mixed evidence: • Higher life expectancy raises growth (Jamison, Sachs, and Wang 2001), per capita income (Weil 2005), and incentive to acquire schooling (Kalemli-Ozcan, Ryder, and Weil 2000).		• Positive effects of health interventions by aid agencies and non-governmental organizations (NGOs) (see appendix E).

CPIA criteria/indicators	Sustained growth	Poverty reduction	Development effectiveness
Building Human Resources (0.05) (cont.)	• Major international health improvements since 1940s have led to a larger increase in population than incomes, hence there is no evidence that health improvements raised income per capita (Acemoglu and Johnson 2007).		• Randomized literature has found a number of aid interventions to be effective in education (see appendix E).
Education (0.017) • Sustained progress toward universal basic education, literacy, and more equitable access to early child development program services. • Standards for teacher preparation, student learning, and oversight of private/NGO providers. • Systematic tracking of school performance and student learning outcomes and feedback to schools and parents. • Policies for post-basic education and training services. • Quality, equity of access, and efficiency of resource use.	• Educational attainment (Easterly 2001). • Primary enrollment rate (Hanushek and Kimko 2000; Barro and Sala-i-Martin 2003; Doppelhofer, Miller, and Sala-I Martin 2004; Hanushek and Woessmann 2008). • Secondary and tertiary education (World Bank 1999; Vandenbussche, Aghion, and Meghir 2006; Aghion and Howitt 2009).	• Adequate and effective delivery of education, health, and social infrastructure (World Bank 2004e). • Education enables people to make use of economic opportunities created by the growth process (Dreze and Sen 2002). • Improving literacy facilitates more pro-poor growth (Chhibber and Nayyar 2007). • Poor educational outcomes reduce the poverty-reducing impact of growth (Menezes-Filho and Vasconcellos 2004). • Investment in education can be used to attack poverty as a method to redistribute to the poor (Besley and Burgess 2003).	
Human immunodeficiency virus/acquired immunodeficiency syndrome (HIV/AIDS), tuberculosis, malaria • Prevention, treatment, care and support of HIV/AIDS, tuberculosis, and malaria. • Track disease prevalence, resources, and program implementation.	Mixed evidence: • Greater the prevalence of malaria, lower the per capita income (Sachs 2003).		

(*continued on next page*)

CPIA criteria/indicators		Sustained growth	Poverty reduction	Development effectiveness
Building Human Resources (0.05) (cont.)	• Quality and timeliness of services. • Focus on the poor. • Cost-effective use of public resources.	• Short-run eradication of malaria lowers per capita income (because malaria affects mainly young children) whereas it raises per capita income only slightly over long run (Ashraf, Lester, and Weil 2008). • Eradication of tuberculosis raises per capita income slightly in both short and long run (Ashraf, Lester, and Weil 2008). • HIV/AIDS associated with small reduction in per capita income over long-run (Kambou, Devarajan, and Over 1992; Over 1992; Cuddington 1993; Cuddington and Hancock 1994; Haacker 2002). • HIV/AIDs has no impact on per capita income (Bloom and Mahal 1997). • HIV/AIDS has large negative impact on per capita income (Bell, Devarajan, and Gersbach 2006). • HIV/AIDS increases per capita income of survivors (Young 2004).		
Social Protection and Labor (0.05)	*Social safety net programs* (0.01) • Social protection programs provide income support to poor and vulnerable groups. *Protection of basic labor standards* (0.01) • Ratification and implementation of international core labor standards.	• Getting the labor market right to foster growth and, at the same time, protecting people (not jobs) through establishing social safety nets (World Bank 2008a; Ocampo 2003).	Child labor may lead to intergenerational transmission of poverty: "child labor traps" (Barham and others 1995; Ilahi, Orazem, and Sedlacek 2001; Emerson and Souza 2003; Edmonds 2007).	

CPIA criteria/indicators		Sustained growth	Poverty reduction	Development effectiveness
Social Protection and Labor (0.05) (cont.)	*Labor market regulations* (0.01) • Labor market regulations on health and safety, working conditions, and hiring and firing. *Community-driven initiatives* (0.01) • Encourage and support communities' own development initiatives or local accountability mechanisms. *Pension and old-age savings programs* (0.01) • Pension and savings programs provide income security to most potentially vulnerable groups.	• Empowerment of communities as a determinant of sustained growth (Stern 2001; World Bank 2000c, 2004e).		
Policies and Institutions for Environmental Sustainability (0.05)	• Regulations and policies (and implementation thereof) for pollution and natural resources. • Information widely available. • Priority setting. • Sector ministries incorporate environmental concerns.	• Debate on whether environmental regulation can raise growth rate (Bovenberg and Smulders 1995, 1996; Hettich 1998; and Esty and Porter 2005; versus Fullerton and Kim 2006).	• Policies reducing environmental risk not necessarily progressive (Parry and others 2005; Fullerton 2008).	

Water supply in Marracuene, Mozambique. Photo by Eric Miller/World Bank

A. Aid → Growth with No Conditions

Article (year)	Type of aid	Short /Long-term impact	Period of analysis
Hansen and Tarp (2000)	All aid	Short-term (4 years)	1974–1993
Dalgaard and Hansen (2001)	All aid	Short-term (4 years)	1974–1993
Hansen and Tarp (2001)	All aid	Short-term (4 years)	1974–1993
Ram (2003)	Bilateral	Short-term (4 years)	1970–1993
Clemens, Radelet, and Bhavnani (2004)	Short impact aid (budget support or "program" aid for any purpose, and project aid given for real sector investments for infrastructure or to directly support production in transportation, communications, energy, banking, agriculture, and industry).	Short-term (4 years)	1970–2001
Headey (2005)	Multilateral and bilateral, separately	Short-term (4 years)	1970–2001
Reddy and Minoiu (2006)	Developmental (multilateral and bilateral)	Long-term (2 decades)	1960–2000

B. Aid → Growth with Conditions

Article (year)	Type of aid	Short /Long-term impact	Period of analysis	Conditions
Burnside and Dollar (2000)	All aid (net flow)	Short-term (4 years)	1970–1993	Index of policies: trade openness (Sachs-Warner), fiscal policy (budget surplus), monetary policy (inflation rate).
Guillaumont and Chauvet (2001)	All aid	Long-term (12 years)	1970–1993	Index of environment/vulnerability: climatic shocks (stability of agricultural value added), trade shocks (stability of real value of exports, trend of terms of trade), and structural exposure to these shocks (population size).
Collier and Dehn (2001)	All aid (net flow)	Short-term (4 years)	1970–1993	Countries suffering sharp price drops in key commodity exports.
Collier and Dollar (2002)	All aid	Short-term (4 years)	1974–1997	Country Policy and Institutional Assessment (CPIA) (overall for 20 components).
Collier and Hoeffler (2004)	All aid	Short-term (4 years)	1974–1997	A few years after civil war with good policies (first social, then sectoral, then macro).
Dalgaard, Hansen, and Tarp (2003)	All aid	Short-term (4 years)	1970–1993	Countries outside of the tropics.

C. Aid Has No Impact on Growth

Article (year)	Type of aid	Short/Long-term impact	Period of analysis
Boone (1994)			
Easterly, Levine, and Roodman (2004)	All aid	Short-term (4 years)	1970–1997
Easterly (2003)	All aid	Long-term (12 or 24 years)	1970–1993
Roodman (2007a)	All aid	Tested Hansen and Tarp (2001) in section A and all six papers in section B above	
Rajan and Subramanian (2008)	All aid	Medium (10–20 years) and long-term (30–40 years)	1960–2000

D. Aid Has Negative Impact on Growth

Article (year)	Type of aid	Short/Long-term impact	Period of analysis
Ram (2003)	Multilateral	Short-term	1970–1993
Reddy and Minoiu (2006)	Geopolitical (all aid-developmental aid)	Long-term (2 decades)	1960–2000

APPENDIX E. EXAMPLES OF POSITIVE IMPACTS OF AID PROJECTS FROM RANDOMIZED EVALUATIONS IN EDUCATION, HEALTH, INFRASTRUCTURE, AND AGRICULTURE

Education

Angrist and others (2002) find that lottery winners of vouchers for private schools in Colombia had 0.12–0.16 additional years of schooling, test scores that were higher by 0.2 standard deviations, and higher secondary school completion (the last finding was confirmed in a follow-up study by Angrist, Bettinger, and Kremer (2006). Vermeersch and Kremer (2003) find that a school meals program in preschools in Kenya raised attendance rates from 21 to 29 percent. Kremer and Holla (2008) find that a merit scholarship for high school girls in Kenya seemed to induce greater study effort and raised the girls' test scores, and even had some externalities to boys' performance in the same classroom.

More generally, as underlined by Kremer and Holla (2008), evidence is accumulating on the effectiveness of certain school inputs such as extra teachers and textbooks (for example, see Banerjee and others 2005; Duflo, Kremer, and Robinson 2007; and Glewwe, Kremer, and Moulin 2007); provider incentives (Glewwe, Holla, and Kremer 2008 and Muralidharan and Sundara-raman 2007); remedial education (Banerjee and others 2007; Duflo, Kremer, and Robinson 2007; He, Linden, and MacLeod 2007); citizens' report cards; the hiring of contract teachers; or increased oversight of local school committees (Bjorkman and Svensson 2009; and Duflo, Kremer, and Robinson 2007); and school choice programs (Angrist, Bettinger, and Kremer 2002, 2006; Bettinger, Kremer, and Saavedra 2008).

Health

Gertler (2004) finds that the Programa de Educación, Salud y Alimentación (PROGRESA) cash-for-schooling program in Mexico, which had health components, also had a major health impact. The Bobonis, Miguel, and Puri-Sharma (2006) study on anemia and school participation finds that iron supplements and de-worming drugs were effective in increasing children's weight-for-height and weight-for-age scores. Another area in which randomized evaluations found success is in preventing or treating infant diarrhea (Zwane and Kremer 2007).

Infrastructure

Ashraf, Berry, and Shapiro (2007) find that water purification tablets in Zambia are an inexpensive way of avoiding waterborne illness. Kremer and others (2008) show that investment in protecting naturally occurring springs from contamination led to dramatic improvements in water quality in rural Kenya.

Agriculture

Duflo, Kremer, and Robinson (2007) find that selling vouchers earmarked for fertilizer purchases to the farmers right after harvest solved the problem of the farmers not setting aside funds for fertilizer for the next season. Duflo, Kremer, and Robinson (2008) find a large positive return to fertilizer use in maize farms in Kenya, whereas too little or too much fertilizer renders the return unfavorable. Conley and Udry (2007) find that farmers learn how much fertilizer to apply from their successful neighbors in a new technology for pineapple growing in Ghana.

Fisherman, Colombia. Photo by Edwin Huffman/World Bank

A review of the literature indicates that the *financial sector* criterion does cover the dimensions along which finance is currently thought to be important: stability, that is, depth and efficiency; and access. However, not all three finance dimensions are equally important for growth and poverty reduction. Further, the way some of the dimensions are currently being assessed can be strengthened.

Financial Stability

There is considerable evidence of a large impact of banking crises on output losses (Hoggarth, Reis, and Saporta 2002)[1] as well as on the national budget (Laeven and Valenciana 2008; Honohan 2008b).[2] On the other hand, the evidence as to which policies work to limit banking crises is ambiguous and controversial (discussed below). In light of the controversies over what constitute appropriate policies for financial stability, the fact that the Country Policy and Institutional Assessment (CPIA) assesses intermediate outcomes in addition to policies and institutions (it is supposed to only assess the latter) is perhaps reasonable.

There is quite a lot of controversy in the literature on the current CPIA indicators used for assessing the stability of the financial system. The indicator on the banking sector's vulnerability to shocks, although relevant, is extremely vague. It evokes the concept of stress testing,[3] which has not been very effective, as clearly demonstrated by the recent wave of systemic failures in mature economies, all of whose prudential regulators were using stress tests.

The indicator for banking system soundness specifies two alternative intermediate outcome measures related to non-performing loans (NPLs).[4] Although NPLs may predict crises to some extent, they are typically a lagging indicator, with high values suggestive of a problem that has already crystallized. Hence these NPL measures are crude and inadequate even as indicators of current or imminent problems. This is clearly reflected to the fact that NPLs for residential mortgages did not provide a sensitive early warning system in the recent crisis in advanced economies.

The indicator on adherence to Basel Core Principles (BCP) does embody a set of regulatory policies and practices on most points on which there is broad consensus.

However, the econometric evidence between BCP compliance and financial sector performance is not very strong.

The indicator on tools and resources for banking supervision is subject to a lot of controversy. An extensive data collection and econometric exercise (Barth, Caprio, and Levine 2006) fails to uncover any statistically significant relationship between their measures of banking supervision and regulation on the one hand, and financial sector performance including stability on the other. The alternative approach that emphasizes market discipline (enforced through regulations that provide market participants with information and incentives to monitor firms) has not worked either as evidenced by the current financial crisis.

What is clearly missing in the CPIA is explicit attention to the information (for example, accounting and disclosure requirements) and incentive structures (for example, deposit

95

insurance) for market discipline. This is supported by an extensive literature on moral hazard of deposit insurance schemes and other crisis management policies which show that fiscal costs of crises are higher in cases where policy design neglects moral hazard (Honohan and Klingebiel 2003; Demirguc-Kunt, Kane, and Laeven 2006).

Financial Sector Efficiency, Depth, and Resource Mobilization

There is a convincing literature that financial depth (usually measured as outstanding bank credit to the private sector as a share of gross domestic product [GDP] drives economic growth (Honohan 2009). At the same time, there is a wide range of policies both in finance and in other sectors that influence the depth and efficiency of finance. In this light, it is perhaps not unreasonable that most of the indicators under this dimension are outcome indicators. Yet many of the indicators specified in the CPIA are problematic.

The indicator "size and reach of financial markets" is vague, and is already captured by another indicator "private sector credit as a share of GDP." The latter corresponds directly to the measure of financial depth most commonly used in empirical analyses of the finance-growth link. However, private sector credit as a share of GDP is not an ideal measure. Rapid increases in financial depth are often unsustainable, and yet can be mistaken for finance-supported sustainable growth (Honohan 2004b). Further, the term "reach" normally refers to access, which is covered in the third dimension of the CPIA *finance* criterion.

The indicator "development of capital markets" is typically measured in terms of overall stock market capitalization. But the free-float of shares may be a tiny fraction of total capitalization, so some correction needs to be made to address this. Also there is little or no empirical evidence that confirms a causal link between market capitalization and subsequent economic growth. One paper (Levine and Zervos 1998) finds a relationship between stock market turnover and growth, although this is also not very strongly supported by the evidence.

The indicator "interest rate spreads" measures efficiency of intermediation, which is affected by both administrative efficiency as well as the degree of competition in the sector. Policy in the form of taxation of financial intermediation (implicit or explicit) and in the form of administrative controls (such as holding interest spreads below breakeven rates) can strongly influence the spread, so there is no unambiguous link between spreads and sustainable growth.

The indicator efficiency of microfinance is vague, as efficiency presumably relates to the cost of achieving some goal. Yet the CPIA instructions neither specify the goal nor how to judge the cost. Further, this indicator might fit better under the access dimension.

In addition to these problems with the outcome indicators, this dimension has also neglected the policies that are important for achieving financial depth. A recent paper (Tressel and Detragiache 2008) using a large cross-country panel finds that policies that facilitate entry, liberalize pricing and the provision of services, and reduce state ownership in finance do help deepen finance— although only where complementary deep legal institutions protecting private property from expropriation are present.

Access to Financial Services

There are individual success stories of microfinance (Littlefield, Morduch, and Hashemi 2003), but because of the formidable selection biases in the data, there is little firm evidence of a sizeable growth or poverty reduction impact of microfinance. Indeed, the indications are that overall financial development, as measured by financial depth, has had a larger and more certain impact not just on growth but also on poverty reduction than the expansion of microfinance (World Bank 2008b).

Aside from the lack of strong empirical evidence of this dimension on growth and poverty reduction, the indicators specified under this dimension also suffer from a lack of clarity and specificity. The indicator on the payments system is unclear. To the extent that it refers to the wholesale payments system, it is not an access issue but rather relates to the cost and security of a minor part of the banking system (Honohan 2009). At the same time, however, there is no empirical evidence that a wholesale payments system failure could trigger a banking collapse. To the extent that the payments system refers to the retail system, it relates to access but it is not clear what is being assessed in the CPIA.

The indicator on the credit reporting system is relevant, as credit registries are known to have the potential to expand access to finance, particularly to small and medium enterprises (SMEs) (Miller 2003; Berger, Frame, and Miller 2005; Djankov, McLiesh, and Shleifer 2007). However, the CPIA falls short in specifying how this is to be assessed, although the literature has established a standard set of good practices. Such good practices include facilitating entry of private providers of registries where possible, including as wide a set of information providers as possible, and ensuring privacy laws do not unduly constrain reporting of "positive information" (Miller 2003). There is also evidence that quality matters in ensuring that a credit registry does expand availability of finance (Brown, Jappelli, and Pagano 2009, and Lutoto, McIntosh, and Wydick 2007).

Regarding the indicators on access, cross-country regressions do not suggest any strong influence of *household* financial access on growth or on poverty (taking into account the average level of income) (Honohan 2008a). However, access of small and medium enterprises (SMEs) to formal sector financial services has been found to be important for firm entry, firm growth, innovation, and size distribution of firms (Beck, Demirguc-Kunt, and Levine 2005; Ayyagari, Demirguc-Kunt, and Maksimovic 2007).

The indicator regarding the legal and regulatory framework supporting access to finance is vague. Also, the cross-country empirical literature suggests that although legal and political institutions that protect private property against the state are important for financial *depth*, the protection of contracts between private agents is important for determining *access* (Beck, Demirguc-Kunt, and Levine 2005; World Bank 2008b).

Recommendations

The above review suggests that the CPIA indicators for all three dimensions could be strengthened. Suggestions for such strengthening are presented in appendix box F. 1.

Appendix Box F.1: Suggestions for Strengthening of the Country Policy and Institutional Assessment (CPIA) Indicators for the Financial Sector

Each of the three dimensions currently covered by the CPIA *financial sector* criterion can be revised and strengthened, as follows:

Financial Stability

Whether policy creates good incentives for prudential management of financial firms. This would include enforcement of prudential regulations and the safety net policy (including the nature and extent of deposit insurance).

How good are supervisory powers and effectiveness (including the tools and resources for risk assessment)? This would entail assessment of the compliance with Basel Core Principles (BCP) (already included in the CPIA), which is a useful summary for banking. However, non-bank finance also needs to be considered where it is sizeable.

The vulnerability of financial institutions to shocks. This can be informed by measures of bank capitalization (for example, whether regulatory minima sufficient for the economy's risk, well measured and enforced; whether all banks satisfy regulatory minima; how is capital measured). Non-performing loans (NPLs) (especially net of provision) should be taken into account but supplemented by exposure to foreign exchange risk. Rapid growth of credit should be monitored as a possible warning sign.

Financial Depth and Efficiency

Depth. The key measure is the size of private sector credit as a share of gross domestic product (GDP), adjusted for the country's overall level of development. (However, rapid growth in this indicator should be assessed as negative). Other measures are market capitalization (total and free-float) and stock market turnover.

Efficiency of intermediation. The measures are intermediation spreads (ideally distinguishing what is attributable to taxes and quasi-taxes, inadequate legal protection, exogenous risk and market power), and bank operating costs (for example as a share of total assets).

Policy barriers to efficiency and depth. Among the relevant indicators are: distorting financial sector taxes and quasi-taxes on intermediation including binding interest rate ceilings; and directed credit programs. The preconditions for the BCP (which are not graded) also provide a useful summary of key policy dimensions as relevant to depth and efficiency as to stability.

Access

Policy. Has policy created an enabling environment for expanding outreach of the financial system? For example, is the legal framework for debt recovery and insolvency economically and administratively efficient (including time taken and cost of insolvency and debt recovery)? Is there a good credit reporting system? Are there legal or regulatory barriers to creating one? Is there an adequate legal basis for the leasing industry? Is the regulatory framework for microfinance supportive? Is anti-money laundering and combating the financing of terrorism (AML-CFT) policy well adapted to protecting financial service providers focusing on the poor from undue costs (for example, are microfinance firms able to operate depository and money transmission services without crippling regulatory burden?) (Isern and others 2005).

Outcomes. Measures could include: the percentage of the population with access to formal financial services; how good the access of small and medium enterprises (SMEs) to financial services is (such as from responses to the Investment Climate Assessment surveys); how financially secure the microfinance industry is; and whether retail money transmission costs (internal and international) are low.

Source: Honohan 2009.

This appendix presents the econometric analysis undertaken to estimate the relationship between the CPIA and Bank loan performance. The methodology draws on a similar exercise by Dollar and Levin (2005) who find a strong association between institutional quality and loan success rate using the property rights/rule of law measure from the International Country Risk Guide and democracy measure from Freedom House as proxies for institutional quality, and (Independent Evaluation Group) IEG's loan outcome ratings as a measure of loan performance. This analysis uses a very similar specification to that of Dollar and Levin, but a different measure of loan performance (see below) and the CPIA for the institutional quality variables.

Data
Policy and institutions
The average overall CPIA rating for the country from 2004–07 was used as the explanatory variable. The average ratings for each of the four CPIA clusters were also used alternatively as explanatory variables. The time period 2004–07 was selected because of the major restructuring of the CPIA in 2004, and in particular because of the change in the definition of the rating scale, which resulted in a discontinuity in the data that year.

Loan performance
This analysis uses the Implementation Status and Results Report (ISR) flags for problem loans as the proxy for loan performance because of the need to match the loan performance data with the CPIA data which confines the analysis to this period of 2004–07. Given this restriction, it is not possible to use IEG loan outcome ratings because the analysis would have been restricted to loans

approved and closed between 2004 and 2007. This, in turn, would have reduced the sample size substantially as well as biased the sample because those loans would have consisted mostly of development policy loans. Estimates based on data for loans approved since 1998 found a relatively good correlation between the share of problem loans and IEG loan outcome ratings (the correlation coefficient is 0.63).

The flags for problem loans are based on self-evaluation by Bank staff of loans where implementation progress or development objective is rated unsatisfactory. For this analysis, a loan is identified as a problem if it has been flagged as a problem loan anytime between 2004 and 2007. The sample is restricted to all countries that had at least three loans approved during the period. For each country the share of loans (approved between 2004 and 2007) that had been flagged as problem loans was used as the dependent variable.[1]

Control variables
The following control variables are used in the econometric analysis:[2]

- Average aid as a share of gross domestic product (following Dollar and Levin 2005) which could influence loan performance in opposite ways. On the one hand, there could be increasing returns in the sense that a lot of aid may create a better environment of supporting services and resources. On the other hand, there could be diminishing returns or absorptive capacity constraints. The data are from the Organisation for Economic Co-operation and Development (OECD) Development Assistance Committee (DAC) database.

- Geographic constraints to development as represented by the share of a country's territory in the tropics that has been found to affect economic performance (Dollar and Levin 2005, following Gallup, Sachs, and Mellinger 1999).
- Extent of ethnic fractionalization that has been found to affect political stability and policies and institutions (see, for example, Mauro 1995; Easterly and Levine 1997; Alesina and others 2003).
- Regional dummies to control for region-specific effects on loan performance.

Econometric Specification and Results

Ordinary least squares regressions[3] are used for the estimations. The results are presented in appendix table G.1. There is a significant negative association between the overall CPIA rating of a country and the percentage of problem loans in that country. The results are similar when each of the four CPIA cluster ratings are used separately instead of using the overall CPIA rating. There is some evidence that a higher level of aid as a share of GDP is associated with better portfolio performance, and countries with a higher proportion of land in tropics are more likely to have a higher proportion of problem loans. However, the respective coefficients are not always significant across the different specifications.

Attempts were made to estimate the relative importance of the four CPIA clusters on the Bank's loan portfolio performance. This was difficult because of the high degree of correlation among the ratings of the four clusters (table G.2). Indeed when all four clusters were included as explanatory variables along with other control variables, none of them are found to be significant and their

signs are not consistent across specifications—a manifestation of multicollinearity.

To reduce the multicollinearity problem, specifications were estimated using ratings from all the possible combinations of two CPIA clusters as explanatory variables, in turn. The coefficients on all the combinations of the two CPIA variables are not significant but their signs are consistently negative across specifications. An F-test of the joint null hypothesis that the coefficients of both CPIA variables are equal to zero was rejected, which implies that one or both CPIA ratings have significant negative association with the share of problem projects. However, their individual contributions cannot be discerned because of their high degree of correlation with each other. Further, an F-test of the null hypothesis that the coefficient of the CPIA rating for one cluster is not different from the coefficient of the rating of the other CPIA cluster cannot be rejected. Similar results were obtained when the share of problem projects in a country was regressed on the average ratings of the first three clusters combined and the ratings for cluster D. In sum, there is not sufficient evidence to conclude that the policies and institutions measured by one cluster are relatively more important than those measured by the other clusters for better project performance.

Conclusions

The analysis finds that higher CPIA ratings are associated with better Bank loan portfolio performance. This association is found for overall CPIA ratings as well as ratings for each of the four CPIA clusters. There is insufficient evidence to conclude that any one of the four CPIA clusters is more important than the others for loan performance.

Table G.1: CPIA and Loan Performance: Ordinary Least Squares Regressions
Dependent Variable: Percent of Problem Loans

Independent Variables	Overall CPIA			CPIA Cluster A			CPIA Cluster B			CPIA Cluster C			CPIA Cluster D		
	(1)	(2)	(3)	(1)	(2)	(3)	(1)	(2)	(3)	(1)	(2)	(3)	(1)	(2)	(3)
CPIA ratings	−13.4***	−16.1***	−17.9***	−9.1***	−9.0**	−10.1***	−11.4***	−14.4***	−16.0***	−9.7**	−13.7**	−14.4***	−10.5**	−11.4**	−13.4***
Aid/GDP		−0.5*	−0.4*		−0.4	−0.3		−0.5	−0.4		−0.4	−0.3		−0.4	−0.3
% Tropical Land		10.5			10.6			12.5			13.6*			10.3	
Ethnic Fractionalization		1.7			6.0			2.5			−0.7			2.8	
Africa Dummy	−18.8***	−18.7**	−16.7***	−16.5***	−17.7***	−14.0**	−18.8***	−19.5**	−17.3***	−17.7***	−18.9**	−16.9***	−16.6***	−16.3**	−14.4**
Europe and Central Asia Dummy	−20.6***	−15.5*	−21.9***	−19.8***	−13.5	−19.8***	−21.1***	−14.3	−22.4***	−20.5***	−13.3	−21.9***	−22.2***	−16.9*	−23.6***
East Asia and Pacific Dummy	−25.2***	−25.7***	−23.6***	−21.6***	−21.6***	−19.5**	−26.5***	−27.4***	−26.1***	−23.7***	−25.1***	−23.0***	−24.2***	−24.7***	−22.8***
Middle East and North Africa Dummy	−26.2***	−16.3	−28.0***	−25.0***	−14.4	−25.5***	−25.7***	−15.2	−27.6***	−25.2***	−13.6	−27.2***	−24.2***	−13.4	−25.1***
South Asia Dummy	−22.8***	−17.2*	−22.5***	−20.0**	−13.9	−18.8**	−23.9***	−16.4	−24.5***	−21.5*	−15.8	−21.7***	−21.1**	−15.2	−20.4**
Constant	85.5***	90.9***	104.1***	71.1***	63.1***	75.9***	78.9***	83.6**	98.5***	71.0***	79.3***	89.9***	71.0***	68.6***	82.5***
Observations	92	79	87	92	79	87	92	79	87	92	79	87	92	79	87
R-squared	0.23	0.29	0.26	0.22	0.26	0.22	0.21	0.28	0.24	0.19	0.26	0.22	0.21	0.25	0.23

Source: IEG estimates.
Note: *** significant at 1% level; ** significant at 5% level; * significant at 10% level.

Table G.2: Correlations among Average 2004–07 CPIA Ratings for the Four Country Policy and Institutional Assessment (CPIA) Clusters

CPIA	Cluster A	Cluster B	Cluster C	Cluster D	Overall CPIA
Cluster A	1.00				
Cluster B	0.61	1.00			
Cluster C	0.66	0.74	1.00		
Cluster D	0.74	0.81	0.84	1.00	
Overall CPIA	0.86	0.87	0.90	0.94	1.00

Source: IEG estimates.

Notes: a. Based on 92 observations. b. All correlations are significant at 1% level

APPENDIX H: COMPARING COUNTRY POLICY AND INSTITUTIONAL ASSESSMENT RATINGS BY THE WORLD BANK, AFRICAN DEVELOPMENT BANK, AND ASIAN DEVELOPMENT BANK

Comparison of the CPIA ratings (rather than relative rankings implied by the ratings) can only be done for the CPIA ratings by the World Bank, the AfDB, and the ADB. Ratings by these three development banks are on the exact same scale, with each rating having the exact same meaning, which is not the case with the other indicators.

Generally speaking, it is found that the 2007 CPIA ratings by the AfDB and ADB are higher than the CPIA ratings by the Bank. Specifically, the ratings by the AfDB were higher than those by the Bank for all 16 CPIA criteria; for 12 of the 16, the ratings were statistically significantly higher at the 5 percent level. The ratings by the ADB were higher than those of the Bank for 14 of the 16 CPIA criteria; for 5 of the 14, the ratings were statistically significantly higher. For the two criteria for which the Bank's ratings were higher than those of the ADB, the differences in the ratings were not significantly different (see appendix table H.1).

Appendix H.1: 2007 CPIA Ratings by the World Bank, AfDB and ADB

Criterion	Average for common World Bank and AFDB member countries		Average for common World Bank and ADB member countries	
	World Bank	AfDB	World Bank	ADB
q1	3.64	3.99	3.83	4.00
q2	3.38	3.74	3.44	3.67
q3	3.31	3.67	3.90	4.00
q4	3.58	3.62	3.87	3.65
q5	3.20	3.48	3.17	3.42
q6	3.25	3.38	3.35	3.27
q7	3.24	3.55	3.56	3.62
q8	3.24	3.53	3.58	3.63
q9	3.31	3.45	3.48	3.58
q10	3.01	3.22	3.23	3.29
q11	3.24	3.45	3.13	3.25
q12	2.90	3.23	3.00	3.21
q13	3.16	3.52	3.29	3.60
q14	3.46	3.55	3.35	3.58
q15	3.02	3.27	3.10	3.13
q16	2.85	3.24	2.87	3.06

Sources: World Bank, AfDB, and ADB.

Note: Bold figures denote ratings that are significantly different at the 5 percent level between the World Bank and the AfDB, and the World Bank and the ADB. ADB= Asian Development Bank; AfDB= African Development Bank.

Comparator Indices	Trade (q4)	Financial Sector (q5)	Business Regulatory Environment (q6)	Gender Equality (q7)	Equity of Public Resource Use (q8)	Building Human Resources (q9)	Social Protection and Labor (q10)	Policies and Institutions for Environmental Sustainability (q11)	Property Rights and Rule Based Governance (q12)	Quality of Budgetary and Financial Management (q13)	Efficiency of Revenue Mobilization (q14)	Quality of Public Administration (q15)	Transparency, Accountability, and Corruption in the Public Sector (q16)
Worldwide Governance Indicator			Regulatory quality						Rule of Law			Government effectiveness	Control of corruption
Doing Business		(5) Getting credit (Strength of legal rights index, depth of credit information index).	Doing Business Indicators: (1) Starting a Business (2) Dealing with construction permits (3) Employing workers (6) Protecting investors (7) Paying taxes (10) Closing a business										
Index of Economic Freedom: Heritage Foundation			Business freedom (data from Doing Business)						Property Rights				Freedom from Corruption (data from Transparency International); property rights
International Country Risk Guide (ICRG): PRS Group									Investment profile (contract viability; profit repatriation; payment delays; law and order			Bureaucracy Quality	Corruption
Global Gender Gap Report (World Economic Forum)				Gender Gap Index									
Transparency International													Corruption Perception Index

CPIA CRITERIA

CPIA CRITERIA

Comparator Indices	Trade (q4)	Financial Sector (q5)	Business Regulatory Environment (q6)	Gender Equwality (q7)	Equity of Public Resource Use (q8)	Building Human Resources (q9)	Social Protection and Labor (q10)	Policies and Institutions for Environmental Sustainability (q11)	Property Rights and Rule Based Governance (q12)	Quality of Budgetary and Financial Management (q13)	Efficiency of Revenue Mobilization (q14)	Quality of Public Administration (q15)	Transparency, Accountability, and Corruption in the Public Sector (q16)
Gender Empowerment Measure United Nations Development Programme (UNDP) Human Development Report				Gender Empowerment Measure									
Ibrahim Index of African Governance													Rule of law, transparency, and corruption
Bertelsmann Transformation Index			Private property				Social safety nets		Private property				Q3.2 Does an independent judiciary exist? Q3.3 Are there legal or political penalties for officeholders who abuse their position?
Global Enabling Trade Report (World Economic Forum)	Enabling Trade Index: (1) Market access—tariffs and non-tariff barriers, (2) Border administration		Enabling Trade Index: (4) the business environment—regulatory environment										
2005 Environmental Sustainability Index								Social and institutional capacity					
Global Competitiveness Index	Prevalence of trade barriers	Interest rate spread (hard data)	Burden of government regulation			Business impact of malaria			Property rights				
	Trade-weighted tariff rate (hard data)	Financial market sophistication	Strength of auditing and reporting standards			Malaria incidence (hard data)			Efficiency of legal framework				
	Burden of customs procedures	Financing through local equity market	Efficacy of corporate boards			Business impact of tuberculosis			Business costs of crime and violence				

(continued on next page)

107

Comparator Indices	Trade (q4)	Financial Sector (q5)	Business Regulatory Environment (q6)	Gender Equwality (q7)	Equity of Public Resource Use (q8)	Building Human Resources (q9)	Social Protection and Labor (q10)	Policies and Institutions for Environmental Sustainability (q11)	Property Rights and Rule Based Governance (q12)	Quality of Budgetary and Financial Management (q13)	Efficiency of Revenue Mobilization (q14)	Quality of Public Administration (q15)	Transparency, Accountability, and Corruption in the Public Sector (q16)
Global Competitiveness Index (cont.)		Ease of access to loans	Protection of minority shareholders' interests			Tuberculosis incidence (hard data)			Reliability of police services				
		Soundness of banks	Intensity of local competition			Business impact of HIV/AIDS							
		Regulation of securities exchanges	Extent of market dominance			Human immunodeficiency virus (HIV) prevalence (hard data)							
		Legal rights index (hard data)	Effectiveness of anti-monopoly policy			Infant mortality (hard data)							
			Extent and effect of taxation			Life expectancy (hard data)							
			Total tax rate (hard data)			Quality of primary education							
			Number of procedures required to start a business (hard data)			Primary enrollment (hard data)							
			Time required to start a business (hard data)			Education expenditure (hard data)							
			Strength of investor protection (hard data)			Secondary enrollment (hard data)							
			Cooperation in labor-employer relations			Tertiary enrollment (hard data)							
			Flexibility of wage determination			Quality of the educational system							
			Hiring and firing practices										

CPIA CRITERIA

Source: IEG.

APPENDIX J. NUMBER OF IDA AND IBRD COUNTRIES FOR WHICH EXTERNAL DATA ARE AVAILABLE

CPIA		ICRG	GCI	ETI	DB	Bertelsmann Transformation Index	Index of Economic Freedom	WGI	Corruption Perception Index	Ibrahim Index of African Governance	Environmental Sustainability Index	Gender Gap Index	Gender Empowerment Measure
q1	IDA												
	IBRD												
q2	IDA												
	IBRD												
q3	IDA												
	IBRD												
q4	IDA		39	37									
	IBRD		52	48									
q5	IDA		39	37	75								
	IBRD		52	48	64								
q6	IDA		38	37	75	56	55	75					
	IBRD		52	48	64	55	59	65					
q7	IDA											40	17
	IBRD											53	43
q8	IDA												
	IBRD												
q9	IDA		39			56							
	IBRD		52			55							
q10	IDA					56							
	IBRD					55							
q11	IDA										57		
	IBRD										53		
q12	IDA	42	40			56	55	75					
	IBRD	53	52			55	59	65					
q13	IDA												
	IBRD												
q14	IDA												
	IBRD												
q15	IDA	42						75					
	IBRD	53						65					
q16	IDA	42				56	55	75	74	38			
	IBRD	53				55	59	65	61	8			

Source: IEG.

Note: DB= Doing business; ETI=Enabling Trade Index; GCI= Global Competitiveness Index; IBRD= International Bank for Reconstruction and Development; ICRG= International Country Risk Guide; IDA= International Development Association; WGI= World Governance Indicators.

CPIA criterion	IBRD		IDA		Total	
	Number of network comments	Share of countries with network comments (%)	Number of network comments	Share of countries with network comments (%)	Number of network comments	Share of countries with network comments (%)
q1	59	90.8	62	82.7	121	86.4
q2	59	90.8	62	82.7	121	86.4
q3	59	90.8	62	82.7	121	86.4
q4	43	66.2	37	49.3	80	57.1
q5	10	15.4	8	10.7	18	12.9
q6	7	10.8	7	9.3	14	10.0
q7	16	24.6	25	33.3	41	29.3
q8	12	18.5	10	13.3	22	15.7
q9	50	76.9	48	64.0	98	70.0
q10	34	52.3	38	50.7	72	51.4
q11	4	6.2	7	9.3	11	7.9
q12	13	20.0	11	14.7	24	17.1
q13	10	15.4	19	25.3	29	20.7
q14	14	21.5	13	17.3	27	19.3
q15	7	10.8	6	8.0	13	9.3
q16	10	15.4	14	18.7	24	17.1
Total	**407**	**39.1**	**429**	**35.8**	**836**	**37.3**

Source: IEG calculations based on World Bank information.
Note: IBRD= International Bank for Reconstruction and Development;; IDA= International Development Association.

Elephants, Kenya. Photo by Curt Carnemark/World Bank

Chapter 1

1. This is an evaluation of the implementation of the IDA10–12 Replenishment Agreements.

2. The previous name of the Independent Evaluation Group (IEG) name was the Operations Evaluation Department (OED). The name changed from OED to IEG in December 2005. Relevant documents pertaining to the CPIA and other evaluations from the earlier period may still be catalogued under OED in some databases.

3. The external panel consisted of nine academics and public officials from developed and developing countries. The panel met at the Bank on February 17–18, 2004, and reviewed the coverage of the CPIA system, methodology, database, and cross-country comparability. The panel submitted its final report to Management on April 2, 2004. See World Bank 2004a.

4. The cluster was renamed from "public finance/ civil administration" in 1997.

5. The criteria on *financial stability* and *financial sector depth, efficiency and resource mobilization* were collapsed into a new *financial sector* criterion, and the *competitive environment for the private sector* and *goods and factor markets* criteria were collapsed into the new *business regulatory environment* criterion.

6. One of these is the criterion on *management and sustainability of the development program*, which is covered in almost all of the other criteria. The other is the criterion on *monitoring and analysis of poverty outcomes and impacts*. This criterion covers the availability of up-to-date household surveys and analysis, which is necessary for the criterion on *equity of public resource use*, and the criterion on *building human resources*. (World Bank 2004d).

7. There were some changes in the instructions for some criteria mainly aimed at reducing overlap between criteria, and improving consistency.

8. World Bank (2008e, annex 1, p. 2).

Chapter 2

1. These are some of the key elements of the so-called Washington Consensus view.

2. The point of view of Rodrik and others seems to be accepted by the majority of the economists today (even if this consensus is obviously quite recent). Aghion and Howitt (2009) reconcile new growth theory with what they call "Gerschenkron's views," thereby addressing development economists' concern that growth theory can only deliver universal, one-size-fits-all policy prescriptions (legal reform to enforce property rights, investment climate favorable to entrepreneurship, education, macrostability, and so on) to maximize the growth prospects of a country or sector, and does not apprehend structural transformations in the process of convergence. (New growth theory calls for better property rights protection and higher education investment in all countries under all latitudes. Gerschenkron's view is the idea that relatively backward economies could more rapidly catch up with more advanced economies by introducing appropriate institutions that are growth enhancing at an early stage of development but may cease to be so at a later stage). More specifically, they analyze some general implications of the notion of "distance-dependent" appropriate institutions, by which they mean institutions that are growth enhancing only for countries at a certain stage of technological development. In particular, they show how the failure to adapt institutions to technological development may generate non-convergence traps whereby a country's average productivity (or per capita GDP) remains bounded away from frontier levels.

3. The theoretical and empirical analyses of Vandenbussche, Aghion, and Meghir (2006) suggest that countries with productivities far from the technological frontier should put more emphasis on primary/ secondary education, whereas countries closer to the frontier should put more emphasis on tertiary education.

4. See Aghion and Howitt (2009) for a discussion. For the neoclassical and endogenous growth theories, it is investment in physical and human capital that drives growth, whereas for the product variety and Schumpeterian theories, it is investment in technology (in the form of research). In the hybrid model, investment in capital and technology are both important.

5. The discussion in this paragraph is drawn from World Bank (2008a).

6. Bourguignon (2004) indicated that a serious evaluation of Mexico's PROGRESA/Oportunidades and Brazil's Bolsa Escola/Bolsa Families, essentially means-tested income transfer programs with conditionalities, finds that these programs were effective in raising school enrollment rates and health outcomes in targeted populations. The sources cited for this were Skoufias (2001) on PROGRESA, and Bourguignon, Ferreira, and Leite (2003) on Bolsa Escola; and World Bank (2004g).

7. This has especially been the case with East Asian countries. See World Bank (1993).

8. An early study of Grameen Bank finds that it generated employment and income for the poor, especially women (Hossain 1988). The most comprehensive impact studies of microfinance, a joint research project of the Bangladesh Institute of Development Studies and the World Bank find strong evidence that the programs help the poor through asset building (and consumption smoothing) (Khandker 1998; Pitt and Khandker 2003).

9. A very recent paper (Freund and Rocha 2010) estimates that for African exports, a one-day reduction in inland travel times translates into nearly a 3 percentage point reduction in all importing country tariffs.

10. This is in accordance with the so-called Lerner's symmetry, whereby taxing imports has the same effect on international trade as taxing exports.

11. The phenomenon is called the "environmental Kuznets curve" whereby pollution levels, initially fairly low, rise as national income increases up to a certain point, then begin to decline with further economic growth as cleaner technologies are adopted and environmental sanitation infrastructure investments begin to catch up with expanding local needs (IEG 2008, chapter 1, footnote 3).

12. The allocations were calculated using the PBA formula. The GNI per capita and population data are from World Development Indicators, and the portfolio performance ratings are constructed using data from The World Bank's internal database. Because the simulations focused on changes in allocations, they did not require data on the overall IDA envelope.

13. In fiscal 2009, the post-conflict countries are Afghanistan, Angola, Burundi, Democratic Republic of Congo, Republic of Congo, Côte d'Ivoire, Eritrea, Liberia, and Timor-Leste. The re-engaging countries are Central African Republic, Haiti, and Togo. The capped countries are India and Pakistan.

14. References are cited in Kanbur (2004).

15. A 1 percent rate of growth in average household income or consumption brought anything from a modest drop in the poverty rate of 0.6 percent to a more dramatic 3.5 percent annual decline. (Ravallion 2001).

16. This is a term coined by Ghura, Leite, and Tsangarides (2002).

17. Besley and Burgess (2003) underline that expanding access to credit for the poor may increase the elasticity between economic growth and poverty reduction, in addition to being a form of redistribution.

18. Honahan (2004b), based on analysis of a cross-section of some 70-odd developing countries.

19. According to Winters, McCulloch, and McKay (2004), these channels are: (i) job opportunities and wages of the poor; (ii) prices that poor consumers pay for the goods they buy; (iii) government revenues and in turn social expenditures; (iv) income instability and workers' chances of becoming poor. Goldberg and Pavcnik (2004) identify three other channels: (i) participation of household members in the labor market; (ii) household consumption; and (iii) household production.

20. Porto (2005) shows that reducing such barriers would reduce poverty from an initial headcount ratio of 48.3 percent to a poverty rate from 43.3 to 45.5 percent. In other words, it would lift between 100,000 to 180,000 Moldovan citizens (out of a population of 3.5 million) out of poverty.

21. Notably, this has followed Amartya Sen's work on poverty and freedom (Sen 1997, 1999).

22. It is recognized that economic development encompasses more dimensions than just growth, although growth is certainly the key dimension, and moreover the only dimension for which a theoretical foundation exists. Poverty reduction is another dimension of economic development, and it is also recognized that although growth is not sufficient for poverty reduction, it is necessary. Therefore, the

discussion on the theoretical and empirical literature of the impact of aid on growth also pertains to the impact of aid on reduction of income poverty.

23. These are the Harrod-Domar model and its extension the Solow growth model.

24. Boone (1994). According to Clemens, Radelet, and Bhavnani (2004), parts of the analysis of Boone (1994) were published in Boone (1996) without the growth regressions.

25. The exception was small countries, where aid flows which made up a large share of GDP were found to lead to higher investments, which Boone attributed to the lack of fungibility of aid flows. Boone provided an example that in a small country one dam or a large public infrastructure project can represent a sizeable portion of GNP, and the project is unlikely to be fungible.

26. Other innovations in this later generation of empirical literature include: larger datasets that cover more countries and more years; accounting for the endogeneity of aid (that is, in addition to growth being an outcome of aid, aid can also be influenced by the growth performances of countries); and allowing for a non-linear aid-growth relationship (in particular diminishing returns to aid, or in other words, decreasing impact of aid on growth after reaching a point of maximum impact).

27. In Burnside and Dollar (1997, 2000), fiscal policy is measured by the budget surplus (following Easterly and Rebelo 1993), monetary policy by the inflation rate (following Fischer 1993) and trade by trade openness (as measured by Sachs and Warner 1995).

28. Including the relative size of the donor versus the recipient (the larger the ratio, the greater the influence, and presumably the larger amounts of aid), commonality of language, and colonial ties (either current or past).

29. Roodman (2007a). He performed the tests on Burnside and Dollar (2000), Collier and Dehn (2001), Collier and Dollar (2002), Collier and Hoeffler (2004), Hansen and Tarp (2001), Dalgaard, Hansen, and Tarp (2004), and Guillaumont and Chauvet (2001). The tests were designed to minimize arbitrariness and were derived mainly from the differences among the papers themselves. The tests included: (i) changing the control set (using the control sets of other papers being tested); (ii) redefining aid; (iii) redefining good policy; (iv) changing periodization; (v) changing outliers; and (vi) expanding the sample.

30. Such problems include difficulties with: (i) accounting for endogeneity (in particular, which instruments to use); (ii) the specification of the regression equation (including the timing of the impact of aid on growth); and (iii) the treatment of outliers; data limitations, among others.

31. Headey (2005) and Reddy and Minoiu (2006) find that multilateral or developmental aid has a positive impact on growth, whereas geopolitical and bilateral aid do not (except for bilateral aid that is not politically motivated). Ram (2003) finds that bilateral but not multilateral aid has a large and positive impact on growth (although this paper has been criticized for not taking the endogeneity of aid into account).

32. Clemens, Radelet, and Bhavnani (2004) also find that the impact on growth is somewhat larger in countries with stronger institutions or longer life expectancies.

33. The concept of such evaluations originates from the scientific/medical realm of randomized trials, whereby the effects of medicines are tested by comparing the group of patients who received the medicine with a group who received the placebo. The selection of the "comparable" group is therefore key and, in the context of aid project evaluations, needs to ensure that the differential effects between the two groups could not be due to some characteristic of the recipient group that is not present in the control group.

34. A request made by the IEG team to the network on April 23, 2009, for the number of responses to the environment questionnaire for 2008 was not answered.

35. This is constructed by applying the relevant weights to the ratings for market access and border administration, respectively, of the Enabling Trade Index.

36. Although the rank correlation coefficient with one based on the Global Competitiveness Index (GCI) will remain unchanged at 0.70. The one based on the GCI is constructed by applying the relevant weights to the combined rating for tariffs and trade barriers (50 percent each) and the rating for burden of customs administration.

37. As in the simulation on dropping q8, this simulation is conducted based on a CPIA implied by the IDA allocation formula—that is, 25 percent weight given to CPIA clusters A through C, and 75 percent weight on cluster D.

38. There is room for debate as to the causality between every banking crisis and output losses, as

115

there have certainly been instances in the past where fiscal or political crises have triggered banking crises, such as Argentina in 1981, in the transition countries, and in several African countries.

39. At the same time, however, what evidence there is does not suggest that crises systematically worsen the Gini coefficient (Honohan 2004a), that is, that banking crises have a disproportionate effect on the poor, although the poor are likely less able than others to absorb adverse shocks.

40. One is the stock of NPLs as a share of total loans; the other, the "level of capital at risk," is a net figure which subtracts provisions already taken against these NPLs.

Chapter 3

1. For the criteria on *gender* (q7), *property rights and rule-based governance* (q12), and *quality of budgetary and financial management* (q13), the 2007 AfDB questionnaire is identical to the pre-2005 Bank CPIA questionnaire that has since been updated, although the differences are not substantial. Further, the Bank's ratings for the criterion on *policies and institutions for environmental sustainability* (q11) are relatively stringent compared with those of the AfDB. For example, the Bank gives a "1" rating on q11 if "For both pollution and natural resource issues: regulations and policies are lacking. Environmental information is not published. Environmental Assessment legislation is lacking. No data are available for priority setting. Sector ministries do not incorporate environmental concerns." A "1" rating is given by AfDB if "For two years or more, government policies have a negative effect on environment (for example agriculture policies that stimulate expansion into marginal land or tropical forest; subsidized prices on the exploitation of scarce and/or non-renewable resources). Government has no environmental action plans or similar national framework, and no institutions to sustainably manage the environment and support the various dimensions of sustainable development."

2. It is difficult to find good comparators for the economic management criteria because both outcomes and policies are taken into account in the CPIA ratings, whereas other indicators focus only on outcomes (such as the economic risk index produced by the International Country Risk Guide).

3. The IEG team examined two indicators that are possible comparators for q13. These are one of the global integrity indicators produced by Global Integrity that rate the budget process, and the Open Budget Index produced by the Open Budget Initiative that rates the transparency of the budget. However, both these indicators comprise only part of what is being assessed under q13, so are not strictly comparable with q13, and hence the team did not include them as comparators.

4. Rank correlations are used instead of pair-wise correlations for comparing the different indicators because of the less restrictive assumption underlying rank correlations (they do not require the assumption of a linear relationship between the indicators). Nonetheless, the IEG team for this evaluation performed both types of correlations and obtained very similar results from them.

5. A better correlation denotes a rank correlation coefficient that is at least 5 percent higher.

6. Ratings from ADB are excluded from this comparison because only 3 IBRD countries are rated by ADB, whereas 12 are rated by AfDB.

Appendix F

1. There is room for debate as to the causality between every banking crisis and output losses, as there have certainly been instances in the past where fiscal or political crises have triggered banking crises, such as Argentina in 1981, in the transition countries, and in several African countries.

2. At the same time, however, what evidence there is does not suggest that crises systematically worsen the Gini coefficient (Honohan 2004a), that is, that banking crises have a disproportionate effect on the poor, although the poor are likely less able than others to absorb adverse shocks.

3. Stress tests model the impact of extreme but plausible shocks, and measure the capacity of banks to absorb the shocks with available liquidity and capital.

4. One is the stock of NPLs as a share of total loans; the other, the "level of capital at risk," is a net figure which subtracts provisions already taken against these NPLs.

Appendix G

1. For loans approved from 1998 onward, the correlation between the share of problem projects in a country and the share of loans receiving an unsatisfactory IEG outcome rating for that country is 0.63.

2. The level of per capita GDP was not included as a control variable due to its high correlation with

the overall CPIA rating. The percent of problem loans might also depend on the quality of the Bank staff working on those loans; ratings on task team quality are provided by the Quality Assurance Group (QAG) in its quality at entry ratings for loans. However, due to limited data availability, the quality of Bank staff was not included as a control variable.

3. To account for the possible endogeneity of both the CPIA ratings and the *Aid to GDP* variable, two-stage least square specifications were estimated. The CPIA and *Aid to GDP* variable were instrumented using the share of population speaking English, the share of population speaking a continental European language, distance from equator, level of population, and each of the above four instruments multiplied by population (see Dollar and Levin 2005). The first-stage regressions suggest that the instruments are weak (the F-statistics are relatively low). The Durbin-Wu-Hausman test for endogeneity suggests that both variables are exogenous and the OLS estimates are consistent.

Women preparing food, Nigeria. Photo by Curt Carnemark/World Bank

Acemoglu, Daron, and Simon Johnson. 2007. "Disease and Development: The Effect of Life Expectancy on Economic Growth." *Journal of Political Economy* 115 (61): 925–985.

Acemoglu, Daron, and James A. Robinson. 2000. "Political Losers as a Barrier to Economic Development." *American Economic Review Papers and Proceedings* 90: 126–44.

Acemoglu, Daron, and Thierry A. Verdier. 2000. "The Choice Between Market Failures and Corruption." *American Economic Review* 90 (1): 194–211.

———. 2001. "The Colonial Origins of Comparative Development: An Empirical Investigation." *American Economic Review* 91 (5): 1369–401.

Acemoglu, Daron, Simon Johnson, and James A. Robinson. 2005. "The Rise of Europe: Atlantic Trade, Institutional Change, and Economic Growth." *American Economic Review* 95 (3): 546–79.

Adsera, Alicia, Carles Boix, and Mark Payne. 2003. "Are You Being Served? Political Accountability and Quality of Government." *Journal of Law, Economics, & Organization* 19 (2): 445–90.

Agenor, Pierre-Richard. 2004. "Does Globalization Hurt the Poor?" *International Economics and Economic Policy* 1 (1): 21–51.

Aghion, Philippe, and Peter Howitt. 2009. *The Economics of Growth*. Cambridge, Mass.: The MIT Press.

Aghion, Philippe, Eve Caroli, and Cecilia García-Peñalosa. 1999. "Inequality and Economic Growth: The Perspective of the New Growth Theories." *Journal of Economic Literature* 37 (4): 1615–60.

Aghion, Philippe, Peter Howitt, and David Mayer-Foulkes. 2005. "The Effect of Financial Development on Convergence: Theory and Evidence." *Quarterly Journal of Economics* 120 (1): 173–222.

Ahmad, Ehtisham, and Nicholas Stern. 1987. "Alternative Sources of Government Revenue: Illustrations from India, 1979–80." In *The Theory of Taxation for Developing Countries*. David M. G. Newbery, and Nicholas H. Stern (editors), New York: Published for The World Bank by Oxford University Press.

Ahrend, Rudiger. 2001. "Press Freedom, Human Capital and Corruption." Mimeo.

Alesina, Alberto. 1997. "Politics, Procedures and Budget Deficits." Background Paper prepared for *The World Development Report* 1997. World Bank, Washington, DC.

Alesina, Alberto, and George-Marios Angeletos. 2005. "Corruption, Inequality and Fairness." National Bureau of Economic Research (NBER) Working Paper No. 11399.

Alesina, Alberto, and Roberto Perotti. 1996. "Income Distribution, Political Instability, and Investment." *European Economic Review* 40 (6): 1203–28.

Alesina, Alberto, and Dani Rodrik. 1994. "Distributive Politics and Economic Growth." *Quarterly Journal of Economics* 109 (2): 465–90.

Alesina, Alberto, and Beatrice Weder. 2002. "Do Corrupt Governments Receive Less Foreign Aid?" *The American Economic Review* 92 (4): 1126–37.

Alesina, Alberto, Arnaud Devleeschauwer, William Easterly, Sergio Kurlat, and Romain Wacziarg. 2003. "Fractionalization." *Journal of Economic Growth* 8 (2): 155–94.

Ames, Brian, Ward Brown, Shanta Devarajan, and Alejandro Izquierdo. 2001. "Macroeconomic Policy and Poverty Reduction." Prepared by

The International Monetary Fund and The World Bank.

Anderson, Kym. 2003. "Trade Liberalization, Agriculture, and Poverty in Low-income Countries." WIDER Discussion Paper No. 2003/25. United Nations University.

Andvig, Jens, and Odd-Helge Fjeldstad. 2008. "Crime, Poverty and Police Corruption in Developing Countries." Christian Michelsen Institute (CMI) Working Paper No. 2008:7.

Angrist, Joshua, Eric Bettinger, and Michael Kremer. 2006. "Long-Term Educational Consequences of Secondary School Vouchers: Evidence from Administrative Records in Colombia." *American Economic Review* 96 (3): 847–62.

Angrist, Joshua, Eric Bettinger, Erik Bloom, Elizabeth King, and Michael Kremer. 2002. "Vouchers for Private Schooling in Colombia: Evidence from a Randomized Natural Experiment." *American Economic Review* 92 (5): 1535–58.

Ashraf, Nava, James N. Berry, and Jesse Shapiro. 2007. "Can Higher Prices Stimulate Product Use? Evidence from a Field Experiment in Zambia." NBER Working Paper No. 13247.

Ashraf, Quamrul, Ashley Lester, and David Weil. 2008. "When Does Improving Health Raise GDP?" NBER Working Paper No. 14449.

Ayers, Robert. 1997. "Crime and Violence as Development Issues in Latin America and the Caribbean." Paper prepared for a World Bank Seminar on Urban Criminal Violence, Rio de Janeiro, March 2–4.

Ayyagari, Meghana, Asli Demirguc-Kunt, and Vojislav Maksimovic. 2007. "Firm Innovation in Emerging Markets: Role of Governance and Finance." Policy Research Working Paper No. 4157. World Bank, Washington, DC.

Azfar, Omar, Young Lee, and Anand Swamy. 2001. "The Causes and Consequences of Corruption." *Annals of the American Academy of Political and Social Science* 573: 42–56.

Bahl, Roy, and Richard Bird. 2008. "Tax Policy in Developing Countries: Looking Back and Forward." Institute for International Business Working Paper No. 13. Joseph L. Rotman School of Management, University of Toronto.

Balat, Jorge, Irene Brambilla, and Guido Porto. 2007. "Realizing the Gains from Trade: Export Crops, Marketing Costs, and Poverty." NBER Working Paper No. 13395.

Banerjee, Abhijit, Paul Gertler, and Maitresh Ghatak. 2002. "Empowerment and Efficiency: Tenancy Reform in West Bengal." *The Journal of Political Economy* 110 (2): 239–80.

Banerjee, Abhijit, Shawn Cole, Esther Duflo, and Leigh Linden. 2005. "Remedying Education Evidence from Two Randomized Experiments in India." NBER Working Paper No. 11904.

———. 2007. "Remedying Education: Evidence from Two Randomized Experiments in India." *Quarterly Journal of Economics*, 122 (3): 1235–64.

Bardhan, Pranab. 1997. "Corruption and Development: A Review of Issues." *Journal of Economic Literature* 35 (3): 1320–46.

———. 2000. "Social Justice in the Global Economy." International Labor Organization Social Policy Lecture, University of the Western Cape, South Africa. September 1–6.

———. 2006a. "The Economist's Approach to the Problem of Corruption." *World Development* 34 (2): 341–48.

———. 2006b. "Institutional Economics of Development: Some General Reflections." Opening Lecture at CESifo/BREAD Conference on Institutional Economics at San Servolo, Italy.

———. 2006c. "Institutions, Trade and Development." Paper prepared for UNCTAD, Geneva, Switzerland.

Barham, Vicky, Robin Boadway, Maurice Marchand, and Pierre Pestieau. 1995. "Education and the Poverty Trap." *European Economic Review* 39 (7): 1257–75.

Barro, Robert. 1999. "Determinants of Democracy." *Journal of Political Economy* 107 (6) 2.

———. 2003. "Determinants of Economic Growth in a Panel of Countries." *Annals of Economics and Finance* 4: 231–74.

Barro, Robert, and Xavier Sala-i Martin. 2003. *Economic Growth*. Cambridge, Mass.: The MIT Press.

Barth, James, Gerard Caprio, and Ross Levine. 2006. *Rethinking Bank Regulation: Till Angels Govern*. New York: Cambridge University Press.

Beck, Paul, and Michael Maher. 1986. "A Comparison of Bribery and Bidding in Thin Market," *Economics Letters* 20: 1–5.

Beck, Thorsten, Asli Demirguc-Kunt, and Ross Levine. 2004. "Finance, Inequality, and Poverty: Cross-Country Evidence." NBER Working Paper No. 10979.

———. 2005. "Law and Firms' Access to Finance." *American Law and Economics Review* 7 (1): 211–52.

Becker, Gary, and George Stigler. 1974. "Law Enforcement, Malfeasance and the Compensation of Enforcers." *Journal of Legal Studies* 3 (1): 1–19.

Bell, Clive, Shantayanan Devarajan, and Hans Gersbach. 2006. "The Long-Run Economic Costs of AIDS: A Model with an Application to South Africa." *The World Bank Economic Review* 20 (1): 55–89.

Berger, Allen N., W. Scott Frame, and Nathan H. Miller. 2005. "Credit Scoring and the Availability, Price, and Risk of Small Business Credit." *Journal of Money, Credit, and Banking* 37 (2): 191–222.

Besley, Timothy. 1995. "Property Rights and Investment Incentives: Theory and Evidence from Ghana." *The Journal of Political Economy* 103 (5): 903–37.

Besley, Timothy, and Robin Burgess. 2000. "Land Reform, Poverty Reduction, and Growth: Evidence from India." *Quarterly Journal of Economics* 115 (2): 389–430.

———. 2002. "The Political Economy of Government Responsiveness: Theory and Evidence." *Quarterly Journal of Economics* 117 (4): 1415–51.

———. 2003. "Halving Global Poverty." *The Journal of Economic Perspectives* 17 (3): 3–22.

Besley, Timothy, and Anne Case. 1995. "Does Electoral Accountability Affect Economic Policy Choices? Evidence from Gubernatorial Term Limits." *Quarterly Journal of Economics* 110 (3): 769–98.

Besley, Timothy, Robin Burgess, and Andrea Prat. 2002. "Mass Media and Political Accountability." In *The Right to Know: Institutions and the Media*, Roumeen Islam (ed.). World Bank, Washington, DC.

Bettinger, Eric, Michael Kremer, and Juan Saavedra. 2008. "Are Educational Vouchers Only Redistributive?" Draft, prepared for the CESifo/PEPG joint conference "Economic Incentives: Do They Work in Education?" Munich, Germany, May 16–17.

Bird, Richard. 2003. "Administrative Dimensions of Tax Reform." International Tax Program Paper No. 0302. Joseph L. Rotman School of Management, University of Toronto.

———. 2005. "Value-Added Taxes in Developing and Transitional Countries: Lessons and Questions." International Tax Program Paper No. 0505. Joseph L. Rotman School of Management, University of Toronto.

———. 2008. "Tax Challenges Facing Developing Countries." Institute for International Business Working Paper No. 12.

Bird, Richard, and Duanjie Chen. 1998. "The Fiscal Framework for Business in Asia." In *Fiscal Framework and Financial System in East Asia: How Much Do They Matter?*, Wendy Dobson (ed.). Toronto: University of Toronto Press.

Bird, Richard, and Pierre-Pascal Gendron. 2006. "Is VAT the Best Way to Impose a General Consumption Tax in Developing Countries?" International Tax Program Paper No. 0602. Joseph L. Rotman School of Management, University of Toronto.

———. 2007. *The VAT in Developing and Transitional Countries*. New York: Cambridge University Press.

Bird, Richard, and Barbara Miller. 1989. "The Incidence of Indirect Taxation on Low-Income Households in Jamaica." *Economic Development and Cultural Change* 37 (2): 393–409.

Bird, Richard, and Enid Slack. 2002. "Land and Property Taxation around the World: A Review." *Journal of Property Tax Assessment and Administration* 7 (3): 31–80.

Bird, Richard, and Eric Zolt. 2007. "Tax Policy in Emerging Countries." International Tax Program Paper No. 0707. Joseph L. Rotman School of Management, University of Toronto.

Bjorkman, Martina, and Jakob Svensson. 2009. "Power to the People: Evidence from a Randomized Field Experiment of Community-Based Monitoring in Uganda." Policy Research

Working Paper No. 4268. World Bank, Washington, D.C.

Bloom, David E. and Ajay S. Mahal. 1995. "Does the AIDS Epidemic Really Threaten Economic Growth?" NBER Working Paper No. 5148.

———. 1997. "Does the AIDS Epidemic Threaten Economic Growth?" *Journal of Econometrics* 77 (1): 105–24.

Bobonis, Gustavo J., Edward Miguel, and Charu Puri-Sharma. 2006. "Anemia and School Participation." *Journal of Human Resources* 41 (4): 692–721.

Bodewig, Christian, and Akshay Sethi. 2005. *Poverty, Social Exclusion and Ethnicity in Serbia and Montenegro: The Case of Roma*. World Bank, Washington, DC.

Boex, L., F. Jameson, Jorge Martinez-Vazquez, and Robert McNab. 2000. "Multi-Year Budgeting: A Review of International Practices and Applications for Developing and Transitional Economies." *Public Budgeting and Finance* 20 (2).

Boone, Peter. 1994. "The Impact of Foreign Aid on Savings and Growth." Center for Economic Performance Working Paper No. 677, London School of Economics.

———. 1996. "Politics and the Effectiveness of Foreign Aid." *European Economic Review* 40 (2): 289–329.

Boskin, Michael. 2006. "Eight Lessons for Public Finance in Developing Economies." China Development Forum, State Council of the PRC, Beijing, March.

Bourguignon, Francois. 1998. "Crime as a Social Cost of Poverty and Inequality: A Review Focusing on Developing Countries." DELTA, Paris. Mimeo.

———. 1999. "Crime, Violence and Inequitable Development." Paper prepared for the Annual World Bank Conference on Development Economics, Washington, D.C., April 28–30.

———. 2004. "The Poverty-Growth-Inequality Triangle." Paper presented at the Indian Council for Research on International Economic Relations, New Delhi, February 4.

Bourguignon, Francois, Francisco Ferreira, and Phillippe Leite. 2003. "Conditional Cash Transfers, Schooling and Child Labor: Micro-simulating Brazil's *Bolsa Escola* Program." *World Bank Economic Review* 17 (2).

Bovenberg, A. Lans, and Sjak Smulders. 1995. "Environmental Quality and Pollution-Augmenting Technical Change in a Two-Sector Endogenous Growth Model." *Journal of Public Economics* 57 (3): 369–91.

———. 1996. "Transitional Impacts of Environmental Policy in an Endogenous Growth Model." *International Economic Review* 37 (4): 861–93.

Braithwaite, Valerie. 2003. *Taxing Democracy. Understanding Tax Avoidance and Evasion*. Aldershot and Burlington, VT: Ashgate.

Brautigam, Deborah. 2000. *Aid Dependence and Governance*. Stockholm: Almqvist & Wiksell. International for the Swedish Ministry of Foreign Affairs.

Breen, Richard, and Cecilia García-Peñalosa. 2005. "Income Inequality and Macroeconomic Volatility: An Empirical Investigation." *Review of Development Economics* 9 (3): 380–98.

Brown, Michael, Tulio Jappelli, and Marco Pagano. 2009. "Information Sharing and Credit: Firm-Level Evidence from Transition Countries." *Journal of Financial Intermediation* 18 (2): 151–72.

Brunetti, Aymo, and Beatrice Weder. 1999. "A Free Press is Bad News for Corruption." Mimeo. Basel, Switzerland: University of Basel.

Burgess, Robin, and Rohini Pande. 2005. "Do Rural Banks Matter? Evidence from the Indian Social Banking Experiment." *American Economic Review* 95 (3): 780–95.

Burgess, Robin, and Nicholas Stern. 1993. "Taxation and Development." *Journal of Economic Literature* 31 (2): 762–830.

Burnside, Craig, and David Dollar. 1997. "Aid, Policies, and Growth." Policy Research Working Paper No. 1777. World Bank, Washington, DC.

———. 2000. "Aid, Policies, and Growth." *American Economic Review* 90 (4): 847–68.

———. 2004. "Aid, Policies, and Growth: Reply." *American Economic Review* 94 (3): 781–84.

Buvinic, Mayra, and Andrew R. Morrison. 2000. "Living in a More Violent World." *Foreign Policy* 118: 58–72.

Buvinic, Mayra, Andrew R. Morrison, and Michael Shifter. 1998. "Violence in Latin America and the Caribbean: A Framework for Action." Paper presented at an Inter-American Development Bank (IDB) Seminar on "Building Peaceful Societies: A Framework for Action." Cartagena, Columbia.

Cagé, Julia. 2009a. "Literature Review for a Special Study by the Independent Evaluation Group on the Country Policy and Institutional Assessment of The World Bank." Background Paper for this CPIA evaluation.

———. 2009b. "Asymmetric Information, Rent Extraction and Aid Efficiency." Agence Française de Développement Working Paper.

Calderon, Cesar, and Luis Serven. 2003. "The Output Cost of Latin America's Infrastructure Gap." In *The Limits of Stabilization: Infrastructure, Public Deficits and Growth in Latin America*, William Easterly and Luis Serven (editors). Palo Alto, CA: Stanford University Press, and The World Bank.

———. 2004. "The Effects of Infrastructure Development on Growth and Income Distribution." Policy Research Working Paper No. 3400. World Bank, Washington, DC.

Call, Charles. 2000. "Sustainable Development in Central America: The Challenges of Violence, Injustice and Insecurity." Hamburg Institut für Iberoamerika-Kunde, CA 2020 Working Paper No. 8.

Campos, Edgardo, and Sanjay Pradhan. 1996. "Budgetary Institutions and Expenditure Outcomes. Binding Governments to Fiscal Performance." Policy Research Working Paper No. 1646. World Bank, Washington, DC.

Cardenas, Enrique, Jose. Ocampo, and Rosemary Thorp. 2000. *The Export Age: The Latin American Economies in the Late Nineteenth and Early Twentieth Centuries*. (Vol. 1, *An Economic History of Twentieth Century Latin America*). New York: Palgrave Press.

Cashin, Paul Anthony, and Rupa Duttagupta. 2008. "The Anatomy of Banking Crises." IMF Working Paper WP/08/93.

Chand, Sheetal, and Karl Moene. 1999. "Controlling Fiscal Corruption." *World Development* 27(7): 1129–40.

Chetwynd, Eric, Frances Chetwynd, and Bertram Spector. 2003. "Corruption and Poverty: A Review of Recent Literature." United States Agency for International Development (USAID) Final Report.

Chhibber, Ajay, and Gaurav Nayyar. 2007. "Pro-Poor Growth: Explaining the Cross-Country Variation in the Growth Elasticity of Poverty." Brooks World Poverty Institute (BWPI) Working Paper No. 14, The University of Manchester.

Chong, Alberto, and Cesar Calderon. 2000. "Causality and Feedback between Institutional Measures and Economic Growth." *Economics and Politics* 12 (1): 69–81.

Christiaensen, Luc, Lionel Demery, and Stefano Paternostro. 2002. "Growth, Distribution, and Poverty in Africa: Messages from the 1990s." Policy Research Working Paper No. 2810. World Bank, Washington, DC.

Clemens, Michael, Steven Radelet and Rikhil Bhavnani. 2004. "Counting Chickens when They Hatch: The Short Term Effect of Aid on Growth." Center for Global Development Working Paper No. 44.

Cnossen, Sijbren. 2004. "VAT in South Africa: What Kind of Rate Structure?" *International VAT Monitor* 15 (1): 19–24.

Collier, Paul. 2007. *The Bottom Billion: Why the Poorest Countries Are Failing and What Can Be Done About It*. New-York and Oxford: Oxford University Press.

Collier, Paul, and Jan Dehn. 2001. "Aid, Shocks and Growth." Policy Research Working Paper No. 2688. World Bank, Washington, DC.

Collier, Paul, and David Dollar. 2002. "Aid Allocation and Poverty Reduction." *European Economic Review* 46 (8): 1475–1500.

———. 2004. "Development Effectiveness." *Economic Journal* 114 (496): F244–F271.

Collier, Paul, and Anke Hoeffler. 2002. "Aid, Policy and Peace: Reducing the Risks of Civil Conflict." *Journal of Defense Economics and Peace* 13 (6): 435–50.

———. 2004. "Aid, Policy and Growth in Post-Conflict Societies." *European Economic Review* 48 (5): 1125–45.

Conley, Timothy G., and Christopher R. Udry. 2007. "Learning About a New Technology: Pineapple in Ghana." Economic Growth Center Discussion Paper No. 817, Yale University.

Cuddington, John T. 1993. "Modeling the Macroeconomic Effects of AIDS, with an Application to Tanzania." *The World Bank Economic Review* 7 (2): 173–189.

Cuddington, John T., and John D. Hancock. 1994. "Assessing the Impact of AIDS on the Growth Path of the Malawian Economy." *Journal of Development Economics* 43 (2): 363–68.

Dalgaard, Carl-Johan, and Henrik Hansen. 2001. "On Aid, Growth and Good Policies." *Journal of Development Studies* 37 (6): 17–41.

Dalgaard, Carl-Johan, Henrik Hansen, and Finn Tarp. 2003. "On the Empirics of Foreign Aid and Growth." *The Economic Journal* 114 (496): F191–F216.

Dehejia, Rajeev, and Roberta Gatti. 2002. "Child Labor: The Role of Income Variability and Access to Credit across Countries." NBER Working Paper No. 9018.

De la Croix, David, and Clara Delavallade. 2006. "Growth, Public Investment and Corruption with Failing Institutions." Center for Operations Research and Econometrics (CORE) Discussion Paper No. 2006/101.

Demirgüç-Kunt, Asli, Edward J. Kane, and Luc Laeven. 2006. "Deposit Insurance Design and Implementation: Policy Lessons from Research and Practice." Policy Research Working Paper No. 3969. World Bank, Washington, DC.

De Nicoló, Gianni, Patrick Honohan, and Alain Ize. 2005. "Dollarization of Bank Deposits: Causes and Consequences." *Journal of Banking and Finance* 29 (7): 1697–1727.

Deolalikar, Anil, Alex Brillantes Jr., Raghav Gaiha, Ernesto Pernia, and Mary Racelis. 2002. "Poverty Reduction and the Role of Institutions in Developing Asia." Asian Development Bank Economics and Research Department Working Paper No. 10.

De Soto, Hernando. 2000. *The Mystery of Capital: Why Capitalism Triumphs in the West and Fails Everywhere Else*. New York: Random House.

Devas, Nick, Simon Delay, and Michael Hubbard. 2001. "Revenue Authorities: Are They the Right Vehicle for Improved Tax Administration?" *Public Administration and Development* 21 (3): 211–22.

Dillinger, William. 1992. *Urban Property Tax Reform. Guidelines and Recommendations*. World Bank, Washington, DC.

Di Tella, Rafael, and Ernesto Schargrodsky. 2003. "The Role of Wages and Auditing during a Crackdown on Corruption in the City of Buenos Aires." *Journal of Law and Economics* 46 (1): 269–92.

Dixit, Avinash. 2007. "Evaluating Recipes for Development Success." *World Bank Research Observer* 22 (2): 131–57.

Djankov, Simeon, Rafael La Porta, Florencio Lopez-de Silanes, and Andrei Shleifer. 2009. "Disclosure by Politicians." NBER Working Paper No. 14703.

Djankov, Simeon, Caralee McLiesh and Andrei Shleifer. 2007. "Private Credit in 129 Countries." *Journal of Financial Economics* 84 (2): 299–329.

Dollar, David, and Aart Kraay. 2002. "Growth is Good for the Poor." *Journal of Economic Growth* 7 (3): 195–225.

Dollar, David, and Victoria Levin. 2005. "Sowing and Reaping: Institutional Quality and Project Outcomes in Developing Countries." Policy Research Working Paper No. 3524. World Bank, Washington, DC.

Doppelhofer, Gernot, Ronald Miller, and Xavier Sala-i Martin. 2004. "Determinants of Long-Term Growth: A Bayesian Averaging of Classical Estimates (BACE) Approach." *American Economic Review* 94 (4): 813–35.

Dreze, Jacques, and Amartya Sen. 1989. *Hunger and Public Action*. New York: Oxford University Press.

———. 1995. *India: Economic Development and Social Opportunity*. New Delhi: Oxford University Press.

———. 2002. *India Development and Participation*. New Delhi: Oxford University Press.

Duncan-Waite, Imani, and Michael Woolcock. 2008. "Arrested Development: The Political Origins and Socio-Economic Foundations of Common Violence in Jamaica." Brooks World Poverty Institute (BWPI) Working Paper 46, University of Manchester, U.K.

Due, John. 1988. *Indirect Taxation in Developing Countries*. Baltimore: Johns Hopkins University Press.

Duflo, Esther, Michael Kremer, and Jonathan Robinson. 2007. "Why Don't Farmers Use Fertilizer? Experimental Evidence from Kenya." Massachusetts Institute of Technology and Harvard University, Working Paper.

———. 2008. "How High Are Rates of Return to Fertilizer? Evidence from Field Experiments in Kenya." *American Economic Review* 98 (2): 482–88.

Dyck, Alexander, David Moss, and Luigi Zingales. 2008. "Media versus Special Interests." NBER Working Paper No. 14360.

Easterly, William. 2001. *The Elusive Quest for Growth: Economists' Adventures and Misadventures in the Tropics*. Cambridge, Massachusetts: MIT Press.

———. 2003. "Can Foreign Aid Buy Growth?" *Journal of Economic Perspectives* 17 (3): 23–48.

———. 2006. "Inequality Does Cause Underdevelopment: Insights from a New Instrument." Mimeo.

Easterly, William, and Stanley Fischer. 2001. "Inflation and the Poor." *Journal of Money, Credit and Banking* 33 (2): 160–78.

Easterly, William, and Ross Levine. 1997. "Africa's Growth Tragedy: Policies and Ethnic Divisions." *Quarterly Journal of Economics* 112 (4): 1203–50.

———. 2003. "Tropics, Germs, and Crops: How Endowments Influence Economic Development." *Journal of Monetary Economics* 50 (1): 3–39.

Easterly, William, Ross Levine, and David Roodman. 2004. "Aid, Policies, and Growth: Comment." *American Economic Review* 94 (3): 774–80.

Easterly, William, and Sergio Rebelo. 1993. "Fiscal Policy and Economic Growth: An Empirical Investigation." NBER Working Paper No. 4499.

Easterly, William, Carlos Rodriguez, and Klaus Schmidt-Hebbel (editors). 1995. *Public Sector Deficits and Macroeconomic Performance*. New York: Oxford University Press.

Eastwood, Robert, and Michael Lipton. 2001. "Pro-Poor Growth and Pro-Growth Poverty Reduction: Meaning, Evidence, and Policy Implications." *Asian Development Review* 18 (2): 22–58. The Asian Development Bank.

Edmonds, E.V. 2007. "Child Labor." NBER Working Paper No. 12926.

Eijffinger, Sylvester, and Petra Geraats. 2005. "How Transparent Are Central Banks?" *European Journal of Political Economy* 22 (1): 1–21.

Emerson, Patrick, and Andre Souza. 2003. "Is There a Child Labor Trap? Intergenerational Persistence of Child Labor in Brazil." *Economic Development and Cultural Change* 51 (2): 375–98.

Epaulard, Anne. 2003. "Macroeconomic Performance and Poverty Reduction." IMF Working Paper WP/03/72.

Esty, David C., and Michael E. Porter. 2005. "National Environmental Performance: An Empirical Analysis of Policy Results and Determinants." *Environment and Development Economics* 10 (4): 391–434.

Evans, Peter, and James Rauch. 1999. "Bureaucracy and Growth: A Cross-National Analysis of the Effects of 'Weberian' State Structures on Economic Growth." *American Sociological Review* 64 (5): 748–65.

Ferraz, Claudio, and Federico Finan. 2008. "Exposing Corrupt Politicians: The Effects of Brazil's Publicly Released Audits on Electoral Outcomes." *Quarterly Journal of Economics* 123 (2): 703–46.

Fischer, Stanley. 1991. "Growth, Macroeconomics and Development." NBER Working Paper No. 3702.

———. 1993. "The Role of Macroeconomic Factors in Growth." *Journal of Monetary Economics* 32 (3): 485–512.

Field, Erica. 2002. "Entitled to Work: Urban Property Rights and Labor Supply in Peru." Princeton, N.J.: Princeton University.

Fields, Gary, Paul Cichello, Samuel Freije, Marta Menéndez, and David Newhouse. 2002. "Escaping Poverty: Household Income Dynamics in Indonesia, South Africa, Spain, and Venezuela." In *Pathways Out of Poverty: Private Firms and Economic Mobility in Developing Countries*. Gary S. Fields, and Guy Pfefferman (editors). Washington D.C.: International Finance Corporation.

Fjeldstad, Odd-Helge, and Mick Moore. 2007. "Taxation and State-Building: Poor Countries in a Globalised World." Chr. Michelsen Institute Working Paper No. 2007:11.

Fleisig, Heywood. 1995. "The Right to Borrow: Legal and Regulatory Barriers that Limit Access to Credit by Small Farms and Businesses." Public Policy for the Private Sector Note 44. The World Bank, Washington DC.

Foster, James, and Miguel Székely. 2008. "Is Economic Growth Good for the Poor? Tracking Low Incomes Using General Means." *International Economic Review* 49 (4): 1143–72.

Foster, Mick, Adrian Fozzard, Felix Naschold, and Tim Conway. 2002. "How, When and Why Does Poverty Get Budget Priority? Poverty Reduction Strategy and Public Expenditure in Five African Countries." Overseas Development Institute Working Paper No. 168.

Fozzard, Adrian, and Mick Foster. 2001. "Changing Approaches to Public Expenditure Management in Low-Income Aid Dependent Countries." World Institute for Development Economics Research (WIDER) Discussion Paper No. 2001/17.

Freund, Caroline, and Nadia Rocha. 2010. "What Constrains Africa's Exports?" The World Bank, Washington, DC.

Fullerton, Don. 2008. "Distributional Effects of Environmental and Energy Policy: An Introduction." NBER Working Paper No. 14241.

Fullerton, Don, and Seung-Rae Kim. 2006. "Environmental Investment and Policy with Distortionary Taxes and Endogenous Growth." NBER Working Paper No. 12070.

Gallup, John L., and Jeffrey D. Sachs, with Andrew Mellinger. 1999. "Geography and Economic Development." Center for International Development Working Paper No. 1, Harvard University.

Gemmell, Norman, and Oliver Morrissey. 2003. "Tax Structure and the Incidence on the Poor in Developing Countries." Centre for Research on Economic Development and International Trade Research Paper No. 03/18.

Gertler, Paul. 2004. "Do Conditional Cash Transfers Improve Child Health? Evidence from PROGRESA's Control Randomized Experiment." *American Economic Review Papers and Proceedings* 94 (2): 336–41.

Ghura, Dhaneshwar, Carlos Leite, and Charalambos Tsangarides. 2002. "Is Growth Enough? Macroeconomic Policy and Poverty Reduction." IMF Working Paper WP/02/118.

Glewwe, Paul, Alaka Holla, and Michael Kremer. 2008. "Teacher Incentives in the Developing World." Mimeo.

Glewwe, Paul, Michael Kremer, and Sylvie Moulin. 2007. "Many Children Left Behind? Textbooks and Test Scores in Kenya." NBER Working Paper No. 13300.

Goldberg, Pinelopi, and Nina Pavcnik. 2004. "Trade, Inequality, and Poverty: What Do We Know? Evidence from Recent Trade Liberalization Episodes in Developing Countries." NBER Working Paper No. 10593.

———. 2005. "The Effects of the Colombian Trade Liberalization on Urban Poverty." NBER Working Paper No. 11081.

Guillaumont, Patrick, and Lisa Chauvet. 2001. "Aid and Performance: A Reassessment." *The Journal of Development Studies, Taylor and Francis Journals* 37 (6): 66–92.

Gupta, Sanjeev, Benedict Clements, Emanuele Baldacci, and Carlos Mulas-Granados. 2005. "Fiscal Policy, Expenditure Composition, and Growth in Low-Income Countries." *Journal of International Money and Finance* 24 (3): 441–63.

Gupta, Sanjeev, Benedict Clements, Alexander Pivovarsky, and Erwin Tiongson. 2003. "Foreign Aid and Revenue Response: Does the Composition of Aid Matter?" IMF Working Paper WP/03/176.

Gupta, Sanjeev, Hamid Davoodi, and Rosa Alonso Terme. 1998. "Does Corruption Affect Income Equality and Poverty?" IMF Working Paper WP/98/76.

———. 2002. "Does Corruption Affect Income Distribution?" *Economic Governance* 3 (1): 23–45.

Gupta, Sanjeev, Luis de Mello, and Raju Sharan. 2000. "Corruption and Military Spending." IMF Working Paper WP/00/23.

Gyimah-Brempong, Kwabena, and Samaria Munoz de Camacho. 2006. "Corruption, Growth, and Income Distribution: Are There Regional Differences?" *Economics of Governance* 7 (3): 245–69.

Haacker, Markus. 2002. "The Economic Consequences of HIV/AIDS in Southern Africa." IMF Working Paper WP/02/38.

———. 2004. "HIV/AIDS: The Impact on the Social Fabric and the Economy." In *The Macroeconomics of HIV/AIDS,* Markus Haacker, editor. Washington D.C.: The International Monetary Fund.

Hall, Robert, and Charles Jones. 1999. "Why Do Some Countries Produce So Much More Output per Worker Than Others?" *The Quarterly Journal of Economics* 114 (1): 83–116.

Hansen, Henrik, and Finn Tarp. 2000. "Aid Effectiveness Disputed." *Journal of International Development* 12 (3): 375–98.

———. 2001. "Aid and Growth Regressions." *Journal of Development Economics* 64 (2): 547–70.

Hanushek, Eric, and Dennis Kimko. 2000. "Schooling, Labor-Force Quality, and the Growth of Nations." *American Economic Review* 90 (5): 1184–1208.

Hanushek, Eric, and Ludger Woesmann. 2008. "The Role of Cognitive Skills in Economic Development." *Journal of Economic Literature* 46 (3): 607–68.

Harrison, Ann. 2006. "Globalization and Poverty." NBER Working Paper No. 12347.

Hashemi, Syed M., Sidney Ruth Schuler, and Ann P. Riley. 1996. "Rural Credit Programs and Women's Empowerment in Bangladesh." *World Development* 24 (4): 635–53.

Hausmann, Ricardo, and Michael Gavin. 1996. "Securing Stability and Growth in a Shock-Prone Region: The Policy Challenges for Latin America." In *Securing Stability and Growth in Latin America,* Ricardo Hausmann and Helmut Reisen (eds.). Paris: Organization for Economic Cooperation and Development (OECD).

Hay, Jonathan R., Andrei Shleifer, and Robert W. Vishny. 1996. "Privatization in Transition Economies, Toward a Theory of Legal Reform." *European Economic Review* 40 (3–5): 559–67.

Hazell, Peter, and Lawrence Haddad. 2001. "Agricultural Research and Poverty Reduction." Food, Agriculture, and the Environment Discussion Paper 34. International Food Policy Research Institute (IFPRI), Washington, D.C.

He, Fang, Leigh L. Linden, and Margaret MacLeod. 2007. "Helping Teach What Teachers Don't Know: An Assessment of the Pratham English Language Program." Columbia University. Mimeo.

Heady, Christopher. 2001. "Taxation Policy in Low-Income Countries." WIDER Discussion Paper No. 2001/81.

Headey, Derek. 2005. "Foreign Aid and Foreign Policy: How Donors Undermine the Effectiveness of Overseas Development Assistance." Centre for Efficiency and Productivity Analysis Working Paper Series No. 05/2005, Australia, School of Economics, University of Queensland.

Heinemann, Alessandra, and Dorte Verner. 2006. "Crime and Violence in Development. A Literature Review of Latin America and the Caribbean." Policy Research Working Paper 4041. The World Bank, Washington, DC.

Hellman, Joel, Geraint Jones, and Daniel Kaufmann. 2000. "Seize the State, Seize the Day: State Capture, Corruption, and Influence in Transition." Policy Research Working Paper No. 2444. The World Bank, Washington, DC.

Hettich, Frank. 1998. "Growth Effects of a Revenue-Neutral Environmental Tax Reform." *Journal of Economics* 67 (3): 287–316.

Hoff, Karla, and Joseph Stiglitz. 2001. "Modern Economic Theory and Development." In *Frontiers of Development Economics: The Future in Perspective.* New York: Oxford University Press.

Hoggarth, Glenn, Ricardo Reis, and Victoria Saporta. 2002. "Costs of Banking System Instability: Some Empirical Evidence." *Journal of Banking and Finance* 26 (5): 825–55.

Holmes, K.R., B. T. Johnson, and M. Kirkpatrick. 1997. *The 1997 Index of Economic Freedom.* New York, New York: The Heritage Foundation, Dow Jones and Company, Incorporated.

Honohan, Patrick, editor. 2003. *Taxation of Financial Intermediation: Theory and Practice for Emerging Economies.* New York: Oxford University Press and Washington, D.C.: The World Bank.

Honohan, Patrick. 2004a. *Financial Sector Policy and the Poor*. World Bank Working Paper No. 43. The World Bank, Washington, DC.

———. 2004b. "Financial Development, Growth and Poverty: How Close are the Links?" In *Financial Development and Economic Growth: Explaining the Links,* Charles Goodhart (ed.). London: Palgrave.

———. 2008a. "Cross-Country Variation in Household Access to Financial Services." *Journal of Banking and Finance* 32 (11):2493–2500.

———. 2008b. "Risk Management and the Costs of the Banking Crisis." *National Institute Economic Review* 206 (1): 15–24.

———. 2009. "Country Policy and Institutional Assessment (CPIA) Indicators and the Role of Finance in the Development Process." Draft background paper for *The CPIA: An Evaluation*, Independent Evaluation Group, The World Bank.

Honohan, Patrick, and Daniela Klingebiel. 2003. "The Fiscal Cost Implications of an Accommodating Approach to Banking Crises." *Journal of Banking and Finance* 27 (8):1539–60.

Hossain, Mahabub. 1988. "Credit for Alleviation of Rural Poverty: The Grameen Bank in Bangladesh." Research Report 65. International Food Policy Research Institute, Washington, DC.

Huntington, Samuel. 1968. *Political Order in Changing Societies*. New Haven: Yale University Press.

Ilahi, Nadeem, Peter Orazem, and Guilherme Sedlacek. 2001. "The Implications of Child Labor for Adult Wages, Income and Poverty: Retrospective Evidence from Brazil." The International Monetary Fund. Mimeo.

IEG (Independent Evaluation Group). 2008. *Environmental Sustainability: An Evaluation of World Bank Group Support*. Washington, D.C.: The World Bank.

Inter-American Development Bank. 1997 "Studies of the Magnitude, Costs and Policies Against Violence in Six Places: Lima, Rio de Janeiro, San Salvador, Mexico, Venezuela and Colombia." Prepared for the Chief Economic Officer of the Inter-American Development Bank. Inter-American Development Bank, Washington, DC.

International Monetary Fund. 2000. "Mozambique Fiscal Transparency Study." Aide Memoire.

Irz, Xavier, Lin Lin, Colin Thirtle, and Steve Wiggins. 2001. "Agricultural Productivity Growth and Poverty Alleviation." *Development Policy Review* 19 (4): 449–66.

Isern, Jennifer, David Porteous, Raul Hernandez-Coss, and Chinyere Egwuagu. 2005. "AML/CFT Regulation: Implications for Financial Service Providers That Serve Low-Income People." The Consultative Group to Assist the Poor (CGAP) Focus Note 29.

Jamison, Dean, Jeffrey Sachs, and Jia Wang. 2001. "The Effect of the AIDS Epidemic on Economic Welfare in Sub-Saharan Africa." World Health Organization Commission on Macroeconomics and Health, Working Group 1, Working Paper No. 13.

Jenkins, Glenn. 1994. "Modernization of Tax Administration: Revenue Boards and Privatization as Instruments of Change." *Bulletin for International Fiscal Documentation* 48 (2): 75–81.

Johnson, Simon, John McMillan, and Christopher Woodruff. 2002. "Property Rights and Finance." *The American Economic Review* 92 (5): 1335–56.

Kalemli-Ozcan, Sebnem, Harl E. Ryder, and David N. Weil. 2000. "Mortality Decline, Human Capital Investment, and Economic Growth." *Journal of Development Economics* 62 (1): 1–23.

Kambou, Gerard, Shantayanan Devarajan, and Mead Over. 1992. "The Economic Impact of AIDS in an African Country: Simulations with a Computable General Equilibrium Model of Cameroon." *Journal of African Economies* 1 (1): 109–130.

Kanbur, Ravi. 2004. "Growth, Inequality and Poverty: Some Hard Questions." Mimeo.

———. 2005. "Reforming the Formula: A Modest Proposal for Introducing Development Outcomes in IDA Allocation Procedures." Revised version published in *Revue d'Economie du Developpment*.

Kaufmann, Daniel. 2003. "Rethinking Governance: Empirical Lessons Challenge Orthodoxy." Discussion draft. The World Bank.

Kaufmann, Daniel, Aart Kraay, and Pablo Zoido-Lobaton. 1999. "Governance Matters." Policy

Research Working Paper No. 2196. The World Bank, Washington, DC.

———. 2002. "Governance Matters II: Updated Indicators for 2000/01." Policy Research Working Paper No. 2772. The World Bank, Washington, DC.

Kaufmann, Daniel, Aart Kraay, and Massimo Mastruzzi. 2003. "Governance Matters III." Policy Research Working Paper No. 3106. The World Bank, Washington, DC.

Kerekes, Carrie, and Claudia Williamson. 2008. "Unveiling de Soto's Mystery: Property Rights, Capital Formation, and Development." *Journal of Institutional Economics* 4 (3): 299–325.

Khandker, Shahidur. 1998. *Fighting Poverty with Microcredit: Experience in Bangladesh.* New York: Oxford University Press.

Khandker, Shahidur, 2005. "Microfinance and Poverty: Evidence Using Panel Data from Bangladesh." *The World Bank Economic Review* 19 (2): 263–86.

Khandker, Shahidur, and Mark Pitt. 2003. "The Impact of Group-Based Credit on Poor Households: An Analysis of Panel Data from Bangladesh." The World Bank, Washington, DC.

Kiser, Edgar, and Audrey Sacks. 2007. "Improving Tax Administration in Contemporary African States: Lessons from History." Prepared for *The Thunder of History: Taxation in Comparative and Historical Perspective.* Northwestern University, May 4–5.

Klapper, Leora, Luc Laeven, and Raghuram Rajan. 2006. "Entry Regulation as a Barrier to Entrepreneurship." *Journal of Financial Economics* 82 (3): 591–629.

Klasen, Stephan. 2002. "Low Schooling for Girls, Slower Growth for All?" *World Bank Economic Review* 16 (3): 345–73.

Klasen, Stephan, and Francesca Lamanna. 2003. "The Impact of Gender Inequality in Education and Employment on Economic Growth: Updated Estimates." Mimeo.

Knack, Stephen, and Philip Keefer. 1995. "Institutions and Economic Performance: Cross Country Tests Using Alternative Institutional Measures." *Economics and Politics* 7 (3): 207–27.

Knowles, Stephan, Paula Lorgelly, and Dorian Owen. 2002. "Are Educational Gender Gaps a Brake on Economic Development: Some Cross-Country Empirical Evidence." *Oxford Economic Papers* 54 (1): 118–49.

Krebs, Tom. 2003. "Human Capital Risk and Economic Growth." *Quarterly Journal of Economics* 118 (2):709–44.

Kremer, Michael, and Alaka Holla. 2008. "Pricing and Access: Lessons from Randomized Evaluations in Education and Health." Center for Global Development Working Paper No. 158.

Kremer, Michael, Jessica Leino, Edward Miguel, and Alix Peterson Zwane. 2008. "Spring Cleaning: A Randomized Evaluation of Source Water Quality Improvement." Harvard University, Department of Economics. Mimeo.

Krusell, Per, and Jose-Voctor Ríos-Rull. 1996. "Vested Interests in a Positive Theory of Stagnation and Growth." *The Review of Economic Studies* 63 (2): 301–29.

Kuznets, Simon. 1955. "Economic Growth and Income Inequality." *American Economic Review* 45 (1): 1–28.

Landes, David. 1983. *Revolution in Time.* Cambridge, MA: Harvard University Press.

Laeven, Luc, and Fabian Valencia. 2008. "The Use of Blanket Guarantees in Banking Crises." IMF Working Paper WP/08/250.

La Porta, Rafael, Florencio Lopez-de-Silanes, and Andrei Shleifer. 2008. "The Economic Consequences of Legal Origins." *Journal of Economic Literature* 46 (2): 285–332.

La Porta, Rafael, Florencio Lopez-de-Silanes, Andrei Shleifer, and Robert W. Vishny. 1998. "Law and Finance." *Journal of Political Economy* 106 (6): 1113–55.

———. 1999. "The Quality of Government." *Journal of Law, Economics and Organization* 15: 222–79.

———. 2000. "Investor Protection and Corporate Governance." *Journal of Financial Economics* 58: 3–27.

Leff, Nathaniel. 1964. "Economic Development through Bureaucratic Corruption." *The American Behavioural Scientist* 8 (3): 8–14.

Levine, Ross. 1997. "Financial Development and Economic Growth: Views and Agenda."

Journal of Economic Literature 35 (2): 688–726.

———. 1998. "The Legal Environment, Banks, and Long-Run Economic Growth." *Journal of Money, Credit, and Banking* 30 (3): 596–613.

———. 2003. "More on Finance and Growth: More Finance, More Growth?" The Federal Reserve Bank of St. Louis.

———. 2005. "Law, Endowments and Property Rights." *Journal of Economic Perspectives* 19 (3):61–88.

Levine, Ross, Norman Loayza, and Thorsten Beck. 2000. "Financial Intermediation and Growth: Causality and Causes." *Journal of Monetary Economics* 16 (46).

Levine, Ross, and Sara Zervos. 1998. "Stock Markets, Bank and Economic Growth." *American Economic Review* 88 (3): 537–58.

Lewis, W. Arthur. 1954. "Economic Development with Unlimited Supplies of Labour." *Manchester School of Economic and Social Sciences* 22 (2): 139–91.

Lien, Da Hsiang Donald. 1986. "A Note on Competitive Bribery Game." *Economics Letters* 22: 337–41.

Lin, Justin Yifu. 1992. "Rural Reforms and Agricultural Growth in China." *American Economic Review* 82 (1): 34–51.

Littlefield, Elizabeth, Jonathan Morduch, and Syed Hashemi. 2003. "Is Microfinance an Effective Strategy to Reach the Millennium Development Goals?" CGAP Focus Note 24.

Loayza, Norman. 1996. "The Economics of the Informal Sector: A Simple Model and Some Empirical Evidence from Latin America." *Carnegie-Rochester Conference Series on Public Policy* 45 (1): 129–62.

Londono, Juan Luis. 1996. "Violencia y Capital Social." Paper presented at the Second Annual Conference of the World Bank on Development in Latin America and the Caribbean. Bogotá, Colombia.

Lopez de Silanes Florencio, Simon Johnson, Rafael La Porta, and Andrei Shleifer. 2000. "Tunnelling." NBER Working Paper No. 7523.

Lui, Francis. 1985. "An Equilibrium Queuing Model of Bribery." *Journal of Political Economics* 93 (4): 760–81.

Luoto, Jill, Craig McIntosh, and Bruce Wydick. 2007. "Credit Information Systems in Less-Developed Countries: A Test with Microfinance in Guatemala." *Economic Development and Cultural Change* 55 (2): 313–34.

Maine, Henry. 1980. *Popular Government*. London: John Murray.

Martinez-Vazquez, Jorge, and Jameson Boex. 2001. "Russia's Transition to a New Federalism." World Bank Institute, Washington, DC.

Mauro, Paolo. 1995. "Corruption and Growth." *Quarterly Journal of Economics* 110 (3): 681–712.

Mazingo, Christopher. 1999. "Effects of Property Rights on Economic Activity: Lessons from the Stolypin Land Reform." Massachusetts Institute of Technology. Mimeo.

McGillivray, Mark, Simon Feeny, Niels Hermes, and Robert Lensink. 2005. "It Works; It Doesn't; It Can, But That Depends? 50 Years of Controversy over the Macroeconomic Impact of Development Aid." World Institute for Development Economics Research Paper No. 2005/54. United Nations University.

McGillivray, Mark, and Oliver Morrissey. 2001a. "Aid Illusion and Public Sector Fiscal Behaviour." *The Journal of Development Studies* 37 (6): 118–36.

———. 2001b. "Fiscal Effects of Aid." World Institute for Development Economic Research Discussion Paper No. 2001/61, United Nations University.

McLure, Charles. 1999 "Tax Holidays and Investment Incentives: A Comparative Analysis." *Bulletin for International Fiscal Documentation* 53(8–9) 326–39.

Menezes-Filho, Naercio, and Ligia Vasconcellos. 2004. "Operationalising Pro-Poor Growth: A Case Study on Brazil." Prepared as part of the Operationalizing Pro-Poor Growth research program.

Mikesell, John. 2003. *International Experiences with Administration of Local Taxes: A Review of Practices and Issues*. School of Public and Environmental Affairs, Indiana University.

Miller, Margaret, editor. 2003. *Credit Reporting Systems and the International Economy*. Cambridge, Massachusetts: MIT Press.

Mocan, Naci. 2004. "What Determines Corruption? International Evidence from Micro Data." NBER Working Paper No. 10460.

Mokyr, Joel. 1990. *The Lever of Riches: Technological Creativity and Economic Progress*. New York: Oxford University Press.

Montiel, Peter, and Luis Servén. 2006. "Macroeconomic Stability in Developing Countries: How Much Is Enough? "*World Bank Research Observer* 21 (2): 151–78. Oxford University Press.

Mookherjee, Dilip. 1995. "Reforms in Income Tax Enforcement in Mexico." IRIS-India Working Paper No. 6. University of Maryland.

Mookherjee, Dileep, and Arindam Das-Gupta. 1995. "Reforming Indian Income Tax Enforcement." IRIS-India Working Paper No. 3, University of Maryland.

Moore, Mick. 2004. "Taxation and the Political Agenda, North and South." *Forum for Development Studies* 31 (1): 7–32.

Moser, Caroline. 1996. "Urban Poverty and Violence: Consolidation or Erosion of Social Capital?" Second Annual World Bank Conference on Development in Latin America, Bogota.

Moser, Caroline, and Jeremy Holland. 1997. *Urban Poverty and Violence in Jamaica*. Washington, DC.: The World Bank.

Muralidharan, Karthik, and Venkatesh Sundararaman. 2007. "Teacher Incentives in Developing Countries: Experimental Evidence from India." The World Bank, Washington, DC. September. Mimeo.

North, Douglas. 1990. *Institutions, Institutional Change and Economic Performance*. New York: Cambridge University Press.

Ocampo, Jose. 2003. "Structural Dynamics and Economic Growth in Developing Countries." Mimeo.

Olken, Benjamin. 2007. "Monitoring Corruption: Evidence from a Field Experiment in Indonesia." *Journal of Political Economy* 115 (2): 200–49.

OED (Operations Evaluation Department). 2001. "Review of the Performance-Based Allocation System, IDA10–12." The World Bank, Washington, DC, February 14.

Otsuka, Keijiro. 2002, "Poverty Reduction Issues: Village Economy Perspective."*Asian Development Review* 19 (1): 98–116.

Over, Mead. 1992. *The Macroeconomic Impact of AIDS in Sub-Saharan Africa*. Working Paper. Population and Human Resources Department. The World Bank, Washington, DC.

Panday, Pranab Kumar. 2008. "Representation Without Participation: Quotas for Women in Bangladesh." *International Political Science Review* 29 (4): 489–512.

Parry, Ian, Hilary Sigman, Margaret Walls, and Roberton Williams. 2005. "The Incidence of Pollution Control Policies." Rutgers University, Department of Economics, Departmental Working Paper No. 2005–04.

Perotti, Roberto. 1992. "Fiscal Policy, Income Distribution, and Growth." *Review of Economics and Statistics* 60 (4): 755–76.

———. 1993. "Political Equilibrium, Income Distribution, and Growth." *Review of Economic Studies* 60 (4): 755–56.

———. 1996. "Growth, Income Distribution, and Democracy: What the Data Say."*Journal of Economic Growth* 1 (2): 149–87.

Persson, T., and G. Tabellini. 1994. "Is Inequality Harmful for Growth?" *The American Economic Review* 84 (3): 600–21.

Porto, Guido. 2005. "Informal Export Barriers and Poverty."*Journal of International Economics* 66 (2): 447–70.

Posner, Richard. 1981. "The Economics of Privacy." *American Economic Review Papers and Proceedings* 71 (2): 405–9.

———. 1998. "Creating a Legal Framework for Economic Development." *The World Bank Research Observer* 13 (1): 1–11.

Rajan, Raghuram, and Arvind Subramaniam. 2008. "Aid and Growth: What Does the Cross-Country Evidence Really Show?" *The Review of Economics and Statistics* 90 (4): 643–65.

Rajkumar, Andrew, and Vinaya Swaroop. 2002. "Public Spending and Outcomes: Does Governance Matter?" Policy Research Working Paper No. 2840. The World Bank, Washington, DC.

Ram, Rati. 2003. "Roles of Bilateral and Multilateral Aid in Economic Growth of Developing Countries." *Kyklos* 56 (1):95–110.

Rauch, James, and Peter Evans. 2000. "Bureaucratic Structure and Bureaucratic Performance in Less Developed Countries." *Journal of Public Economics* 75: 49–71.

Ravallion, Martin. 2001. "Growth, Inequality and Poverty: Looking Beyond Averages." *World Development* 29 (11): 1803–15.

———. 2004. "Looking Beyond Averages in the Trade and Poverty Debate." Policy Research Working Paper No. 3461. The World Bank, Washington, DC.

Ravallion, Martin, and Gaurav Datt. 2002. "Why Has Economic Growth Been More Pro-Poor in Some States of India than Others?" *Journal of Development Economics* 68: 381–400.

Reddy, Sanjay, and Camelia Minoiu. 2006. "Development Aid and Economic Growth: A Positive Long-Run Relation." Working Paper No. 29. United Nations, Department of Economics and Social Affairs.

Reinikka, Ritva, and Jakob Svensson. 2004. "Local Capture: Evidence from a Central Government Transfer Program in Uganda." *Quarterly Journal of Economics* 119: 679–705.

Rigobon, Roberto, and Dani Rodrik. 2004. "Rule of Law, Democracy, Openness, and Income: Estimating the Interrelationships." NBER Working Paper No. 10750.

Rodrik, Dani. 1999. "Institutions for High-Quality Growth: What They Are and How to Acquire Them." Draft paper prepared for The International Monetary Fund Conference on Second-Generation Reforms. Washington, D.C., November 8–9.

———. 2000. "Comments on "Trade, Growth, and Poverty" by David Dollar and Aart Kraay (editors). Mimeo.

———. 2003. "Growth Strategies." NBER Working Paper No. 10050.

Rodrik, Dani, Arvind Subramanian, and Francesco Trebbi. 2002. "Institutions Rule: The Primacy of Institutions over Geography and Integration in Economic Development." NBER Working Paper No. 9305.

Roodman, David. 2007a. "The Anarchy of Numbers: Aid, Development, and Cross-Country Empirics." *The World Bank Economic Review* 21 (2): 255–77.

———. 2007b. "Macro Aid Effectiveness Research: A Guide for the Perplexed." Working Paper No. 134. Center for Global Development, December.

Rosegrant, Mark, and Peter Hazell. 2000. "Transforming the Rural Asian Economy: The Unfinished Revolution." In *Study of Rural Asia* (Vol. 1), Asian Development Bank, copublished by the Oxford University Press.

Rosenstein-Rodan, Paul. 1943. "Problems of Industrialisation of Eastern and South-Eastern Europe." *The Economic Journal* 53 (210/211): 202–11.

Rostow, W. Walt. 1960. *The Stages of Economic Growth: A Non-Communist Manifesto*. Cambridge: Cambridge University Press.

Sachs, Jeffrey. 2003. "Institutions Don't Rule: Direct Effects of Geography on Per Capita Income." NBER Working Paper No. 9490.

———. 2005. *The End of Poverty: Economic Possibilities for Our Time*. New York: Penguin USA.

———. 2008. *Common Wealth: Economics for a Crowded Planet*. New York: Penguin USA.

Sachs, Jeffrey D., and Andrew Warner. 1995. "Economic Reform and the Process of Global Integration." *Brookings Papers on Economic Activity*. (1): 1–118.

Schneidman, Miriam. 1996. "Targeting At-Risk-Youth: Rationales, Approaches to Service Delivery, and Monitoring and Evaluation Issues." Latin America and Caribbean Human and Social Development Group Paper Series No. 2. The World Bank, Washington, DC.

Sen, Amartya. 1992. *Inequality Re-examined*. Cambridge: Harvard University Press.

———. 1997. *On Economic Inequality*. Oxford: Clarendon Press.

———. 1999. *Development as Freedom*. Oxford: Oxford University Press.

Shavell, Steven. 2003. "Economic Analysis of Property Law." NBER Working Paper No. 9695.

Shleifer, Andrei, and Robert Vishny. 1993. "Corruption." *The Quarterly Journal of Economics* 108 (3): 599–617.

Skoufias, Emmanuel, Benjamin Davis, and Sergio de la Vega. 2001. "Targeting the Poor in Mexico: An Evaluation of the Selection of Households into PROGRESA." *World Development* 29 (10): 1769–84.

Steets, Julia. 2008. "Adaptation and Refinement of the World Bank's Country Policy and Institutional Assessment." Global Public Policy Institute on behalf of the German Federal Ministry for Economic Cooperation and Development.

Stern, Nicholas. 2001. *A Strategy for Development*. Washington, D.C.: The World Bank.

Stevens, Michael. 1999. "Interview." The World Bank, Washington, DC, January 6.

Summers, Lawrence. 2003. "Godkin Lectures." Harvard University. Mimeo.

Tanzi, Vito. 1998. "Corruption around the World: Causes, Scope, and Cures." IMF Working Paper WP/98/63.

Todaro, Michael. 1997. *Economic Development*. London: Longman.

Topalova, Petia. 2004. "Factor Immobility and Regional Effects of Trade Liberalization: Evidence from India." MIT. Mimeo.

———. 2005. "Trade Liberalization, Poverty and Inequality: Evidence from Indian Districts." NBER Working Paper No. 11614.

Treisman, Daniel. 2000. "The Causes of Corruption: A Cross-National Study." *Journal of Public Economics* 76 (3): 399–457.

Tressel, Thierry, and Enrica Detragiache. 2008. "Do Financial Sector Reforms Lead to Financial Development? Evidence from a New Dataset." IMF Working Paper WP/08/265.

Van Rijckeghem, Caroline, and Beatrice Weder. 1997. "Corruption and the Rate of Temptation: Do Low Wages in the Civil Service Cause Corruption?" IMF Working Paper WP/97/73.

———. 2001. "Bureaucratic Corruption and the Rate of Temptation: Do Wages in the Civil Service Affect Corruption, and by How Much?" *Journal of Development Economics* 65 (2): 307–31.

Vandenbussche, Jerome, Philippe Aghion, and Costas Meghir. 2006. "Growth, Distance to Frontier and Composition of Human Capital." *Journal of Economic Growth* 11 (2): 97–127.

Vermeersch, Christel, and Michael Kremer. 2003. "School Meals, Educational Achievement and School Competition: Evidence from a Randomized Evaluation." University of Oxford.

Wei, Shang-Jin. 2000. "How Taxing Is Corruption on International Investors?" *Review of Economics and Statistics* 82 (1): 1–11.

Weil, David N. 2005. "Accounting for the Effect of Health on Economic Growth." NBER Working Paper No. 11455.

Welch, Karen Horn, Margaret McMillan, and Dani Rodrik. 2004. "When Economic Reform Goes Wrong: Cashews in Mozambique." Brookings Trade Forum 2003.

Werlin, Herbert. 1979. "The Consequences of Corruption: Ghanaian Experience." In *Bureaucratic Corruption in Sub-Saharan Africa*, Monday U. Ekpo, editor,. Washington, D.C.: University Press of America.

White, H., and E. Anderson. 2002. "Growth versus Distribution: Does the Pattern of Growth Matter?" *Development Policy Review* 19 (3): 267–89.

Williamson, John. 1990. "What Washington Means by Policy Reform." In *Latin American Adjustment: How Much Has Happened?* Washington D.C.: Institute for International Economics.

———. 2004. "The Washington Consensus as Policy Prescription for Development." A lecture in the series "Practitioners of Development" delivered at The World Bank on January 13, 2004.

Winters, Alain, Neil McCulloch, and Andrew McKay. 2004. "Trade Liberalization and Poverty: The Evidence So Far." *Journal of Economic Literature* 42 (1): 72–115.

Woolard, Ingrid, and Stephan Klasen. 2005. "Determinants of Income Mobility and Household Poverty Dynamics in South Africa." *The Journal of Development Studies* 41 (5): 865–97.

World Bank. 1992. *Development and Environment*. New York: Oxford University Press.

———. 1993. *The East Asian Miracle: Economic Growth and Public Policy*. New York and Oxford: Oxford University Press for The World Bank.

———. 1994. *World Development Report, 1994: Infrastructure for Development*. Washington, D.C.: The World Bank.

———. 1997. *World Development Report, 1997: The State in a Changing World*. Washington, D.C.: The World Bank.

———. 1998. *Beyond the Washington Consensus: Institutions Matter*. New York: Oxford University Press.

———. 1999. *World Development Report 1998/99: Knowledge for Development*. New York: Oxford University Press.

———. 2000a. *Can Africa Claim the 21st Century?* New York: Oxford University Press.

———. 2000b. *World Development Report 2000/2001: Attacking Poverty*. New York: Oxford University Press.

———. 2000c. *Poverty Reduction and Strategy Paper Source Book*.

———. 2001a. *Engendering Development*. New York: Oxford University Press.

———. 2001b. "Enhancing IDA's Performance-Based Allocation System." September

———. 2001c. *Poverty Reduction Strategy Sourcebook: A Resource to Assist Countries in Developing Poverty Reduction Strategies*. Washington, D.C.: The World Bank.

———. 2002a. *Globalization, Growth and Poverty*. Washington, D.C.: The World Bank.

———. 2002b. "Linking IDA Support to Country Performance." Third Annual Report on IDA's Country Assessment and Allocation Process. April 30.

———. 2002c. *World Bank Group Work in Low-Income Countries Under Stress: A Task Force Report*. Washington, D.C.: The World Bank.

———. 2003a. "Country Policy and Institutional Assessment 2003: Assessment Questionnaire." Washington, D.C.: The World Bank.

———. 2003b. "IDA's Performance-Based Allocation System: Current and Emerging Issues." October.

———. 2004a. "Country Policy and Institutional Assessment: An External Panel Review." The World Bank, April 5.

———. 2004b. "IDA's Performance-Based Allocation System: IDA Rating Disclosure and Fine-Tuning the Governance Factor." September.

———. 2004c. "IDA's Performance-Based Allocation System: Update on Outstanding Issues." February.

———. 2004d. "Disclosing IDA Country Performance Ratings." Washington, D.C.: The World Bank. Operations Policy and Country Services.

———. 2004e. "Reducing Poverty: Sustaining Growth." Scaling up Poverty Reduction. A Global Learning Process and Conference in Shanghai, The World Bank, May 25–27.

———. 2004f. *2003 Annual Review of Development Effectiveness. The Effectiveness of Bank Support for Policy Reform*.

———. 2004g. *World Development Report 2004: Making Services Work for Poor People*. New York, NY: Oxford University Press.

———. 2004h. *Building State Capacity in Africa: New Approaches, Emerging Lessons*. Washington, D.C.: World Bank Institute, The World Bank.

———. 2005. *Economic Growth in the 1990s: Learning from a Decade of Reform*. The International Bank for Reconstruction and Development/The World Bank.

———. 2006a. "Chairman's Summary: IDA 14 Mid-Term Review Meeting." November.

———. 2006b. *World Development Report*. New York: Oxford University Press.

———. 2007. "Country Policy and Institutional Assessment 2007: Assessment Questionnaire." The World Bank, Washington, DC.

———. 2008a. Commission on Growth and Development: "The Growth Report. Strategies for Sustained Growth and Inclusive Development." Discussion Paper. The World Bank, Washington, DC.

———. 2008b. "Country Policy and Institutional Assessment 2008: Assessment Questionnaire." Operations Policy and Country Services. September 5. World Bank, Washington, DC

———. 2008c. Demirguc-Kunt, Asli, Thorsten Beck, and Patrick Honohan, *Finance for All? Policies and Pitfalls in Expanding Access*. Washington, D.C.

———. 2008d. *Environmental Health and Child Survival: Epidemiology, Economics, Experiences*. Washington, D.C.: The World Bank.

———. 2008e. "IDA: The Platform for Achieving Results at the Country Level." Additions to IDA Resources: the Fifteenth Replenishment. February.

———. 2008f. *Poverty and the Environment: Understanding Linkages at the Household*

Level. Washington, D.C.: The World Bank.

World Economic Forum. 2008. *Global Competitiveness Report 2008–2009.*

Young, Alwyn. 2004. "The Gift of the Dying: The Tragedy of AIDS and the Welfare of Future African Generations." NBER Working Paper No. 10991.

Zwane, Alix Peterson, and Michael Kremer. 2007. "What Works in Fighting Diarrheal Diseases in Developing Countries? A Critical Review." NBER Working Paper No. 12987.

www.ingramcontent.com/pod-product-compliance
Lightning Source LLC
Chambersburg PA
CBHW080332270326
41927CB00014B/3195